the handbook of
cage and aviary
birds

the handbook of
cage and aviary
birds

Matthew M. Vriends, Ph.D.
Tanya M. Heming-Vriends

© 2014 Magnet & Steel Ltd

This edition published by Magnet & Steel Ltd

Printed 2014

This book is distributed in the UK by
Magnet & Steel Ltd
Unit 6,
Vale Business Park
Cowbridge
CF71 7PF

sales@magnetsteel.com

ISBN: 978-1-907337-75-8

DS0107. Handbook of Cage & Aviary Birds

Creative Director: Sarah King
Editor: Judith Millidge
Project editor: Clare Haworth-Maden
Designer: Debbie Fisher
All photographs by Pieter van den Hooven

Body text font: Plantin
Fact File font: Kabel

Printed by Printworks Global Ltd., London/Hong Kong

3 5 7 9 10 8 6 4 2

Contents

Introduction	6
Housing for birds	6
Care of birds	16
Purchasing birds	22
The feeding and management of companion birds	31

The Bird Directory	52
Quail	52
Doves	54
Budgerigar or Parakeet	60
Lories and Lorikeets	63
Cockatoos	75
Cockatiel	84
Eclectus Parrot	86
Parakeets and Parrots	88
Canary	183
Finches and Weavers	188
Barbet, Toucan and Touraco	240
Bulbul	244
Pekin Robin and White-eye	246
Sunbird	245
Mynah, Thrush, TANAGER, starling and jay	248
Index	254
Credits and Acknowledgements	256

The Handbook of Cage and Aviary Birds

The Monk parakeet is famous for its extensive nests.

Stella lorikeet

INTRODUCTION

Aviculture is a hobby which provides many opportunities to observe and study birds at close range, and to enjoy their lively songs and brilliant colours. If birds are made to feel comfortable and at ease they show themselves at their finest, so it is important to know about their characteristics, habits and general requirements. Their captive conditions should represent, as closely as possible, those they are accustomed to in the wild.

HOUSING FOR BIRDS

The housing requirements of different birds vary and it would be wrong to assume that any commercial cage or aviary, indoors or out, is suitable for every bird. The golden rule for the aviculturist and bird fancier is to find out the requirements of their favourite birds, prepare a suitable cage and only then purchase the birds.

Most birds can be housed indoors as well as outdoors. There is much to be said for offering your feathered friends fresh air and (especially) sunlight. On the other hand, remember that nothing is as bad for birds as drafts, fog and smog. Many bird fanciers have created satisfactory conditions for wild birds by building housing in garages, basements or even in the attic where you can make good use of all the space under the roof.

Building housing indoors can work well thanks to the availability of artificial equipment, such as full-spectrum natural lighting (Vita Lite and Ott-Lite, for example), sophisticated watering systems and numerous other accessories that have recently become available. Attics and unused rooms are useful spaces for housing and breeding canaries, lovebirds, parrotlets, Australian grass finches (zebra finches etc.), parakeets (budgerigars) and insect- and fruit-eating tropical birds (the so-called soft-billed birds). People who live in flats have to use indoor housing unless they can get permission to build a small outdoor flight cage on a balcony or other outdoor area. Many commercial companies can help advise on custom-made indoor or outdoor flight cages, and the style and size is limited only by funds and space. Read through the guidelines below to ensure happy and healthy birds.

Outdoor Aviaries

Most aviculturists and bird fanciers prefer aviaries located in the garden or backyard. The model and dimensions of such facilities are a question of personal preference and available space.

Aviaries should be situated with the front facing south whenever possible. If a front-facing southern exposure is not available the aviary should face west. Use the best materials you can afford as they will last longer and you will avoid extensive repairs and on-going renovations.

Use the narrowest wooden boards possible when building an aviary because they are less likely to shrink and warp. For wire mesh, use the familiar hexagonal small-gauge mesh. Square welded mesh, which is available in several wire thicknesses, is preferable for large parakeet species. You can buy these supplies in any home improvement center.

Cover the wire mesh of the aviary roof with a second layer of mesh with wider openings to discourage cats and native wildlife from sitting on the roof and harassing the aviary birds. Keep a space of at least 4 in. (10 cm) between the two layers. Clean the wire mesh with petrol, then paint it with a non-toxic dark green or black paint, so that the birds will be more visible. Fasten all the wire mesh to the outside of the wood, so that the birds will not injure themselves on nails or wire. As a further precaution, nail a thin slat along the boards where you have stapled the wire mesh. This protects the birds from all rough edges and fasteners.

The shelter should have at least one window protected with a wire mesh screen which will discourage the birds from flying into the window and suffering broken wings, legs and other injuries. Construct a sturdy screen so that you can open the window when the weather is mild.

Protect the aviary against rats and mice. Anyone who has experienced the damage – and especially the fear – in the aviary caused by rats on a night raid will certainly resolve never to let this happen again. Vermin must be kept out. Use concrete flooring or heavy paving stones to keep them from gnawing their way in from below. If you prefer an earthen floor, extend the wire mesh of the walls at least 16 to 20 in. (40 to 50 cm) into the ground. You can also bury glass splinters, broken bottles, and similar rubble 16 in. (40 cm) deep all along the aviary. In a smaller aviary, dig down 16 in. (40 cm) along the whole floor and bury wire mesh along the bottom. Then you can still have attractive plantings in the earth above the mesh.

The closed part of an aviary.

> ## A functional aviary should have three sections:
>
> 1. A night shelter.
> 2. An open run
>   (also called a flight).
> 3. A closed run.

Modern outdoor aviaries are ideal for keeping and breeding lovebirds, parrotlets and Australian parakeets.

Aviaries are best integrated into the garden by being placed among trees and shrubs, rather than being left looking forlorn and exposed in the middle of the garden. They should be erected facing south. If this is impossible it is better to have it south-east facing than south-west..

Another alternative is to raise the whole aviary floor 10 in. (25 cm) off the ground, leaving enough crawl space for a dog. A good dog such as a dachshund, beagle or small terrier will deal with any rodents. Do not use a cat!

There are rat and mouse poisons on the market that are safe to use around birds. But make sure that children do not come into contact with them and if in doubt don't use them.

Be aware that mice and rats can gnaw their way through concrete – with difficulty – when it has hardened and very easily while it is still setting. So don't put your entire faith in concrete flooring. Keep the aviary clean. Clear away spilt and unused seed and any other food left behind by ground-feeding birds such as quail and pheasants. Always keep watch for vermin, so you can take prompt remedial action. But prevention is always better than cure.

In designing an aviary, length is a more important dimension than width. The longer you can make it, the better. Similarly, height isn't as crucial, but the flight ought to be at least 6 ft. (2 m) high. Don't make it too high, however, because if you have to catch your birds – say, to bring them indoors for the winter – you're going to have difficulties. For a beginner, an aviary of the following dimensions is ideal: 5 ft. wide x 16 ft. long x 6 ft. high (1.2 m wide x 5 m long x 2 m high); and if you are taller than 6 ft. (2 m) add another foot (metre) to the height. If you plan to have a breeding aviary for just one couple, smaller dimensions of 4 ft. x 8 ft. x 6 ft. (1.3 m x 2.2 m x 2 m) would be suitable.

Make aviaries catproof!

Every flight or run needs a night shelter that must be lit to encourage the birds to spend the night there or to use it as shelter in bad weather. Most birds like to sleep as high up as possible – the well-known roosting position – so ensure that the roosts in the run are lower than those in the night shelter, and the birds will accept the shelter as their sleeping and security area.

If your aviary is long enough, cover part of it with waterproof roofing so that the birds can remain outside and still stay dry in rainy weather. There are many birds, however, that like to get wet during a mild rain shower. This won't hurt them, especially not in spring or summer during the breeding season. Breeding hens will rush into the shower and return to the nest without fully drying themselves, a typical behavior trait which prevents the eggs from drying out.

If you can't build a night shelter, cover one end of the flight (run) with corrugated plastic siding on the top and on the sides. This would still give the birds a secure place to be at night and during wet weather.

Build an entry (safety) porch to prevent the birds from escaping, and include hasps for a good padlock. Unfortunately, this is necessary. With the high prices that most birds command today, additional protection against theft is also sensible – consider investing in an alarm system. Fix identity bands to all your birds and keep a record of each individual. True, it is easy for a thief to remove the bands, but prospective buyers tend to be suspicious (and rightly so) if they are offered birds without leg bands (rings).

Design the aviary so you'll never run into problems with filling or cleaning the food and water bowls. Choose a convenient spot away from any plants, so you are less likely to disturb the birds, especially during the breeding season. The ideal method is to build a separate access door from the outside but that, of course, isn't possible in every location.

The floor of the aviary has to be regularly turned over with a shovel or raked loose. Sew some seeds in one corner of the aviary, and as they sprout they will offer a special treat for most birds. Cover another section of the floor (and regularly refill) with a layer of oyster grit mixed with ground cuttlefish bone.

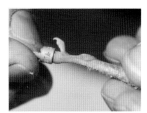

Banding a chick. Take the bird's foot between your fingers so that the back toe points towards the back and the other toes are stretched together towards the front.

Rub a little petroleum jelly on the toes. Place the band over the three front toes (or two in the case of psittacines), slide it backwards, over the toe (toes), and continue a little further up the leg as well.

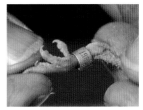

If the back toe (toes) is still 'trapped' under the band, release it with a pointed matchstick. The band is now correctly positioned around the chick's leg. Clean the leg and put the chick back into the nest.

Breeding units are commercially available. Good hygiene is vital as many diseases can spread rapidly via feeding equipment.

An uncovered run can be planted with live trees and shrubs, such as bamboo, boxwood, hawthorn, holly, elderberry, hornbeam, firethorn, Japanese spirea, jasmine, juniper, philodendron, red ribes, snowberry, weeping fig and willow. Landscape the area around the aviary so that it blends in well with your garden as a whole. Choose plants that attract insects as many will fly through the mesh right into the waiting beaks of your birds.

Don't put live plants in an aviary that houses parrots and parakeets as these birds tend to destroy anything they can gnaw at with their destructive beaks. Instead provide some dead fruit trees, willow or other trees with a good supply of branches.

INDOOR HOUSING

It is possible to construct an aviary indoors or to set-up a bird room in an unused room in the house. To protect the birds, there must be wire mesh screens on the windows and you may want to install toughened glass as an extra safety measure.

It is vitally important that indoor housing is properly ventilated. Windows, doors or both, need to be situated so that they can be opened without creating a draught that will disturb and upset the birds.

The principle advantage of indoor housing is that it offers a wealth of options for the breeder. Professionals are known to prefer inside aviaries and rooms over outdoor facilities. Indoor facilities make it easier to check on your birds, unless you build several small outdoor aviaries with a very restricted population. It is also useful to have indoor facilities if you need to bring the birds inside for autumn and winter. Indoor aviaries and bird rooms also appeal to fanciers who don't have a garden or backyard or who don't want to construct housings and vitrines.

Nesting boxes in indoor aviaries should be located against the far wall. Although this will make nest inspection very difficult, the birds will feel more secure. Wooden nest boxes should not be made of any material in which the layers can separate to make space for vermin. Alternatively, you can install commercially produced boxes in your bird room instead of one or more indoor aviaries. These breeding cages (or box cages as they are often called) are primarily used for breeding parakeets, parrotlets, canaries, Gouldian finches and other Australian grass finches, Java sparrows, Bengalese (Society finches), humming birds and similar.

If you intend to breed – and have breeding cages – in a bird room, you obviously need to know which sizes and types of cages you will want to use. A random collection of cages will not do.

To breed song and colour canaries you need a cage at least 18 in. x 14 in. x 16 in. (45 cm x 36 cm x 40 cm). For other canaries, parakeets, Australian grass finches, parrotlets and similar bird species, cages measuring 25 in. x 20 in. x 18 in. (65 cm x 50 cm x 45 cm) will work. For all kinds of tropical birds, we suggest 20 in. x 14 in. x 18 in. (50 cm x 35 cm x 45 cm), although the previous box cage will do nicely. For lovebirds and others of a similar size, cages measuring 33 in. x 23 in. x 20 in. (85 cm x 60 cm x 50 cm) are needed. You can design and make your own box cages as mesh fronts are commercially available in various sizes from petshops.

Home-made breeding cages.

'Creche' cages (top) for independent young and breeding cages (below).

A proper perch will help to deter overgrown nails. (Princess of Wales parakeet.)

Heating element specially designed for bird rooms.

Consider having perches (roosts) custom-made of hardwood in various sizes, although several proper roosts are commercially available to accommodate different bird species. One or two fresh willow and fruit tree branches are welcome. Remember that the toes of perching birds should never be able to close completely around the roost. Also, consider having hand-made nest boxes in several designs. Use hardwood and other quality material whether you make them yourself or have them built.

For insect- and fruit-eating (soft-billed birds) buy bowls and dishes made of hard plastic or glass because they will have to be cleaned more often. Utensils made of steel, hard plastic and similar are useful for psittacines (hookbills). Dishes for drinking, bathing and food should be placed on a low feeding table, about 2 ft. (60 cm) off the ground, and positioned in such a way so that you disturb the birds as little as possible when you see to them.

Indoor housing requires adequate lighting. Although natural daylight is best, fluorescent lighting is a suitable substitute in a garage or basement, for example. The major advantage of fluorescent lights is that they supply the complete spectrum of natural daylight, including health-promoting ultra-violet rays.

You may also want to plan ahead for artificial heating, even though there are few birds that absolutely require it for survival. However, it's always better to be safe than sorry and furnish a little extra heat. An even temperature will help promote successful breeding, also enabling you to start breeding earlier in the season, even in February or March. A constant temperature of 65°F (18°C) is best. Be careful with heaters, however, and remember that oil heaters, electrical heaters and other portable units must be used with great care.

The safest units are heating elements with thermostats. These heaters remove humidity from the air in such a manner that the area doesn't dry out too much. Air that is too dry may interfere with the hatching process. You will definitely need a hygrometer to measure the humidity of the room. If you adhere to the recommended temperature of 65°F (18°C), the relative humidity should be 65 per cent. Keep several large, flat dishes filled with water in the cage, or install a humidifier. If you keep plants in planters or pots, which we recommend, you also will have to spray them with a fogger. Don't worry about wet leaves because birds generally like to slink along wet leaves to wash themselves.

To keep birds active and eating as long as they should, turn the lights on for them around 4 pm, especially on dark days, and keep them on until 9 pm. Then turn them down gradually using a dimmer switch. Always keep a night light on, however, because birds should not be kept in total darkness. They may fly up at night if they get frightened and they could bump into something in the dark, hurting themselves and causing a disturbance among the other birds. The lights should come on gradually at 6 am, so you might find that an automatic timer is useful. They are inexpensive, and save time and trouble. On really dark days however, make sure the lights stay on all day.

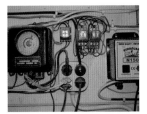

Dimmer switches etc. should always be installed by a licenced electrician.

Commercial (breeding) cages should have proper light, a pull-out drawer, a removable partition and doors on the sides.

CAGES

The basic rule for cages is the bigger, the better. You could build one yourself quite easily, apart from the front section. We like the so-called 'box cages' best among the commercial models. It has a wire mesh front or one made of bars or trellis, and the wall, floor and top are of wood, metal or similar material. Don't use pressed board because it emits poisonous gasses over time, which damages the birds' air passages.

You will be able to hang a brooding box on the sides of most cages. Get nest boxes with removable tops or (better still) sides or front, so you will be able to have a look inside the box if necessary.

Breeding cages for canaries and finches.

There are no strict guidelines for ideal breeding places, so it's often a matter for experiment. Most species have their own preferences, such as the finch nest (middle) and the Australian grassfinch (bottom).

You will need to have several perches for the birds to roost on. Arrange them so the birds won't foul one another with their droppings by setting up a 'three jump' arrangement. Install perches so they can't turn and position them so birds can't hop on, but will have to use their wings to reach them.

Cages with vertical bars are best used for canaries, tropical finches and similar birds. Cages with horizontal trellis are ideal for parrots and parakeets which use the bars to move up and down using their strong beak (often known as their 'third leg').

Glass show cages or vitrines are basically box cages with a glass front and enough mesh on the top and sides for sufficient ventilation. Glass show cages are often very attractive with properly arranged exotic plants and one or two pairs of exotic birds. The cage must be constructed so that the glass plate, which makes up the front, sits at an angle, with the lower edge slanted outward. This prevents the glass from getting caked and spotted from droppings and splashed water. The sides need to be fitted with several small doors for access to feeding dishes and other necessary utensils.

People who like to keep a few colourful, active birds will find cages with glass fronts very convenient housing. It is possible to breed birds in these vitrines, provided the species you select are among those that are known to respond well to breeding in captivity.

Maintenance

A well-furnished aviary will need a variety of bowls, dishes, perches and other utensils. Look at the various types offered in a reputable bird or pet store and ask what each is used for. You will need good food and water bowls for drinking, as well as a flat earthenware dish for bathwater.

Maintenance is essential if you want to keep healthy birds that will breed successfully over a long period. Everything has to be kept clean. Automatic feeders and waterers must be checked daily, since birds cannot survive without food or water for long.

Bowls have to be cleaned at least once a day, and for soft-billed birds they should be cleaned more often. Don't use more bowls and containers than you need as the cage will simply look messy and cluttered. Limit yourself to bowls for water and food plus several racks (commercially available) for green food. You can use several sturdy clothes pegs to hang green food and other extras, like spray millet, at strategic places in the cage or aviary. Cuttlebone is usually sold with a holder, but if not you can always put a strong piece of wire through it and hang it against the side of the cage or in the covered part of the aviary flight next to a perch. In an outside aviary do not hang food where birds might be threatened by their natural enemies while they eat.

Regularly check the condition of all wire mesh. Snip off and replace any rusty areas. Check the woodwork, too. Remember, many tropical birds are quite small and a little hole in the roof or wall often suffices as an exit for the entire aviary population.

Wire should be re-painted with petroleum and then with black or green lead-free paint, as was done on installation. This will ensure the wire mesh will last for years and the birds be more visible.

Schedule an annual housecleaning. This is the time to thoroughly check wire, wood and to repaint. The floor of the aviary should be dug up at least 12 in. (30 cm) deep and turned over. The nest boxes should be thoroughly washed, disinfected and put away for the next breeding season. Sleep boxes (usually some of the present nest boxes) should also be cleaned and disinfected, and once dried, replaced. Don't hang them somewhere else; this will confuse the birds and create stress. The more attention you give to keeping your bird area clean, the more you'll enjoy both the birds and the facilities in which you keep them.

Cages, especially breeding cages, need to be cleaned regularly to deter external parasites. Lice, for example, can cause unsuccessful hatchings. During the breeding season it's difficult to clean a breeding cage but do your best without disturbing the birds.

Note the container drawer which can be pushed inside the cage filled with treats, water and the bird's daily seed or pellet mixture.

You will need a bird net. Get one with a short handle and made of very fine mesh, cloth, or similar material. Catch birds preferably in flight, not when they are hanging against the wire mesh of the aviary. Don't try to catch all the birds in your collection at once. The birds will get exhausted and accidents will occur. You can also catch birds in the night shelter, but be careful. Before you start, take out all nest boxes, bowls and perches. Then guide the birds inside quietly, without yelling or waving. Do the job in the morning, so that the birds have all day to recover. Birds definitely don't like being caught!

CARE OF BIRDS

Novice breeders should not take on too many birds – begin your avicultural career gently. It is best to start out with one or three pairs (never two pairs of the same species).

Avoid housing too many birds in the available space, as overstocking an aviary can cause numerous accidents and illnesses. Birds need to have sufficient space for their natural activities. In the breeding season, for example, a bird must be able to establish its own territory, so give the males a marked-off area in which it alone is the boss and from which it will exclude trespassers.

Most birds must be kept in pairs to maintain control over the heredity of the offspring. If two pairs of the same species are kept together there will be fights and disturbances. Use this rule: either get one pair or three or more, but never two of the same species; hence, one pair or three pairs of Zebra finches, never a duo.

Nandaya conures are less noisy when hand-reared, and become playful and affectionate birds.

Breeders are often warned to give special care to newly acquired birds which have been imported, from Europe, for example, but even locally bred individuals must be given proper attention.

Many bird species have been domesticated, particularly canaries, parakeets (budgerigars), Gouldian finches and Java sparrows. The Bengalese or Society finch, a bird bred in the Orient, is a hybrid variety developed by crossing two species of mannikins, birds which still exist in the wild in Indonesia. (The literature isn't clear about the entire origin of these charming birds, which are bred widely and in many colour varieties.) Many hybrids of these domesticated birds have been developed over the years, such as the many representatives of the dove family notably the turtle dove and diamond dove.

Bird fancying is a dynamic and lively activity, encouraged to an extent by manufacturers of specialist bird food and equipment who have developed a huge variety of excellent foods and snacks, vitamins, minerals and medications now widely available Species that couldn't be kept at all, or only for a short time 30 years ago, can now be bred in captivity with great success. Thanks to specialist equipment, delicate species can be kept at just the right temperature and humidity; many problems associated with soft-billed birds have been solved, and large parrots can be hand-raised quite easily!

Exotic birds that were captured in the wild overseas often arrived in a dreadful condition. Now, most importation has come to a halt and the only birds we still import are domestically bred bird species from Europe. Their trip only takes between several hours to two days, but even so, they are properly cared for and looked after. As soon as they arrive, they are checked by health and customs authorities. They're also examined by an avian veterinarian which helps to prevent the importation of sick birds.

Most transfers take place in spring,so that birds don't have to cope with bad weather soon after arrival. The birds then have an opportunity to become acclimatised during the summer months and breeding can be attempted the following year.

After the quarantine period, the birds will be sold to distributors and dealers. A reputable dealer will provide proper food and allow the birds to recover in spacious cages. After several days the birds should be given lukewarm bath water. They should be kept in a comfortable place at about 65°F (18°C) and disturbed as little as possible. Gradually the temperature can be reduced to the normal outdoor temperature. This is when dealers can start selling their birds to pet shops and fanciers. If you buy a pair of birds at this stage, you still shouldn't put them in an outside aviary right away. Keep them inside awhile and give them special care in a separate

Gouldian finches (the Red-headed form [left] and the Yellow form [right]) require a relatively high mineral intake; cuttlefish bone, rock salt (available from pet shops and supermarkets), iodine blocks and grit should also be available to them at all times.

Make sure that the seed you purchase is not too old. Always buy your seed from a reputable supplier. To test the seed yourself, leave it to germinate. Old seed loses its germination strength and nothing will happen. Fresh seed should germinate in three to four days.

roomy cage – don't place them with other birds yet. Newly purchased birds should obviously get the best possible care including the right food. Almost all birds like to eat insects, and even the so-called seed-eating birds feed their young on small insects (or a substitute, like commercial egg food) almost exclusively during their first days of life. Provide the newly purchased birds with ant pupae, cut-up mealworms, spiders and similar food. Most birds will not be familiar with the insects that will be available for you to feed them, so we have developed a method to get the birds used to the new fare. Cut open an orange and put the insects on the cut surface. (Or you can hollow out the orange and put the insects in the hollow.) The orange juice gets absorbed by the insects, making them taste much more acceptable. Also consider boiling the ant pupae for half a minute.

After the birds have become accustomed to their new environment, get dry or soaked grass seed, millet spray and a high quality brand of enriched (seed mixed with vitamins and minerals) tropical seed mixture, greens and pellets. Don't give your birds any sand or grit until they are completely accustomed to their surroundings and food. And take note of the suggestions elsewhere in this book on how to introduce new birds to the existing collection (see page 26).

To keep birds healthy and lively maintain a properly balanced diet and provide adequate housing. In the autumn, put most species in a light room that is draught-free. In winter, provide a varied diet, and in the breeding season make sure the birds have protein-rich food of animal origin.

Always handle and deal with your birds quietly. Don't loose your patience and especially don't start chasing birds that you aren't able to catch quickly.

If you work in aviaries, put on special work clothes. This will keep your good clothes from getting dirty and helps the birds get used to you. Don't keep on entering the aviary in a new, unfamiliar garment - once in a skirt, then in shorts, with or without a hat or cap, then with (sun-) glasses, then without. Birds stay quieter if you're always dressed the same – they will recognise you!

Don't ever let friends and visitors inside the aviary. Keep them outside the enclosure, preferably several yards (metres) away as lots of visitors may upset the birds. In the breeding season, a time when absolute quiet is of prime importance, enter the aviary as little as possible and as quietly as possible, preferably at set hours, and keep visitors at a respectable distance and quiet!

A special word for fanciers with very limited space. We have seen caged birds kept in living rooms, entry halls and hallways. This can be done successfully if the birds are guarded from draughts. Be sure to cover the bottom of the cages with a solid layer of river sand or bird grit, which is available commercially, once the birds are familiar with their surroundings. Large birds, like toucans and parrots, should have the opportunity to fly loose in the room for a while every day; dangerous obstacles should be removed from the room and stoves and such turned off.

Household dangers

 Bathrooms: watch out for open windows; cleaners and chemicals; open toilet bowls (birds could drown). *Keep bathroom doors closed.*

Cages and aviary mesh with wrong-sized openings: most birds which stick their heads through mesh or between bars, get trapped, suffer injury or strangle to death. *Check mesh size with a pet dealer.*

Water containers (sinks, tubs, aquariums, vases): birds fall in and drown. Birds can mistake foam on the surface as a firm landing-place. *Keep containers empty and/or covered.*

Direct sunlight can cause heatstroke, which is manifested by heavy panting, extended wings, weakness and collapse. *Get the bird into shade at once to prevent heart failure. Give the sick bird some water and see an avian veterinary surgeon immediately.*

Doors: birds can get caught in them and become crushed or may escape. *Close doors before releasing birds.*

 Draughts: open doors and windows, airing the room, etc., can cause colds that produce nasal discharges, runny eyes, sneezing and pneumonia. *Avoid draughts – remove birds when the room is being aired.*

Drawers and cupboards: most birds are very curious and like to explore open drawers and cabinets. If a bird is accidentally shut inside it can starve to death or suffocate. *Keep drawers and cupboards closed.*

 Easy chairs, sofas etc.: birds can be crushed when accidentally sat on. *Get into the habit of checking chairs, cushions etc. before sitting down.*

If you are rearing Chinese Painted quail, you must ensure that drinking water is always available in a very shallow container – remember a chick is not much bigger than a bumblebee and could easily drown in a small amount of water. Feeding and drinking containers should not be placed near the walls of the aviary or cage, because quail tend to run up and down the edges and would keep running through their food and water.

 Electrical wires and sockets: shock or even death from biting through wires (especially parrots and parakeets). *Conceal wires under mouldings, carpets, etc.*

 Hard floors: parrots and parakeets with clipped wings lack full powers of flight. Such birds can break a leg or bruise themselves in a hard landing. *See information on page 21 about clipped wings.*

 Human feet: free birds may be accidentally trodden on. *Look before you walk.*

 Kitchen: never keep your bird in an area that is polluted by gas and cooking fumes. Fumes given off by overheated or burning Teflon pans are toxic to birds. Also dangerous are steam and heat from cooking; open pots containing hot liquids; hot stoves and household cleansers, all of which are potentially poisonous. *Keep birds out of the kitchen.*

 Knitted or crocheted items, wool, string, chains: birds' toes can get entangled and a trapped bird could strangle itself. *Remove jumpers, wool, etc. from the birds' room.*

 Large decorative vases: birds can slip in and become trapped, resulting in suffocation, starvation or heart failure. *Fill these containers with sand or paper.*

 Nicotine, sprays, etc.: smoke-laden air is harmful and nicotine is lethal. Other dangerous air pollutants for birds are paint fumes, carbon monoxide, insecticide sprays, deodorizer sprays and insecticidal pest strips. *Do not smoke, use sprays, etc., near your birds.*

 Perches that are too small in diameter may result in the excessive growth of toenails. *Use hardwood perches of correct diameter.* (See page 47.)

 Pesticides: all pesticides are lethal for birds. *Never spray plants in the room where your bird is kept or bring sprayed plants into that room.*

Poisons: a wide variety of common household items can be deadly: lead, pans coated with plastics, mercury, all household cleaners. Harmful: pencil leads, inserts for ballpoint pens, magic markers, alcohol, coffee, hot spices. Other poisons: acetone, amphetamines, aspirin, antifreeze, arsenic, bleach, carbon tetrachloride, chlordane, cosmetics, crayons, DDT,

deodorants, drain cleaners, fabric softeners, fireworks,
fluoroacetates, garbage toxins, hair dye, linoleum, lye,
matches, ('safety matches' are non-toxic), medicines,
mothballs, various wild mushrooms, lead based paint, perfume,
petrol products, pine oil, rat and mouse poison, red squill,
roach poison, shellac, sleeping pills, snail bait, strychnine,
suntan lotion, thallium, warfarin and weed killers and
wood preservatives. ***Remove all harmful and lethal
substances.***

Sharp objects, nails, splinters, ends of wire: may cause cuts or
puncture wounds. ***Remove all sharp objects.***

Temperature changes: most birds will do well in 50-75°F
(10-24°C). Abrupt changes in temperature can be disastrous
for your birds. ***The heating should be even and reliable.***

Windows, picture windows, glass walls: birds fly into them,
resulting in concussion, fractured skull, broken neck, wings or
feet. ***Lower blinds over windows, or cover with curtains.***

Clipped wings

Many bird fanciers clip the wing feathers of their birds (mainly
parrots, cockatoos, macaws, cockatiels, etc.) to prevent them
from flying around the room. Use a sharp pair of scissors and
clip off all but the two outermost flight and six or seven of
the secondary feathers of each wing as near to the base as
possible. If you are inexperienced consult an avian veterinary
surgeon. The decision for or against wing clipping may
depend on the temperament of the individual bird (especially
in the case of an older one). You or your vet should take
care not to cut the feathers too short as this can cause
bleeding. It does not hurt a bird to have its feathers clipped,
and after the next moult, the clipped feathers will be replaced
by new ones.

Never assume that a bird with clipped wings cannot escape if
a door or window is left open. Lost-and-found ads are filled
with plaintive reminders of this every summer!

Purchasing Birds

Owners of pet birds typically start with a single canary, finch, budgie, mynah bird or a familiar parrot species. Only later do they think about breeding, and then acquire a second bird of the opposite sex in the hope that it will pair with the first bird. Gradually, the hobby expands to a homemade breeding cage or a simple aviary in the garden, and then several breeding pairs.

Informed purchases

The casual approach to buying birds is far from ideal. Before getting into breeding study as many good books on keeping, breeding and caring for birds as possible. Also read several issues of bird magazines to see where you can most easily acquire the birds and supplies in which you are interested. Fortunately, there are a number of magazines that are well worth reading, and they have a wealth of advertisements. And don't forget a visit to (or take out a membership of) your local bird club. Visit a few reputable pet shops to look at and compare different breeds of birds. Talk to the manager and take notes. Find out what the birds you like are eating so that you can offer the same food. (If necessary, you could gradually change to new and better food. See page 32, The feeding and management of companion birds.)

Red-faced lovebirds are shy, and very sensitive to draughts, changes in temperature and sudden noises. They are easily stressed which can cause them to suffer from a cerebral haemorrhage. These species are only for experienced lovebird aviculturists.

Don't buy birds by mail order. Remember that no species of bird responds well to a long journey. Always look over the birds you are buying. And don't ever buy birds during severe cold, because the birds will only get sick from the stress of the change in climate.

Where to buy birds? The answer to this question is a matter of finding a dealer you can trust. Most dealers strive to make their birds as comfortable as possible in their temporary quarters. The cages should be light and airy, disinfected and large enough to keep birds for long or short periods.

As a buyer, you should be aware that dealers have to really work at keeping a collection free of external parasites, given that new stock is constantly being brought in. Similarly, there may be other problems. Observe the birds carefully from a distance. The birds should conduct themselves normally.

How to Choose Healthy Birds

Also, note the condition of the cages, the food and water dishes. They all should make a well-cared for, clean impression.

In addition to shopping at dealers, consider buying from friends, club members and breeders in your areas. Daily newspapers and bird and pet magazines are full of sales advertisements, especially after the breeding season.

When visiting a private seller, look for the same things as in a commercial establishment. Everything should make a well-cared for, neat impression. The birds should look bright and lively.

Examining the birds

With commercial and private sales alike, the seller must be willing to let you exchange a bird if, for example, it doesn't turn out to be of the sex you want. You should get a clear, written guarantee to cover points like this.

Do take a close look at the birds you consider buying. A healthy bird has a tight covering of feathers, in contrast to sick birds, whose feathers are parted and dull. Look for these signs particularly with the feathers on the bird's head. Individual feather quality is not so important. If the feathers do look somewhat ruffled, they'll improve after the next moult if the birds are well housed and well fed. At breeding time, for instance, most birds feathers can look scruffy! However, don't buy birds that pick their own feathers or scratch between the feathers with their toes. Also, leave birds whose vent feathers look wet and dirty.

In budgies, lovebirds, Neophema species, some 40 other psittacines and hookbills less than three years of age, and young ones among the little parrot-like birds, missing tail- and wing-feathers, feathers that look pinched and clubbed and a beak with fractures and mouth ulcers could be symptoms of Psittacine Beak and Feather Disease Syndrome (FBFDS) – a viral disease.

Healthy birds regularly fluff and ruffle their feathers to form air pockets that insulate them against chills or cold temperatures.

Hookbills share with woodpeckers and cockatoos the so-called climbing zygodactyle foot, which has the first and fourth toe pointing forwards and the second and thrid toe backwards.

The Handbook of Cage and Aviary Birds

Macaws, like all other hookbills, need mental stimulation! Provide some toys and play things such as wooden chew blocks, rawhide bones etc., but don't over crowd the cage. An unhappy bird will hop or fly in an agitated fashion from perch to perch, and will usually start feather picking or toe chewing, become aggressive and loud, and often start making repetitive movements with head or body – bowing, side-to-side motions, or movements in the form of the figure eight.

Budgie breeders often speak of French Moult (FM) and have termed these pitiful birds 'crawlers,' 'creepers' or 'runners'. Some birds with FM will recover their missing tail and wing feathers, but others remain bare in those spots. Some cannot even fly. For others, especially larger hookbills, like cockatoos, macaws, African Grays, conures and rosellas, this disease is a calamitous event, as they are expensive species. The disease is highly contagious and fatal. Contact an avian vet immediately, and separate the sick birds. There is no cure.

If you plan to exhibit your birds, check they do not have missing toes or a deformed beak. Beaks and legs should be free of injury. Dirt shouldn't stick to the body.

Take a careful look at the bird's breastbone, which should not stick out sharply to the front. The eyes should be clear and the birds should not be rubbing themselves against the roost. Watch out for colds, which claim quite a few victims, especially among recently imported birds (from Africa, for example) that have not yet been acclimatised, or received veterinary clearance. To detect possible internal parasites, it is advisable to have the droppings of newly acquired birds examined at a veterinary laboratory.

Hold the bird you are interested in close to your ear (but not too close when you hold a parrot) and listen to its breathing. A squeaking, grating or gasping noise could mean it has a respiratory infection and should not be purchased. There may be a nasal discharge or even vomiting or regurgitating. The latter is the process by which the bird voluntarily brings food (seeds and other eaten materials) and some mucus up from the crop in order to feed another bird, or to welcome its owner; vomiting is an involuntary process in which the bird brings up mucus and a little food.

Blow gently on the breast feathers so that they part and you can see the skin which should be clean and healthy, not red and spotty.

Watch the way the bird sleeps. Very young ones sleep with both feet on the perch, with their head tucked under one of the wings. An adult bird that sleeps this way certainly isn't doing well. Healthy adults sleep with their beaks stuck between their feathers and one leg pulled up to protect it against cold and to conserve energy. Small exotic finches even hunch down, so that the one leg on which they are resting is partially protected by the stomach feathers against the night temperatures. Even in the tropics, the temperatures can differ markedly between night and day.

BRINGING HOME NEW BIRDS

Buy small birds in the morning so that you will have them home by noon. This way they can spend the rest of the day eating, drinking and getting used to their new surroundings. Larger birds, such as parrots and pheasants, can be brought home later in the day. If you transport birds by train or car, wrap the transport cage completely in heavy package wrapping paper. Leave the front partially uncovered, however, to let in air and light.

Get newly purchased birds home as quickly as possible. Small tropical birds cannot do without food and water for very long. Don't put water in the water dish – it will soon spill out. Instead, put a piece of soaked wheat bread in a dish to help the birds slake their thirst. Give them a small dish of seed or put extra seed and moist bread on the bottom of the transport cage – most birds instinctively look for feed on the ground.

You can always keep seed-eating birds happy with a stalk of millet spray. Hang some spray millet up for the birds when you get home, too.

If you have to bring birds home in the winter – which we don't recommend – avoid placing them in a warm room right away. It could literally kill them. The air in their lungs, air sacs and hollow bones expands upon being heated, and this exerts great stress on the body, causing a very painful death. Instead, get the new arrivals used to a higher temperature gradually.

Treat new arrivals very gently whatever the season. Birds understandably get shy and scared when they are shaken about in transport cages, so give them absolute rest after you get them home. Leave them alone in their transport cages for a few hours to give them the opportunity to recover.

25

The best advice can be summarised in a dozen words. Never buy inferior birds; buy the best and healthiest birds you can afford!

Always buy a bird with a legitimate leg band (ring) as this band indicates that the breeder is registered with a bird society or federation.

Do give them water (at room temperature) and food during this time. It is important that the water is at room temperature because the temperature in the transport cage can go up considerably, wrapped as it is in packing paper. Cold water, therefore, could easily bring about illnesses or intestinal problems. Give spring water rather than water from your tap.

Don't put the new arrivals with your existing collection right away. The new birds may be incubating some disease so a quarantine of about 30 days is absolutely necessary. Furthermore, new birds can thoroughly upset the existing pecking order in the aviary. Put the new arrivals in a wire cage for a few days when you first put them in the aviary. This way the new birds and the existing population can safely get used to each other.

After the new arrivals have started to mix with the birds already in your aviary, watch them carefully for a while. Be fully aware of their activities. Who is the hell-raiser? Who gets picked on? Who needs extra food, more nesting material or another partner? Don't leave anything to chance and act immediately if anything untoward happens.

Remember, not all birds get along together. Males can upset the whole aviary once they are no longer needed during brooding. Nor is every species suited for a communal aviary, especially if it is represented by only two breeding pairs. Zebra finches and various small parrots, for example, always live embattled lives if two couples are housed together in the same aviary. It is different if there are three or more pairs.

Caring for more than one bird is a hobby that requires time, dedication and money, so don't over-invest. Buy relatively inexpensive birds to start with and gain experience with them. Then, if you really get hooked, you can buy more expensive, and challenging birds.

Acclimatising birds

Acclimatising birds is a highly important requirement. The term means getting used to a strange climate or, by extension, getting used to a completely new environment. This applies especially to tropical and subtropical birds that are moved to a temperate climate. It is not just the change in temperature that causes problems, it is also the stress birds encounter after being caught – an event which in itself is quite traumatic.

Fortunately, the importation of most birds has come to a complete stop. Most countries are slowly improving their wildlife resource management, strengthening the provisions of existing wildlife laws, and enforcing regulations to protect endangered species.

The overall result of these changes is that the importation of many plants and animals, including birds-of-all-feathers, is being reduced. Most birds coming into our country are imported, captive-bred species. Nevertheless, in the wild, habitat destruction is still reducing the homes of many bird species and in some cases the species' only chance of survival is through captive breeding.

In the past, the birds had to undergo all kinds of deprivation – at least in most cases. From the catchers, birds went to buyers, wholesale exporters and importers, and finally to the retail store and the eventual buyer. Just think about the process! The many times the birds were moved to a new cage? The times they were exposed to extreme temperatures? How they were fed unsuitable foods, kept in inappropriate housing and possibly experienced pain and discomfort. All these changes were extremely stressful, despite the fact that most birds reached their destination reasonably quickly once transportation by air became the norm.

In those days responsible importers made the difference and today, those in charge do an excellent job. They will start the birds gradually on foods that would be acceptable to the retailer and the bird fancier. Food is not a crucial factor with seed-eating birds and most psittacines, but soft-billed birds (fruit- and insect-eating bird species), lories and lorikeets, toucans etc. do face a real challenge in adapting to a new diet, particularly if they aren't fed the same insect and/or fruit to which they have been accustomed in the wild or in breeding facilities. The key to whether such birds have been properly acclimatised or not is whether they eat regularly.

Tubular heaters are safe for a birdroom or aviary shelter.

The Yellow-streaked lory feeds largely on nectar and pollen gathered from flowers, and its tongue is tipped with brush-like protrusions (papillae) that gather the food efficiently.

What a bird eats is actually not all that important – there are many alternatives (pellets, egg food, rearing foods and so on). The important factor is that the food should be properly digestible. Honey has become a standard transition food, as has egg food. Honey stimulates the digestion and even egg feed, for example, has honey in its mix. There are few cage and aviary birds, if any, that will refuse honey.

Stimulating the digestion is important because the bird's digestion can suffer as a result of transportation. Birds need constant access to food and drinking water because they have to maintain a high body temperature and rapid respiration.

If a bird's food intake is disturbed in transit for any reason, the bird's behaviour changes immediately. It becomes nervous, moves anxiously through its cage and pecks at other birds constantly. As the condition worsens, it raises up its feathers, sticks its head under its wings and goes to sleep in a corner.

Reputable importers and retailers constantly work at keeping their birds interested in food. They are careful to provide a diet similar to the one the birds ate before they were put on transport. The familiar food can be changed to a more easily available food by mixing the two and gradually changing proportions. Variety should be maintained in the menu, including a rich assortment of seeds, fruits and insects.

Importers and other bird dealers must also regulate the temperature carefully. It can be difficult, but the good ones do it – if only to keep their losses at a minimum. Indeed, they have reduced their losses considerably, although there is always room for improvement!

Both retailers and fanciers must pay attention to temperature requirements. Birds should be housed at a temperature between 72 and 80°F (22-27°C), in as large a space as possible. This prevents the loss of body heat in the birds, which is desirable, if not essential, for proper acclimatisation.

Green-naped lory.

Birds that won't eat voluntarily despite your best efforts must be force-fed by hand. That is obviously much easier to do with large birds than with small exotics. Be sure to wear gloves if you hand-feed large birds, especially psittacines.

For newly arrived insect- and fruit-eating birds cover the bottom of the cage with heavy wrapping paper with the dull side up, or use newspaper. For seed-eaters, the cage bottom should be covered with a thick layer of coarse sand.

At the start, offer food and water in open dishes, because the birds may not be used to different types of feeders, cups, automatic waterers, etc. Drinking water should be at room temperature. Do not supply bath water in the first week after arrival, and then give bath water in flat dishes at room temperature.

In an aviary or cage, Chinese Painted quail (here two males), will pick at greens and will eat the seed dropped on the ground by other birds. If you give them a daily helping of a good seed mix (such as that for finches), universal food and a few small meal worms, the birds should do well. If you keep quail in an outdoor cage, you should provide one or two grass sods which can be frequently changed, so the birds have something to peck at. In the grassy outdoor aviary, quail should be provided with a fine, clean, dry sand so that they can take a sand bath whenever they wish.

Place cages in a sunny, bright location that is protected from draughts and keep the birds' surroundings peaceful and quiet.

Watch new arrivals closely for the first three to four weeks. Try to introduce them to the main aviary on a warm day at a time when you can be fairly sure that good weather will last for a while. Place the new birds' cage inside the aviary so that the established residents can get to know them without actually being able to harm them. The new birds will get a lot of attention from the established aviary residents during the first few days. During the evening and night, the new birds in their cage, should be taken out of the aviary and back indoors.

After four days, you can open the cages and let the new arrivals join the others. Spread some food on the floor for the new birds, until they have learned to use the aviary seed dishes and hoppers. At first, the new birds will still look for food on the ground.

Moluccan cockatoo.

You may want to release new birds in the sleeping shelter if your aviary has one. The birds might prefer to spend their first days there, especially if you spread their food on the floor. This is less essential if you release birds on a warm day.

It is important, however, to release birds early in the morning, so that they have all day to explore their new surroundings and find enough possibilities for escaping, hiding and sleeping. Plants should be available for this purpose. Many species need special plants in order to begin breeding in their new quarters.

It is best to put birds in the aviary in the spring, given the milder temperatures and longer days. When autumn approaches, move all (or nearly all) tropical and subtropical birds to a frost-free, if not heated, room; preferably a light room with spacious cages in which to spend the winter. Perhaps, you can use breeding cages for this purpose. Be sure to separate the sexes, especially zebra finches, canaries, budgies, Forpus species and similar. Provide artificial lighting (see page 13), so that it will be light at least 13 to 14 hours per day – for example from 8 am to 9 pm.

Provide cod liver oil for seed-eating birds, preferably by mixing five drops into about 2 lbs. (1 kilo) of seed. Also, regularly provide old wheat bread soaked in water (see chapter on feeding, page 32).

An outside aviary is best for birds born and raised in captivity, or those which are thoroughly acclimatised. Absolutely all tropical and subtropical birds should be placed in lightly heated, large enclosures, at about 60°F (15°C). Outside aviaries can be considered only if the birds have access to an absolutely frost-free night shelter, where they can escape from draughts, rain and cool night temperatures. During the day, birds could be released into an outside run, provided the weather is good. Late in the afternoon, they should be shooed back into the night shelter.

Purple glossy starling.

THE FEEDING AND MANAGEMENT OF COMPANION BIRDS

Commercial bird seed can be excellent and some brands have a well-deserved reputation for quality. These seeds are tested in experiment stations – sometimes with hundreds of companion birds – and are chemically analysed and the results printed on the label.

Tropical bird seed mixes are important and can be fed with confidence, especially if the birds are also fed greens, fruits, vitamins and minerals and daily fresh water. There are also excellent pellets that supply all the nutrients a bird needs.

Parakeet seed mix.

Pellets

Green food, such as this chichory, is an essential food item.

Canary seed mix

Experimental analysis has shown that old seeds loose much of their nutritional value. It's a good idea to have fresh seeds on hand and never to buy more than a years supply. It's better to buy fresh seed directly from the mill on a monthly basis.

To see if a new batch of seed is fresh, let it sprout. To do this, put a few (about 20 seeds) on a flat plate and add some lukewarm water. Let the mixture stand, renewing the water daily. In four to five days (not longer) the seeds should have sprouted. If this doesn't happen, change food dealers.

Small (finch/canary) pellets. Some pellets are coloured; they will affect the colour and consistency of the bird's droppings.

Sprouted seeds.

At the beginning of the breeding season start to offer egg food in small quantities so the birds grow accustomed to it. If you do not do this there is a chance that this essential supplement will be withheld from the young. Egg foods are available from good pet shops in various brands.

The following notes are for those who would prefer to prepare their own seed mixtures rather than buy commercial preparations.

CANARIES

Canaries, especially those kept in aviaries, need a wide variety of seeds. This is understandable since they are free to fly around all day in the (garden) aviary and breathe fresh air. Outdoor living creates an appetite.

Most cage birds are kept for their musical ability as singers and not for breeding purposes. However the aviary canary does get used for breeding which also influences its dietary requirements. The menu should therefore consist of canary grass seed (white seed), rape seed (nutsweet summer seed), Hamburg rape seed, niger seed, groats (from oats), hemp (if available), mawseed (poppy seed), lettuce seed, linseed and plaintain seed. The proportions required of these seeds are: 35: 30: 10: 8: 8: 2: 2: 2: 1: 2. This basic seed menu applies to both the aviary canary and the canary in a breeding cage.

Canaries in small cages should preferably receive canary grass seed, rape seed and Hamburg rape seed in the ratio of 5: 70: 25.

In addition, supply a few treats (see page 37) which are packaged as a special seed/fruit/veggie mixtures. You can also make it up yourself by just reading the labels. Another treat mix consists of canary grass seed, hulled oats, white lettuce seed, niger seed and mawseed in a ratio of 50: 25: 5: 15: 2

To reach a full 100 per cent, add three parts of a special mixture of hemp, plaintain seed and linseed. Singing canaries love this special mix and you can actually hear the difference in their singing.

If singing canaries, such as Harz and waterslager and American Singer, sing too quietly, increase the percentage of the treat mix, but temporarily take away rearing and conditioning foods (such as CeDe) and wheat bread soaked in water. Also, provide green food such as lettuce, cabbage, chickweed (very important!), Brussels sprouts and finely chopped spinach and carrots. Give them cuttlefish bone, ant pupae and an assortment of fruit.

TROPICAL AND SUB-TROPICAL SEED EATERS

These are the small exotic birds, such as Zebra finches, Bengalese (Society finches), Red avadats, Nuns (mannikins), etc. Limit them to a mix of Senegal millet, La Plata panicum millet, canary grass seed and niger seed in a ratio of 80: 5: 10: 5. We prefer to feed each type of seed separately for all tropical and sub-tropical seed-eating birds. For bigger species, consider La Plata panicum millet staple food. Provide some canary grass and Senegal millet as well, in a ratio of 60: 25: 15.

Tropical seed-eating birds need more than just millet for a balanced diet, so give some of the variations suggested above to maintain the birds' health. Be sure to furnish the birds regularly with some spray millet and a fresh supply of green food daily. If possible, also provide some insects at least twice a week. Then, give them some old wheat bread soaked in water, especially during the breeding season.

Other excellent food is mosquito larvae, water fleas, tubifex, small cut-up mealworms, ant pupae (sometimes erroneously called ant eggs), and fruits, especially juicy ones. You can also supply universal, egg or rearing food and some commercial hand-feeding formulas during the breeding season.

Grey or Normal Zebra finch.

INSECT EATERS

It is difficult to give a definitive menu for insect-eating (or soft-billed) birds which require a lot of individual attention. The care of these birds really should be left to thoroughly experienced aviculturists. If you are an expert, a separate section in your bird room or special aviaries is necessary.

The Plush-crested jay is omnivorous.

Many species have all but solid droppings, which require special attention for the floor of aviaries and cages. Ordinarily, this means putting down a new floor covering like heavy wrapping paper covered with pine shavings or similar bedding. In aviaries, this means digging up the ground thoroughly at least twice a week.

A number of food products for these birds is available commercially, but they have to be supplemented with insects, small or cut-up mealworms, enchytrae (especially during the breeding season), ant pupae, grasshoppers, flies, spiders, beetles or earthworms etc.

Fire-tufted barbet.

Toco toucan.

Jardine's parrot.

Plum-headed parakeet.

Avoid using any insects from ground where artificial fertiliser has been spread. Meat or fish grubs that have been washed carefully can also be offered, but make sure they are free of spoiled bits of meat. In addition to insects, the birds should consume a wide variety of fruits, especially juicy ones. Sprouted seeds are also good for many species!

FRUIT EATERS

The cages of fruit eaters (also known as soft-billed birds) need maintenance similar to those of insect eaters. They can be fed all kinds of fruits – pears, apples, grapes, soaked raisins and currants, cut-up bananas and grapefruit are all accepted. Provide an orange every day, cut into cross-sections. Impale the fruits on nails driven through a small board and hang it in the cage or aviary. Remove any big pips first.

The birds should also be given a top quality universal food. Some species like to eat sprouted seeds, like millets and canary grass seed. Fruit eaters will also enjoy apple sauce laced with sugar and universal food. In autumn, consider feeding your birds cherries and elderberries. Branches of these can be put into the cage or aviary and renewed periodically.

Birds that have been recently imported (captive-raised from Europe) should be given an orange cut into quarters covered with universal food, so the new arrivals can become acquainted with unfamiliar food. They get accustomed to it quickly, which is convenient if the bird keeper occasionally runs low on fresh fruits.

Always cut large fruits into two or more parts. Put these on separate feeding boards so that all of the birds in the aviary will have access to a full selection of the fruit. This prevents unnecessary fights for favourite foods.

PARAKEETS

These hook bills are not nearly as finicky in their diet as is generally believed. Still, adequate attention to their menu is imperative to maintain truly healthy birds.

Smaller species, like parakeets (or budgerigars, budgies) and lovebirds, can be given a mix of canary grass seed, white millet, La Plata panicum millet, German millet, hemp and hulled (but not broken) oats, in a ratio of 25: 20: 30: 10: 5: 10.

The same mixture can be given to cockatiels and larger parakeets like ring-necks, blue-wings and golden-mantled rosellas. Add a mix of small (black) sunflowers and peeled oats. Furnish the required seeds separately rather than in a mix for these birds. Extra grass seeds and oats are recommended, especially for the larger species.

In addition, supply rearing and conditioning feed, unroasted peanuts and fruits, like apples, pears, raisins, cherries and bananas. Also provide insects like ant pupae, enchytrae and cut-up mealworms.

The Quaker loves soaked and sprouted sunflower seed, fresh and boiled corn and fresh fruits and vegetables.

Larger species of parakeets should get eight to ten mealworms per day, but no more. Smaller birds should get one or two. In breeding periods, cut up large and small mealworms (so that they can be fed to the young) and 'cook' them by holding them in boiling water for a few minutes. An old nylon stocking is very handy for this purpose.

In addition, give green food like lettuce and sprouted seeds and don't forget to supply grit, cuttlebone and mineral blocks.

Larger parakeets and most parrots must be fed from an open bin, which can be a problem because these birds spill a lot of feed. To minimise waste, don't fill feed cups and bins to the rim but only about halfway. The bin itself should be placed in a large, flat earthenware dish so that spilled seeds can be recovered. Clean out dirt and hulls from the spilled seed, and you can put it back into the feed bin.

Put rearing food in porcelain dishes or those made of glazed earthenware (like small food dishes for baby chicks). Supply a relatively small amount of rearing food only because it tends to spoil quickly. If you house your birds in a garden aviary, place the containers in a covered area of the aviary for the same reason.

PARROTS

Be sure that parrots eat a varied diet. If left alone parrots will eat only sunflower seeds and leave their other food untouched. Sunflower seeds lack lysine, an amino acid essential for feather growth, but because they taste sweet, hookbills love them. If this is all they eat, you will soon notice heavy feather loss, especially on wings, tail, breast and lower body. By the time these symptoms occur, it will take considerable effort to bring the birds back to a normal condition.

Rupple's parrot.

The Red-bellied parrot likes cooked beans and pulses, boiled corn and various fresh fruits and vegetables.

Brown-headed parrot.

Even worse, it will be hard to break the birds' habit of consuming only sunflower seeds. You need to be firm and ensure the parrots eat the other food as well.

Give them La Plata panicum millet, canary grass seed, unpeeled or un-hulled oats and hemp in a ratio of 44: 15: 35: 5

Also give them a variety of nuts (pine nuts, peanuts [unsalted], almonds [unsalted], walnuts [unsalted], pecans [unsalted]), 'people food' but not table scraps [they love pasta], legumes [beans, lentils, etc.]), well-done meat, poultry and fish, potatoes, cooked vegetables, rice and a rich variety of fruits. Avoid processed or smoked meat (high in salt), and offer only small amounts of cheese. Mouldy peanuts are a great threat to the health of any parrot or parakeet if they are contaminated by *Aspergillus flavus* as they contain the deadly fungal poison aflatoxin, which has severe effects on liver function and can be fatal.

Never feed parrots any (human) cake or other sweets. Zoos and bird parks have explicit signs warning visitors not to feed sweets to birds and for good reason. Such foods can make them sick.

BIRD TREATS AND SNACKS

There are almost more treats, bird cakes, bird sticks, nuggets and other snacks available than pet bird species! Some are excellent, others are worthless, regardless of all the promising words and the beautiful packaging.

In the bird trade there are all manners of treats and snacks with which the pet bird can be 'spoiled' – mixtures and tidbits containing all kinds of vitamins, minerals, wheat germ, fancy seeds (often coated with various coloured vegetable dyes, which are therefore harmless); pink and blue oats, safflower and unshelled peanuts, for example. In order to understand the products' labels properly, you may as well study enzymes, amino acids, trace elements and the differences between phosphoric and carbonated calcium full-time!

The pet bird fancier who fusses with all these tonics and pick-me-ups does not necessarily have or breed better birds than the owner who just makes sure that his birds get a balanced diet. Pet and companion birds do much better on a healthy diet consisting of pellets, fresh seed mixtures, greens, fruits and fresh water.

By all means indulge your birds' preferences and feed occasional snacks or treats such as honey sticks and nuggets. Many tropical and subtropical finches enjoy niger seed, for example, which is rich in minerals. However, it is also high in fat and should be offered only in small quantities as excessive consumption can cause liver problems. Buy finch seed mixtures for daily use and make sure it does not contain too much niger seed; the same applies to snacks and treats (such as sticks, bells and nuggets). Fortunately, most commercial treats and snacks no longer have large quantities of niger seed. Parrots of all sizes like nuts and fruits – so the products with nuts and dehydrated fruits are excellent treats once or twice a week. Too much of these goodies will result in obese birds.

Germinated and sprouted seeds

In addition to dry food and treats, most pet and companion birds need (and like) germinated and sprouted seeds – and during the winter these are a substitute for green food (although there are dehydrated greens in sticks and bells). Sticks, bells and nuggets with the proper seed mix can also be considered an excellent means of preventing boredom and stress. Germinated and sprouted seeds contain valuable nutrients, including vitamin E, which is particularly important during the mating season.

You can make an excellent mixture of seeds and beans (use the latter for larger parakeets and parrots) for germination. Germinated and sprouted seeds should be given only in small quantities, three times a week, as a supplement to the main diet, so they are a treat of sorts.

It can be mixed with soft and/or rearing food which many pet bird fanciers and breeders still regard as snacks as well, which obviously is not true. These foods are absolutely necessary during the mating, breeding and rearing periods and in many cases, throughout the year.

There are various ways to produce sprouts, but a fresh batch must be started every day. Here are two tested methods for sprouting seeds:

1. Mix two parts small-grained millet and one part canary grass seed ('white seed') in a large pot. Add water to soak so the seeds will swell. To speed up the process, place the pot on a radiator or in a warm room (or outside in the sun). Place the seeds in a sieve and rinse thoroughly under running water two or three times a day. Return them to the pot with fresh water.

Like most rosellas, the Pennant needs seeding grasses on a daily basis.

Take the following seeds and beans in similar amounts:

- Rape seed
- Radish seed
- Lettuce seed
- Mung beans (use only when feeding large parakeets and parrots)
- White milo seed
- Red milo seed

When all these seeds are fresh, germination should take place at the same time when they are mixed together.

Gouldians, here a yellow-headed yellow white-breasted hybrid, not only love millet spray but also the seeeding heads, the flowers and the keaves of the highly nutritious chickweed (*Stellaria media*).

After 24 hours, the seeds are ready for use. Dry them lightly with a clean towel, then mix in a few drops of a vitamin/mineral preparation (various excellent brands are commercially available). A few drops of cod liver oil will do also. This helps the sprouts remain moist longer, adds to their nutritional value and supplies vitamin D.

2. Mix two-thirds small-grained millet, a little large-grained millet and no more than one-fourth canary grass seed in a pot. Add water to soak so the seeds can swell and leave them for 12 hours. Place the seeds in a sieve and rinse thoroughly under running water. Return them to the pot, cover it and let it sit for another 24 hours. The seeds may then be fed to the birds.

The choice of seeds to be sprouted depends, of course, on the tastes of the bird species. For example, exotic finches from Africa like small-grained millet and canary grass seed, while those from Australia (Zebra finch, Gouldian finch, etc.) also enjoy soaked large-grained millet, and so do the majority of budgerigars (parakeets), and other psittacines (cockatiels, conures etc.,).

Millet spray

Millet spray is not only the best treat, but all bird species love it even when they are feeling under the weather! Millet spray can be offered straight from the package (it is also available commercially) or can be sprouted as described above, but it is extremely important to change the water frequently so the ores of the spikes and the ears will not rot.

Discard the water after 24 hours and set the spikes upright in a sturdy glass container (an old jar) with wet sand or fresh water. Let the container stand on a radiator for another day until the sprouts become visible. The sprouts may then be fed to the birds.

Greens

Finches, parakeets, doves and quail should all receive an abundance of fresh green food. This includes chickweed, collard, leaf and bib lettuce, endive, spinach, cabbage, pieces of carrot and carrot tops, celery leaves, chicory, broccoli, dandelion (the whole plant, even the roots), watercress and other green foods.

Most commercial seed mixtures contain dehydrated greens and although dried greens are not as nutritious as fresh greens, they are better than nothing. So, sticks and bells with greens are good substitutes and so are the 'Veggie and Fruit' canned treats which are nitrogen-flushed. Available in cans and polybags (both usually nitrogen-flushed as well), pumpkin seeds, pine nuts, red chilli peppers, miniature ears of colourful Indian corn and carrot tips and slices will do nicely – but present your birds with fresh greens as well.

Fruits

Most pet birds love to nibble on pieces of apple, pears, tomatoes, oranges, melons, pineapple, guavas, bananas, cherries (without the stones), grapes, grapefruit, berries, raisins (which one can find in various sticks, bells, canned treats, etc.) and currants (it is advisable to soak these for 24 hours in water for a real treat). Big, fresh pieces of fruit should be provided on feeding spikes, such as nails hammered into a board, so they will stay clean.

A hen Chinese painted quail shows her chick the art of feeding by picking up and dropping seed and other tidbits.

Fresh greens and fruits can also be provided in wire baskets and are sold commercially for this purpose. Dried fruit and greens, purchased from your petshop should be given to your birds in separate cups, which should be washed thoroughly after 24 hours. The remaining fruit should be discarded to prevent spoilage.

Treats of animal origin

You should not buy a bag of seed that crawls away from the pet shop's counter carried by the moth and worms visible in the seed mixture! Although most birds would not object to an occasional insect, since most seed manufacturers nitrogen-flush their seed mixtures, it is extremely unlikely that any seed mixture will be crawling with insects.

However, practically all pet birds like to eat food of animal origin – insects such as termites, ant pupae ('ant eggs'), small spiders and similar, as well as man-made substitutes such as the above mentioned universal food, egg food, rearing food, and so on.

The amount of animal protein needed on a daily basis, or when young are being raised, varies considerably among different species.

Eggs are the cheapest source of animal protein (that is the reason that most of the rearing foods from Europe are egg-based). Dried mealworms, the larval form of the darkling beetle, are another source of animal protein, as are moths, fly larvae and enchytrea (white worms), with occasional substitutions of tubifex, red mosquito larvae and water fleas (daphnia) for variety. You may enrich the named universal and egg foods with finely diced boiled egg and small insects.

Weeds

Although wild birds instinctively will not eat poisonous plants, this is not necessarily true of birds that have been domesticated for centuries. The assumption that cockatiels, Amazon parrots, Australian grass parakeets, lovebirds, tropical finches and others will avoid all poisonous weeds is still in question. Therefore, play safe and only make available those plants that can be identified. A simple guidebook with clear illustrations, such as *Weeds, A Golden Guide* from St Martin's Press, New York, is an ideal reference book and there are many other titles available.

Chinese Painter quail like to search for small insects in high grass and weeds. Always keep these quail in trios: two hens and one cock, otherwise a single hen is likely to be persecuted, and will be plucked (especially around the neck) by her intended mate.

Safe weeds include mugwort, chicory, yarrow, goldenrods, wild mustard, chickweed, stitchwort and Kentucky blue grass, hedge nettle, Canada thistle, rabbit's foot grass, snowball, false flax, knapweed, common groundsel, dock or sorrel, spear grass and plaintain.

There are several varieties of common chickweed. It is the ideal green food for practically all birds, young and old. Many of these weeds are also suitable as 'greens', or for their seeds.

Plaintains have basal rosettes of large leaves and small, greenish flowers in spikes. Broadleaf plaintain is used a great deal, and blooms from May into the autumn. It is very common, and grows to a height of 18 in. (45 cm).

Other varieties of the *Plantaginaeceae* family (plaintains) include the buckhorn variety with a thick root, pointy leaves and many runners. It is very common and blooms from April to late autumn growing to a height of 18 in. (45 cm). *Plantago media* has leaves attached to short stems with a dense covering of hair. It is common along rivers but can also be found along road sides. *Plantago coronopus* has leaves arranged in a basal rosette, and is particularly common along the seashore, blooming from May to October.

Feeding weeds and grass seeds are vital to achieve successful breeding results. Remember, however, when collecting your own, that towns and many farmers spray insecticides that are extremely dangerous to birds. When looking for weeds, make sure you can see insects flying about. If the area is too quiet, find a different location for your weed source.

Most of you will probably have no shortage of weeds in your own garden or window boxes. However, most garden centres will supply addresses where you can obtain weed seeds that, after they have bloomed, can be stored in a dry, cool place and given to the birds in small amounts.

Bread

We recommend giving birds, especially finches, canaries and parakeets, a slice of old wheat bread soaked in water, especially during the breeding season. Do not give the birds more than they will eat in a day – and not every day – three times a week is the maximum. Outside the breeding season, reduce the bread ration to once or twice a week.

Cod liver oil

Birds do need vitamins and minerals. One of the easiest but rather old-fashioned methods of supplying them is to add cod liver oil to the feed – there are still well-established bird food manufacturers that make it.

Add about five drops per 2 lbs. (0.9 kg) of seed and mix well. Let the seed mixture stand for a day before feeding it to the birds (keep this mix in a dark, cool room). Be careful not to give the birds too much. It is essential food during the breeding season but giving too much is harmful. The same is true of other commercial bird vitamins and vitamin/mineral preparations. If you feed the right diet, you may not have to add vitamins and minerals at all. If you do use them, store them in a dark, cool place to preserve their potency and avoid spoilage.

Cuttlefish bone and grit

The shell or exoskeleton of the cuttlefish, technically known as cuttlebone, which is shed periodically, is the recommended source of calcium for captive birds. It is quite important for all birds, especially young ones and females. Make sure cuttlebone is available in the breeding season and at moulting time.

It is simple to feed and is available, usually with a hanger, in every good bird and petshop. Hang it in the covered part of the aviary or under a special little roof so it stays dry.

You can use cuttlebone that you find on the beach but if you do, soak it for several days to reduce the salt content.

Grit and gravel help grind food in birds' stomachs making it easier to digest, and grit also is a good supply of calcium. The gravel is not digested, but passes through the body once it has worn too smooth to continue its job.

Many avian veterinary surgeons and aviculturists tend to disagree on the necessity of a daily supply of grit and/or gravel. Even seed-eating birds such as psittacines, canaries and quail, for example, seem to need the small amount of gravel and grit they pick up from the soil so that their alimentary systems work efficiently in the digestion of seeds and other foods. Seed-eating birds have a crop in which the seed is softened before it goes into the gizzard or muscular stomach – the gizzard is an enlargement of the alimentary canal with dense, muscular walls. Without gravel or grit (which is often ground-up white oyster shell – grey or dark shells are believed to contain too much lead) a great deal of seed remains unground and whole seeds are passed out in the droppings.

Experiments have shown that birds that have no access to grit eat greater quantities of food than those that have a supply of grit. Also, the health of birds that do not eat grit is not as robust as those that do. In birds that don't eat grit the undigested seeds cause blockages in the intestines resulting in a whitish, watery discharge.

In various commercial grit brands chalk, gravel and calcareous seaweed (or kelp) are mixed, as well as a little charcoal. In the wild some birds take little bits of charcoal before going to nest but the necessity of a daily supply of charcoal is questionable as it may absorb vitamins A, B2 and K from the intestinal tract. If this is correct, charcoal may actually cause vitamin-deficiency disease. Grit also frequently contains crushed quartz, a hard, insoluble substance with sharp edges that grinds seed in the gizzard.

Never use grit as the sole source of certain essential minerals, such as calcium, iron, magnesium and iodine. Give your birds a variety of food to ensure that sufficient quantities of minerals are available. An overdose of mineralised grit can cause kidney damage. Most aviculturists supply a separate dish with grit once every other day for approximately one hour.

Grit is available in various grades: fine or small for finches, canaries, parakeets (budgerigars), parrotlets and other dwarf parrots; medium size to coarse for large parrots and ornamental fowl.

Water

Birds need water for drinking and bathing. Provide rain water for both purposes if your water supply is high in calcium or other minerals. If air pollution in you area is high, bottled spring water is preferable.

Parakeets and parrots drink and bathe little. Instead of bathing, they prefer to roll around in wet grass or let themselves be wet by rain. They also like to get a spray shower from the garden hose. Do this regularly every week – weather permitting. Use very low pressure!

All other birds like to bathe, much like people. Make sure there are enough bathing dishes so all birds have good access. Drinking and bath water must be changed at least once daily, and more often on warm days.

Remove bathing dishes as soon as you expect frost. Don't allow wet feathers to freeze because this means almost certain death. If your drinking dishes are big enough for bathing install some wire or mesh over them to keep the birds out.

The best waterer is a commercially made, rather expensive rock with a trough for the water to flow through. It is good because birds can't get into it, nor can dust or dirt. Regular fountains and automatic waterers can be fouled, but generally less than open dishes.

Honey water is an excellent tonic for exotic birds. Prepare it by dissolving a tablespoonful of honey in warm water and adding this to about 1-2 quarts (500 ml-1,000 ml) of drinking water. During the breeding season add a tablespoon of evaporated milk to the drinking water.

For bathing, use one or more shallow earthenware dishes. Place them on a flagstone or tile away from roosting or sleeping areas so that the water will be contaminated as little as possible by droppings, sand and dirt.

Sand bath

Birds like to take a sand bath. These help to prevent lice and are good for rubbing off new feather sheaths at moulting time. Install fine sand in a dry, clean spot in the aviary or put dry, fine sand in shallow earthenware dishes.

EATING DISORDERS

Constant overeating can occur when birds are given too much sunflower seed or food that is too sweet. Hand-fed young birds may become accustomed to over-eating if they are given too many treats. Dirty aviaries and cages and vitamin and mineral deficiencies can also cause overeating, which can prove to be a very stubborn condition to stop.

Birds which overeat are lethargic, they look ill and spend practically all their time on the feeding dish, often with their wings hanging down. They look thin and undernourished and their breast bone sticks out. Their droppings are greyish-black. The underpart of their bodies looks rather unhealthy, too, sometimes showing a road map of blue and red veins and arteries, as well as being swollen, hard and, in most cases, infected.

If your birds are overeating, menus must be adjusted to the needs of the birds and the season. Avoid sweet foods as much as possible. No egg or universal food, or self-prepared strength foods should be given for about 20 days. However, you can provide stale brown bread soaked in water on a daily basis. Add disinfectant to the drinking water. Contact an avian veterinary surgeon immediately.

Obesity

Birds become obese from a lack of exercise because their cages are too small or because owners have not provided anything to keep them occupied, or because they are not getting the right food. Getting fat is a very slow process and owners must watch very carefully to spot the first signs. When the birds can barely sit on their perches anymore they are already overweight.

Obese birds sit on the bottom of their cage, panting heavily, and do not seem to want to move. The contours of their bodies have become blurred, heavy and cylindrical and the skin appears yellowish when the feathers are blown apart: this is the fat shining through the skin! Just blow on the breast or abdominal feathers of such a bird and you will see what we mean.

Birds suffering from obesity live much shorter lives than those that have plenty of exercise. Hang some strong sisal ropes in the cage or aviary, and add a few bunches of spray millet and/or weed seeds for them to play with.

Improve the birds nutrition immediately, strictly by the book if needs be; provide lots of well-washed greens or fruit free from chemicals and cut out food with a high protein or fat content.

Cage birds must be released every day in aviaries or (when tame, as in parrots and parakeets) allowed to fly freely for at least one to two hours. This will give them sufficient exercise and they will not suffer from grout.

Birds must also get enough exercise inside their cages. This can be achieved by keeping them in larger cages or by putting the perches further apart so that the bird is forced to make a greater effort to get to the other side. Withholding food from a fat bird will not solve the weight problem. Even fat birds must be fed at all times, but with the right kind of feed. However fat a bird may be it will die if it receives no nourishment.

Constipation

Birds, especially parrots and large parakeet species, housed in an under-sized area, have a tendency to become constipated. Not enough exercise, fatty or overly sweet food, and eating too much are also causes. If the droppings are expelled with some difficulty and are dry, large and hard, the bird is constipated.

First, consider whether the bird's menu is in order – adding greens and fruit is advisable, as is adding some Epson or Glauber's salt to the drinking water. It is more effective to put salts into the beak with a medicine dropper. A small amount of an oily laxative, from a good chemist, dissolved in the drinking water or given with a plastic dropper, can help: rape seed rubbed in fat (suet) can also help. Another old-fashioned remedy is to add ten drops of syrup of buckthorn to the cage's water container.

A good general rule is that any bird not feeling up to par should be immediately separated from other birds and shouldn't be returned until it is completely cured. Check with your avian veterinary surgeon and place the patient in a clean hospital cage (see below).

Diarrhoea

Diarrhoea is not a disease, only a sign that something is wrong with the bird's health. Diarrhoea occurs mainly as a result of neglect or malnutrition. When it continues over a long period it can become quite dangerous, even fatal.

Diarrhoea can be caused by some kind of enteritis. Many causes exist: the wrong or contaminated food, a cold caused by sudden changes in temperature, bacteriological infections, etc. Consult an avian veterinary surgeon immediately and place the bird in a hospital cage with a temperature of 86-94°F (30-35°C). Warmth alone is often sufficient to cure a diarrhoea patient.

Infrared radiation treatment can also produce good results. Irradiate one side of the hospital cage so the sick bird has the choice of sitting in the radiation or not. A reliable heating device is recommended because the bird also needs warmth at night. Also, keep a small 15-watt bulb burning so the bird can eat and drink if it wants to.

Give the bird weak black tea or peppermint tea instead of water. Mix some pulverized charcoal through the sick bird's favourite food and seed, and administer some tetracycline HC1, terramycin or aureomycin, as well as preparations which contain vitamins and trace elements. If diarrhoea continues consult an avian vet immediately. He or she will have recourse to stronger antibiotics.

Perches or roosts

Perches must be of two kinds: ordinary rods for sitting and copulation, and swings or branches for amusement. 'Sitting rods' should never be too thin and could be round or flattened out on top for a better grip. They can be swinging or immovable and made of hard wood. 'Swinging roosts' are fun but not essential.

Immovable perches are absolutely necessary for birds that are courting. Thin roosts are purely for diversion, for games and fun, and generally consist of natural vegetation which, if formed and placed properly, also provide natural nesting places.

Birds will use these roosts for sitting and sleeping, too, particularly in the summer but we recommend you provide separate sleeping roosts as well.

Install these perches in the inside aviary or the covered portion of the outside aviary. Use sturdy, thick rods of hard wood. The wood must be hard and free of bark to keep lice out. The perches must be thick because the toes of the birds should not completely encircle the perch to allow the birds to get proper and thorough rest. Furthermore, if the thickness is right the birds' nails will not grow too long, especially if the different roosts are of varying widths. Also, the muscles of the birds' feet will remain supple.

Well-placed perches will make it easier for the birds to enter the nest.

Put perches up high, as in general, birds like to sleep as high up as possible. Be sure there is enough roosting space to avoid fighting at bedtime. And don't install perches above each other otherwise birds on top will foul the birds below with their droppings.

In outside aviaries, make sure there are some wind- and draught-free places for the birds, such as several small half-open sleeping shelters and nest boxes insulated with indoor-outdoor carpet to keep out draughts.

Nesting places

The most important aspect of nesting places is that there should be plenty of them. Each pair of breeding birds should have a variety of options. Birds will only nest and breed if they have a wide selection of potential nesting places.

Black-billed touraco.

Don't assume that birds will always use the nest boxes recommended for their species. We have seen a supposed tree-hole brooder that happily made an open nest or used a half-open nest box. And semi-hole brooders, like Zebra finches, will sometimes select an open nest, such as a coconut half, or a completely closed-in place, like an entire coconut, despite a variety of available sites that it supposedly prefers. Don't be surprised if the bird changes from one to the other in the same breeding season.

Finches can be bred successfully using a broad range of nesting containers, even empty coconuts.

Love bird nest.

Shy but ready to leave the nest any time!

We have seen this happen a number of times and it is precisely because birds do surprise us with their preferences that we need to anticipate the choices available and make the options as broad as possible. Count on providing at least twice as many nesting places as you have breeding pairs.

There are natural and artificial nesting sites. Natural sites are offered by vegetation. In selecting shrubs for the aviary, pick types that form dense branches with forks at several places. If you have shrubs that have too few good branches, prune the bush back to a few promising buds. Meanwhile, you can cut some branches from another tree or bush and tie them together with wire to form a good nesting place. For ground-nesting birds, provide reeds, rushes and low bushes, such as heather. Such vegetation is an integral part of a good, outdoor aviary of the right size.

Do not offer artificial nesting places until early spring and remove them after the breeding season ends. Keep them clean and sanitary. In the winter, give them a thorough cleaning. Then sanitise them inside and out with carbolic acid. Remember, your goal is to produce totally healthy young and nesting places and nests that are infested with vermin or germs will not help.

Artificial nesting places fall into three basic types:

1. Nest boxes – open, half-open and enclosed models. Nesting logs of birch or beech are really 'closed' nest boxes.

2. Nest baskets – coconut shells, woven baskets of various types, bins and bowls.

3. Miscellaneous – cork, heather, woven straw and similar materials. These are for specialised uses and as such indicated in the text.

THE SICK BIRD

It is impossible to cover all bird diseases in detail within this book. If you are worried about any aspect of your birds' health consult an avian veterinary surgeon. Make sure that you have found one before you buy your first bird, but if you cannot find one locally, ask club members, bird shops, or write to the Association of Avian Veterinarians, P.O. Box 811720, Boca Raton, FL 33481-1720, USA (http://www.aav.org/aav.). They should be able to put you in touch with a vet who works with birds. They also have names and addresses of avian veterinary surgeons outside the USA.

Sometimes there are only the smallest clues indicating that a bird is sick. Nevertheless, don't hesitate to take appropriate action. Immediate action may save a lot of trouble, and even the lives of your birds later on.

If you think one of your birds is sick, the first step is to isolate it from the other birds in the collection. It is possible that it is suffering with a communicable disease that poses a danger to all your birds. As soon as a bird has been diagnosed as having an infectious disease the whole aviary, feeding utensils, perches, toys and accessories should be disinfected (using Lysol, One Stroke Environ, Clorox or Betadine, for example; always follow manufacturers' recommendations).

The sick bird is best placed in a special hospital cage, the back and sides of which are enclosed and only the front exposed; various excellent commercial cages are available. Add glucose and a multivitamin preparation or better still a balanced electrolyte (Pedialyte, Gatorade, fruit juice) to the bird's favourite food or drink but again, be sure to follow the manufacturer's instructions. If a large bird (for instance an African grey) refuses to feed or drink for a period of 24 hours, you will have to force feed it every hour or it will die of starvation, even if the disease hasn't killed it by then; smaller birds should be force fed after 10 hours. Give the patient lactose-free baby food with a spatula or syringe, about 3 cc per serving for large birds, and 1 cc for small ones.

The hospital cage may have a thermostatically controlled heating element, otherwise you can use an infrared heating lamp in front or suspended above the cage. By adjusting this up and down and having a thermometer in the cage, you can fix a constant temperature in the cage of 85-90°F (29-32°C). If necessary, cover the front of the cage with a cloth to help retain heat. Seek immediate help. The cage should preferably have a false mesh bottom so that the bird's droppings fall through and thus prevent the bird soiling itself or even re-infecting itself with its own faeces.

Lutino Parakeet

Red-rumped Parakeet

A thermometer should be placed in the cage, out of reach of the bird; hookbills, for example, will make short work of such an instrument. Lower the temperature by turning the lamps down or by increasing ventilation. There are openings in the lower part of the hospital cage through which cold air enters, is heated by lamps, and then rises by convection into the main cage area. Remember that a sick bird requires fresh air and be sure that there is always a vent open both at the bottom and the upper part of the cage. Take note of the following points:

- Do not hesitate to consult an avian veterinary surgeon, should your sick bird fail to respond positively to hospital-cage treatment within 8-10 hours.

- Although this may sound pedantic, always take care of the healthy birds first each day before dealing with the sick bird, thus avoiding contamination via hands or clothing.

- Wash your hands thoroughly before and after handling the patient. Food and water containers also must be cleaned and disinfected several times daily. (The sick bird should be provided with its normal food, in the hope that it will continue to feed. Do not forget to offer its favourite tidbits.)

- After the bird is cured, the hospital cage and all its accessories should be thoroughly cleaned and disinfected.

- When you take your sick bird to a vet do so in its own cage. A bird that comes from an aviary is best carried in a cardboard carton (but be sure there are sufficient ventilation holes for breathing), in a small rectangular cage or in the hospital cage; there are also carriers commercially available.

- Take fresh faeces (droppings) to the vet and also let him or her examine the food that the bird normally eats.

- Before carrying the cage or box to the car, pack it well in paper and cover it with a blanket, to prevent the possibility of chills. On cold days, such rules are obvious. On very cold days, warm up the car for a few minutes by running the engine before the cage is put inside. Birds can loose heat rapidly inside a car that has been standing in the cold for many hours.

- Use petshop medicines only when your avian veterinary surgeon has suggested them. Remember that avian medicines are constantly being re-evaluated and upgraded. Sick birds should have the best available drugs administered in the correct dosage. The administration of 'medicines-for-all ailments' may interfere with the vet's treatment. Avoid using human medicines unless recommended by your avian veterinary surgeon (Kaopectate, for instance, is a good treatment for loose droppings).

FINAL THOUGHTS ON MAINTENANCE AND CARE

Effective maintenance presupposes good facilities. A well-designed aviary has as few corners and sides as possible, and the structure should be properly stained or treated with carbolic acid and such. The floor is either made of natural soil or covered with pure river or sharp sand; do not use beach sand as it is much too salty.

First, make sure the ground is well maintained. The sand on the floors must be replaced and the earth must be turned over and dug up with a spade. The frequency of this chore depends entirely on the size of the aviary and the density of the bird population. Guide yourself by the principle: never have a dirty floor; better too much work done than too little.

Second, every spring, (at the very least) clean and sanitize all roosts, sleeping shelters, hiding places and other furnishings. Natural vegetation needs to be cut back to remove rotting and dying wood. Then clean off everything with spray from a garden hose. Replace plants as needed.

Third, maintain the aviary as a whole. In spring, move the entire bird collection into cages for long enough to thoroughly clean, paint and service the whole aviary inside and out. Check the roof for leaks. Find and seal cracks that promote drafts. Repair tears in wire mesh. Maintain and make any repairs on locks and hinges. In short, check and restore everything. Done every year, preventative maintenance avoids nasty surprises during the coming season and preserves your collection as well as your property.

Fourth, keep up daily chores. When you replace and refresh seed, drinking water and bath water, clean all the dishes, bowls and fountains. Automatic waterers and self-feeders should be cleaned at least once per week.

Altogether, maintenance is a year-round chore, with a major spring-cleaning and a second overhaul in the autumn, if you have birds wintering in outdoor facilities. Inside facilities, of course, should be equally well maintained – including cages, glass show cages (vitrines), breeding cages and all bird-related equipment.

Fact file

DISTRIBUTION:
southeast Asia, from India to southeast China; also Sri Lanka, Formosa, Hainan and Australia (along northern, eastern and southern coasts)

HABITAT:
grassland and swamps

CLUTCH:
4 to 10 brownish-green eggs, with black speckling; generally about 6 to 8 young will hatch

INCUBATION:
16 to 18 days by the female

FLEDGING:
precocial and downy

AVERAGE LIFESPAN:
10 years

SEXING:
female: brownish, without the male's face markings

JUVENILES:
almost completely black-brown; place young in a separate run as soon as they start to moult into adult plumage, which is at about 4 weeks of age

SIZE:
13 cm (5 in)

CHINESE PAINTED QUAIL
Coturnix chinensis

This species, which can now be obtained in several colour mutations (pied, silver and fawn, for example), can be kept indoors or outdoors in aviaries that have plenty of ground cover (such as tussocks of grass) and that contain a collection of 'tree' birds; in the winter, all quails must be kept indoors as they are unable to tolerate damp and misty conditions.

If you keep quails, pheasants or other ground birds in an outdoor aviary, it is important that the floor is well loosened up so that water can quickly drain away. On a concrete floor, a thick layer of sawdust or coarse peat should be put down. Nothing is more dangerous to a ground bird than walking and sleeping on moist ground. Fix a number of strong perches about 50 cm (20 in) above the ground.

Like most quails, this species has a habit of suddenly flying vertically into the air when alarmed. The cock often becomes aggressive towards the young when they reach the age when they can virtually be sexed, so separate the cock from his offspring at this time.

On hatching, the chicks are like small, active, little balls of down, so place boards along the bottom of the aviary to prevent escapes.

Feeding: the young should be fed with a commercial insectile food; during the year, a seed mixture (millets, canary and maw), plenty of greens, grit (very essential) and small insects (maggots and such like) are required. Fresh water is necessary at all times.

*Normal-coloured female
Chinese Painted Quail.*

CALIFORNIAN QUAIL
Callipepla (Lophortyx) california

This quail is a lovely, easily managed, hardy bird, requiring a large aviary, with a lot of running room. This species cannot be kept with fellow galliformes or small birds. The aviary should have plenty of ground cover in which these quails can look for seeds and live food.

The Californian quail is bred professionally in hatcheries, but also with great success in incubators and brooders by aviculturists; even small bantams can be used for this purpose. The aviary should be equipped with well-placed (behind evergreens, for example), high roosting perches in the covered section where they spend the night because these birds are prone to fighting at night.

These birds are very sensitive to moisture, so make sure that they are housed in an aviary that lies a few inches above the ground, so that the floor of the run will not remain wet for very long in the event of heavy rain.

An ideal species for the beginner, Californian quails are prolific layers, although they are somewhat less reliable while incubating, so do not disturb them then.

Feeding: young chicks should have access to a fine-grade insectile mixture or commercial rearing food for soft-billed birds, to which you can add some maw seed and a tablespoon of small maggots or such like. For adults, see Chinese painted quail (left).

Male Californian quail.

Fact file

DISTRIBUTION:
western North America, from Oregon and California, extending into Mexico; introduced on King Island (Australia)

HABITAT:
wide range of habitats: moister forest edges through chaparral regions to scrub desert

CLUTCH:
12 to 17, sometimes 6 to 28, short, oval, to short, elliptical, creamy and glossy white eggs, with fine, oval speckling and irregular spotting and blotching

INCUBATION:
21 to 23 days by the female

FLEDGING:
precocial and downy

AVERAGE LIFESPAN:
12 years

SEXING:
female: smaller crest than the male's; white head plumage is lacking

JUVENILES:
top: yellowish, with blackish cap and back stripes; underside: creamy white

SIZE:
25 cm (10 in)

The Handbook of Cage and Aviary Birds

Fact file

DISTRIBUTION:
Japan to India, Sri Lanka, Burma and other parts of Asia, and across continental Europe and the British Isles; in 3 subspecies

HABITAT:
arid country, cultivated

CLUTCH:
2 elliptical, smooth and glossy white eggs

INCUBATION:
14 to 16 days by both sexes

FLEDGING:
15 to 17 days; the young often return to nest at night to roost for a few days thereafter

AVERAGE LIFESPAN:
8 years

SEXING:
the female is similar to the male

JUVENILES:
similar to the parents; underside browner; neck ring small or lacking

SIZE:
28 cm (11 in)

COLLARED DOVE
Streptopelia decaocto

This well-known dove was first bred in the wild in England in 1955 and has since increased its range tremendously. In fewer than ten years, the English population increased to more than 20,000 birds, and the species has also spread throughout north-western Europe.

Collared doves were first bred successfully in the United States. Wild collared doves pose some difficulties when brought into captivity, but hand-reared or aviary-bred birds are quite tame and charming. There is no difficulty with fostering, especially if Barbary doves (*S. roseogrisea* var. *arisoria*) are used as foster parents. Although collared doves are quite hardy, they will thrive in a slightly warmed winter shelter, or at least one free from cold winds and dampness, which will guard against frostbite of the toes.

During courtship, the cock begins with a bowing ceremony, whereby the beak nearly touches the ground. The neck feathers are fluffed out to form a collar, the tail is spread like a fan, and the wings are usually flapping and clapping. Provide a shallow wooden box, small pen or basket (commercially available) as their nests are rather flimsy.

Feeding: as for laughing dove, see page 56.

Dilute Barbary dove.

Ivory Barbary dove.

Phaeo Barbary dove.

Normal-coloured Barbary dove.

Grey Barbary dove.

White Barbary dove.

BARBARY DOVE *S. roseogrisea* var. *arisoria*

The wild ancestor of the domesticated Barbary dove comes from the savannah regions of north Africa, but the dove as we know it today is unknown in nature. In an aviary, several pairs (but never two, always one or three or more pairs) can be kept together in a community with other species, such as finches, small parakeet species and pheasants. The birds must be kept in slightly warmed quarters in the winter. As foster parents, they are outstanding. They are especially useful in the rearing of bleeding-heart pigeons and other costly and difficult-to-breed species. Once Barbary doves are accustomed to feeding on ant pupae, small, living mealworms, commercial egg food and rearing food for canaries, they will have no problems rearing those difficult species. As soon as the young are independent, the foster parents can be put back on a seed diet consisting of millet varieties, canary grass seed, hemp, milo and wheat, plus greens and a calcium supplement.

At breeding time, provide small nesting platforms or, indoors, cardboard boxes in which you have laid some straw and hay. The hen lays two eggs that are incubated for 14 to 15 days. The young fledge at 14 to 15 days, but are usually still fairly helpless, often sitting in a corner on the aviary floor. After about a month, the parents stop feeding their young or foster young and begin with a new clutch. Various mutations have been cultured over the years.

Fact file

DISTRIBUTION:
Africa, Arabia and southern
and central Asia Minor to India;
well established in and around
Perth, Kalgoorlie and Esperence,
western Australia; in 6 subspecies

HABITAT:
open, dry terrain, and cultivation

CLUTCH:
2 elliptical, glossy white eggs

INCUBATION:
12 to 14 days by both sexes

FLEDGING:
12 to 13 days; are fed by
the parents for about 10
days thereafter

AVERAGE LIFESPAN:
8 years

SEXING:
female: mainly grey and paler,
with less reddish-brown
on the upper parts than the male

JUVENILES:
dullish-brown
areas instead
of red-brown, and grey
where the parents are pink

SIZE:
28 cm (11 in)

LAUGHING or SENEGAL DOVE *Streptopelia s. senegalensis*

This is an inexpensive, quiet, sociable and hardy dove that is easy to manage and therefore very popular. You should plant a conifer or two in the aviary as these birds are free-breeders and seem to prefer these shrubs for nesting in. Their nests are much more substantial than those of other species. To avoid the accidental loss of the eggs or young, it is best either to place nesting platforms, wire mesh or wood among the twigs or to place a wooden plank under the nest after it has been built. Once independent, the young must be separated from the adults as the latter will want to start another brood and can behave very aggressively towards their older offspring.

Tip: we provide our birds with old thrush's nests and flowerpots partly filled with mulch, with great success!

Feeding: provide a good, commercial, small-dove seed mixture (consisting of canary grass seed, millet varieties, maw seed, rape seed and some hemp as a minimum); like other doves, this species swallows seeds without husking them first. Also give these birds greens, fruit (small berries, pieces of apple, pear and so on), grit (essential) and commercial pheasant- and chick-rearing crumbs, plus some finely chopped vegetables during the breeding season. It is also advisable to offer small maggots and similar insects during the breeding season.

Cape or masked dove
Oena c. capensis

The Cape or masked dove (also known as the Namaque dove) is a little larger than the diamond dove (see page 58) and very attractive. The bird is fairly easy to keep, but is somewhat delicate in cold climates, and a well-lit night shelter is therefore essential. It will thrive in a large, communal aviary, where it will not interfere with the other birds.

Cape doves quickly become tame and learn to accept treats from the fancier's hand. In the wild, the doves construct a nest from small roots and grass situated very close to the ground in thick foliage. These birds are fairly intolerant of the cold and damp, and must therefore be brought indoors during the winter. In an outdoor aviary, they must be able to bask in the sun; several spots covered with coarse sand will do fine. Sometimes a pair takes two or more years before breeding. Provide the birds with a basket or else a wooden or wire-mesh nesting platform fixed into the foliage of a shrub.

Many pairs are ready to start on a new brood before they have reared the existing one, when they abandon their young. Diamond doves make excellent foster parents in such cases.

Feeding: as for the laughing dove (left).

Fact file

DISTRIBUTION:
Africa, along the Red Sea to western Saudi Arabia and southern Africa; in Senegal and Sudan; in 2 subspecies

HABITAT:
dry, open terrain; also in cultivations and villages; in small families

CLUTCH:
2 cream-coloured, sometimes white, eggs

INCUBATION:
14 days by both sexes

FLEDGING:
16 days

AVERAGE LIFESPAN:
8 years

SEXING:
female: lacks the male's black mask; face, head, neck and breast whitish-grey

JUVENILES:
speckled appearance; young males sometimes show a few dull-black breast feathers, with light fawn ends

SIZE:
23 cm (9 in)

Fact file

DISTRIBUTION:
central and northern Australia;
sometimes in the south;
in 2 subspecies

HABITAT:
open woodland, often with
mulga scrub, cultivation, gardens
and parks; watercourses

CLUTCH:
2 elliptical, white eggs

INCUBATION:
12 to 15 days by both sexes

FLEDGING:
12 to 14 days

AVERAGE LIFESPAN:
8 years

SEXING:
female: very similar to the male;
the latter has a somewhat
larger head and more prominent
orbital ring; the female has smaller
white spots on the wings

JUVENILES:
similar to the parents, but duller
and browner; appear banded

SIZE:
19 cm (7½ in)

DIAMOND DOVE
Geopelia c. cuneata

The diamond dove is one of the smallest of the doves that are popular in aviculture. Its common name refers to the narrowly black-bordered, white spots on the wings and shoulders. The sexes can be difficult to distinguish, but the cock has a somewhat larger head and a wider orbital, red ring. One positive sign is the cock's courtship dance: he circles around the hen with a fanned-out tail and repeatedly emits a loud, sometimes irritating, call.

Diamond doves are easily managed and are a suitable addition to a mixed aviary collection of seed-eating species; they do not, however, tolerate other doves or fellows. It is also possible to keep a pair successfully in a large cage.

They are quite hardy and can often stay outside all winter, as long as they have a damp- and draught-proof shelter. In very cold weather, however, they are best kept locked in a shelter as they tend to sit for long periods in one spot and could get frostbite or colds outside. As an extra precaution, it is perhaps best to keep them in an unheated indoor area during the winter months.

Cinnamon dilute diamond dove.

The nest platform can consist of mesh or wood; even half a coconut shell may suffice. A few twigs and skeleton leaves and a little moss and grass will serve as nest material.

A number of colour mutations have been bred: silver, brown, yellow, agate, cinnamon, pied and red.

Agate diamond dove.

Tip: offer diamond doves skeleton tobacco leaves as nest material that will even keep lice away!

Feeding: as for the laughing dove, see page 56.

ZEBRA or BARRED GROUND DOVE
Geopelia s. striata

This charming, prolific, versatile, adaptable and colourful dove has increased in popularity in recent years. The female is usually slightly smaller, and perhaps a little more soberly patterned and coloured, than the male.

According to some fanciers, the zebra dove is not very interesting in a communal aviary, but we have found that a pair can give one much pleasure. They are not particularly lively, but move about peacefully and view the activity around them stealthily. Occasionally, but not very often, they may sit in a particular spot for hours. As long as you have lively co-habitants in the aviary, these doves are likely to interact with only minor squabbles and acrobatics. They are generally quiet, even during the breeding period. Ensure that they are not alarmed as they are very sensitive to sudden disturbances, making peace and quiet vital during the breeding season. Experience has shown that these birds must be kept in a warm station indoors in winter.

Tip: when buying these birds, make sure that you will be able to exchange them if you are not satisfied. You can be sure that you have a true pair only when you first see the cock's courtship display (which is rather similar to that of the diamond dove).

Feeding: as for the laughing dove, see page 56.

Fact file

DISTRIBUTION:
southeast Asia and the Indonesian archipelago; introduced into the Malagasy Republic, St Helena, the Hawaiian islands and many other areas; in 6 subspecies

HABITAT:
open country, with strands of trees and scrubs; also close to jungle clearings and edges, agricultural areas, parks and gardens

CLUTCH:
2 elliptical, white eggs

INCUBATION:
13 to 14 days by both sexes

FLEDGING:
12 to 13 days

AVERAGE LIFESPAN:
8 years

SEXING:
the female tends to be somewhat smaller than the male

JUVENILES:
pinkish on breast; barred underparts

SIZE:
22 cm (8½ in)

Fact file

DISTRIBUTION:
Australia, apart from most coastal regions, particularly along the eastern and south-western seaboards and Cape York peninsula; absent from Tasmania; introduced into Florida (USA) during the early 1950s

HABITAT:
a large range of habitats; mainly grassland with spinifex, dry mallee and mulga

CLUTCH:
5 eggs can be considered average, but may be as many as 10

INCUBATION:
18 days by the female, but joined by the male

FLEDGING:
28 to 32 days

AVERAGE LIFESPAN:
8 years, but birds of 15 to 25 years are known

SEXING:
the female has a brown cere during the breeding season (blue in the male)

JUVENILES:
duller plumage than in the parents; dark iris; barred forehead; independent in 5 to 6 weeks; adult plumage after about 4 months

SIZE:
18 cm (7 in)

BUDGERIGAR or PARAKEET
Melopsittacus undulates

The budgerigar, or 'budgie', as it is affectionately known in Britain, while it is called 'parakeet' in the USA, was first seen in Europe during the 1840s, and is one of the most popular pet birds in the world. It is easy to keep, breed, tame and love! It is friendly and able to imitate many sounds, including that of the human voice.

There are two types: the American variety and the slightly larger, English version that is usually bred for shows. Budgerigars are now available in a wide variety of colour mutations, all of which stemmed from the green colouration of the original wild budgerigar (from an aboriginal word meaning 'good bird/food').

Budgerigars are very affordable, but remember to buy all of the items necessary to keep a bird happy in captivity. Toys, a cage or aviary, food and medical care should all be budgeted for. Even birds as small as budgies are intelligent enough to understand how they are being treated. Never become angry with, or shout at, your pet. Be patient, kind and gentle. In time, your new acquaintance will be perching on your finger and interacting with you as though you were long-lost friends.

Tip: select a bird that is about 6 weeks old for training; the sex is immaterial.

Right: spangled dark-green budgerigar.

Lutino budgerigar.

Pied, yellow-masked,
blue budgerigar.

Black-faced, blue
budgerigar.

Crested budgerigar.

Protect budgies in outside aviaries from excessive rain, preferably by covering part of the roof with transparent plastic sheeting or similar. Although the birds quickly acclimatise to cold winter weather, you should ensure that they have a frost-free shelter in which to spend the night.

Budgies breed readily in a variety of boxes (minimum size: 25 cm/10 in long x 15 cm/16 in deep and high; entrance, 6 cm/2 in). It is best (especially in outdoor aviaries) to remove the nest boxes in late August so that the birds cannot try to rear chicks during the colder months of the year. The boxes can then be replaced in spring ready for a new breeding season. The best results are achieved using commercially available breeding or box cages.

Feeding: provide a good commercial seed mixture. In addition, provide vegetables and greens (endives, chickweed, parsley, watercress, spinach, young dandelions, groundsel, aubergines, green peas, carrots, cooked beets, sweet potatoes, courgettes and curly kale); lettuce should only be offered in the smallest amounts because it has limited nutritional value and can cause loose droppings. Your birds will enjoy pecking at a millet spray and will enjoy occasional treats of wheat germ, oats or small sunflower-seed kernels. They also enjoy strawberries, apples, oranges, tangerines, grapes, pears, tomatoes, kiwi fruits, mangoes, apricots and pineapples. Feed each of your birds a teaspoon of hard-boiled egg mixed with cottage cheese once a week. Some grit should always be available, as should cuttlebone, a valuable source of calcium.

DUIVENBODE'S LORY
Chalcopsitta duivenbodei

In the wild, these lories make continual contact with each other by means of their shrill calls. They spend most of the day high in flowering trees; they roost socially.

This unusually coloured lory species was first exhibited in London Zoo in 1929. At present, the bird is being regularly bred, both in bird parks and by private aviculturists.

At first sight, these birds do not seem to be particularly attractively coloured. But birds in good condition can display unusual colours, especially when they spread their wings to show the golden-yellow undersides that are in stark contrast to the mainly brown plumage, with the exception of the lower back, rump and under-tail coverts, which are violet or deep blue.

This bird is one of four species (and nine subspecies) of the *Chalcopsitta* genus. Like the representatives of the white-rumped lories (*Pseudeos*, see page 67), there is a typical, naked, throat spot, which is blackish coloured in this genus and orange in *Pseudeos Chalcopsitta,* or glossy lories, are extremely aggressive towards all other birds, especially during the breeding season, but a pair kept in a roomy aviary, with a heated night shelter in which a sleep/nest box is placed (see black lory, page 64), will soon become tame and trusting towards their owner. The shrill, piercing call that they use frequently at first will be heard less and less as the birds settle.

Feeding: as for black lory (see page 64), with additional greens and a limited amount of seed (the Duivenbodes lory is one of the few lories that will eat some seed, especially millet spray and small, germinated seeds).

Fact file

DISTRIBUTION:
northern New Guinea, between Geelvink Bay (in the west) and Astrolabe Bay (in the east); in 2 subspecies

HABITAT:
forest, secondary growth, lowlands and hills (up to 150 m/500 ft); in flowering trees

CLUTCH:
2 rounded, white eggs

INCUBATION:
24 to 27 days by the female

FLEDGING:
70 to 82 days

AVERAGE LIFESPAN:
20 years

SEXING:
the female is similar to the male, although the latter is generally a bit larger, especially the head and beak; the male's lower back and rump are usually brighter blue

JUVENILES:
similar to the parents, but duller and with less yellow on the face; breast feathers have dull-yellow borders; under-wing coverts are yellow with a brown base; the skin encircling the eyes and lower mandible is white (black in adults)

SIZE:
30 cm (12 in)

Fact file

DISTRIBUTION:
western New Guinea (Irian Jaya), western Vogelkop and the islands of Salawati and Batana; in 4 subspecies

HABITAT:
coconut plantations, flowering trees, savannah, forest edges, lowland and coastal areas

CLUTCH:
2 rounded, white eggs

INCUBATION:
24 to 25 days by both sexes

FLEDGING:
70 to 90 days; mature at about 3 years

AVERAGE LIFESPAN:
30 years

SEXING:
the male is larger than the female, with a more pronounced head and bill

JUVENILES:
duller than the parents; less red on the ear coverts and body; white facial skin; greyish iris; brown beak

SIZE:
30 cm (12 in)

BLACK LORY
Chalcopsitta atra

In the wild, black lories operate in groups of between 18 and 24 individuals, feeding particularly on the pollen and nectar of palms and eucalyptus trees. They have a remarkably loud call, which they use to the full as they fly over open areas.

A rare species, the black lory was first shown in England in 1904 by Walter Goodfellow, while the first breeding success occurred in 1909 in Scotland, for which E J Brooks was responsible.

As these birds' toenails tend to grow long and sharp, provide a variety of rough-barked, natural twigs as perches. A daily bath of fresh water must be available; they also like to take a shower in summer rain. They require a spacious aviary as they like to fly about, which goes for all members of this genus. This inquisitive, intelligent and affectionate, but sometimes aggressive, lory is usually sexually mature in its third year; in any case, it should not be bred before then because breeding too early may result in weak youngsters, or the parents will not look after them properly and may even abandon them. The sleep/nest box should be 45 x 40 x 50 cm; entrance 10 cm (17 x 15 x 19$^{1}/_{2}$ in; entrance 4 in) and well protected from the elements in a well-built night shelter.

Feeding: provide a commercial lory diet (Nekton lory, for example) and extra fruit (apples, berries, sultanas, figs and papayas). A good canary rearing food will also be eagerly accepted.

YELLOW-STREAKED LORY
Chalcopsitta scintillata

This species is the best-known and most widely kept lory of this genus. Given careful acclimatisation, these birds generally have a strong constitution. These lories were first introduced to the public at London Zoo in 1872. When properly cared for, their plumage has a sheen that is seldom seen in other lories and lorikeets. Excellent fliers, they need an aviary with a flight area at least 3 m (10 ft) long, and a sleep/nest box of 40 x 40 x 60 cm; entrance diameter 10 cm (15 x 15 x 24 in; entrance diameter 4 in).

In flight, the bright yellow and red of the under-wings show up in great contrast to the green of the rest of the plumage. With good care, these birds soon become very tame and trusting towards their keeper. They can be aggressive with strangers, however, and typically angrily fluff up their feathers and scream loudly when you approach the aviary with a stranger. During the winter, they must be kept in a room-temperature environment.

Feeding: these lories do really well on a normal lory diet and a variety of greens (see black lory, left). As a treat, give them unripe corn on the cob and boiled rice with honey.

Fact file

DISTRIBUTION:
southern New Guinea; 3 subspecies (4 if one recognises *C. rubrifrons*, from the Aru islands)

HABITAT:
lowland areas (e.g., the coast) and foothills near rivers

CLUTCH:
2 rounded, white eggs

INCUBATION:
25 to 26 days by the female

FLEDGING:
76 to 100 days

AVERAGE LIFESPAN:
30 years

SEXING:
the female is similar to the male; the latter is generally larger (as is the bill), with more scarlet on the forehead

JUVENILES:
duller than the parents; dark-red or black forehead and crown; brownish iris; white upper mandible, with brown-yellow markings near the base

SIZE:
30 cm (12 in)

The Handbook of Cage and Aviary Birds

Fact file

DISTRIBUTION:
Indonesia: Amboina (Ambon), Saparua and Maluku (Moluccas); in 4 subspecies on Buru, Goram, Ceramlaut and Watubela and Kai islands

HABITAT:
coastal areas with flowering trees; also montane forests (up to 1,250 m/4,100 ft)

CLUTCH:
2, sometimes 4, rounded, white eggs

INCUBATION:
24 to 25 days by the female

FLEDGING:
53 to 70 days; watch out for feather-plucking by the parents, as well as by the fledglings

AVERAGE LIFESPAN:
30 years

SEXING:
the female and male are similar, but the male has a more pronounced body and beak

JUVENILES:
variable; some with blue ear coverts and red in the underparts; white eye-ring; greyish iris; brown beak while the birds are still in the nest; orange when fledgling

SIZE:
30 cm (12 in)

RED or MOLUCCAN LORY
Eos borneo

Although red or Moluccan lories (and the five other species of this genus) are in no way delicate, it is advisable to bring them indoors for the winter or to provide them with a heated shelter, at least in colder climates. In general, the red lory is an adept and rapid flier, but its voice cannot be described as attractive: it is loud and very piercing. We would recommend that all *Eos* species be kept in single pairs as they are aggressive towards all other birds, especially other parrot-like birds.

A pair of these lories will usually breed in a roomy aviary (a minimum of 4 m/12 ft in length), indoors or preferably outdoors. For sleep/nest-box requirements, see the dusky lory (right).

Like all *Eos* species, the young are initially covered in a white down, which changes to grey at about eight days. Once independent, the young birds are best separated from their parents, which are likely to become aggressive, sometimes with disastrous results.

Feeding: in addition to a normal commercial lory diet and a variety of soft fruits (see below), these birds will take a lot of live food, especially when rearing their young. During the breeding season, supplement their diet with small mealworms, ant pupae and especially maggots; also provide sweet apples, bananas, grapes, soaked raisins, various berries and such like. They also like unshelled sunflower seeds, which they not only take eagerly, but also shell adeptly! Fledglings are fond of sunflower seeds, too. Grass and weed seeds, both fresh and germinated, are eaten eagerly, but the quantity consumed may vary from day to day.

DUSKY LORY
Pseudeos fuscata

In the wild, this intelligent species occurs in groups of 20 to 100 individuals, but after the breeding season, flocks of several hundred may be seen in flight.

They are regularly available on the market. They soon become tame and trusting towards their keeper, but pairs should not be kept together with other parrot-like birds (including members of their own species) in the relatively small confines of an aviary.

The dimensions of the sleep/nest box should be at least 30 x 30 x 40 cm (11 x 11 x 15 in), with an entrance diameter of 9 cm (3$^1/_2$ in), and should incorporate a layer of absorbent material in the base.

The courtship procedure is interesting. The cock emits whispers and growling noises as he flutters his wings and bows, stretching his neck in front of the hen. Copulation takes a relatively long time; the cock places one foot on the hen's back and holds himself securely on the perch with the other. These lories have a reputation of being fairly consistent breeders in a relatively small cage (1 m²/ 3$^1/_2$ ft²), although they prefer a larger aviary.

Many authorities state that there is a recognisable sexual dimorphism in this species, but the so-called differences are not always visible. However, three of our pairs showed a similar difference between cock and hen: in the cock, the upper part of the tail feathers is reddish-brown, whereas it is dark blue in the hen.

Feeding: commercial lory food; various soft fruits, especially berries; milky and germinated (canary) grass seeds; millet varieties; millet spray; and various greens.

Fact file

DISTRIBUTION:
New Guinea, Salawati and Japen (Geelvink Bay); two colour phases: orange and yellow

HABITAT:
since the species is distributed throughout New Guinea, a variety of habitats; up to 1,800 m (6,000 ft)

CLUTCH:
2 rounded, white eggs

INCUBATION:
24 to 25 days by the female

FLEDGING:
64 to 72 days

AVERAGE LIFESPAN:
28 years

SEXING:
the female is similar to the male, but the male usually has a slightly larger head and beak

JUVENILES:
duller than the adults; the bare skin at the side of the lower mandible becomes respectively grey, brown-yellow and orange; brown iris; brown beak; after about 4 months, orange

SIZE:
24.5 to 26 cm (9$^1/_2$ to 10$^1/_4$ in)

SWAINSON'S RAINBOW or BLUE-MOUNTAIN LORY
Trichoglossus h. moluccanus

DISTRIBUTION:
eastern Australia, Kangaroo Island; rare in Tasmania; introduced to western Australia (Perth area)

HABITAT:
a multitude of habitats: mountainous areas, lowland and artificial food sites, for example, Currumbin Sanctuary, Palm Beach (Queensland) and other areas

CLUTCH:
2, occasionally 3, oval, white eggs

INCUBATION:
22 to 25 days by the female

FLEDGING:
60 to 64 days, sometimes as early as 51 days and as late as 70 days; mature in about 2 years

AVERAGE LIFESPAN:
28 years

SEXING:
the female is similar to the male, but the male usually has a somewhat larger head and beak

JUVENILES:
duller than the adults; more yellow on the breast; white eye-ring; brown iris and bill

SIZE:
29 cm (11½ in)

This hardy, attractive lory, also known in Australia as the rainbow lorikeet, is best housed in a roomy aviary. Some birds do reasonably well in a large cage, however. Many really tame specimens (those raised by hand) can even talk a little. Caged lories really need a daily flight around a room, but their fluid droppings do not make these beautiful birds ideal household companions! At the Currumbin Sanctuary (near Brisbane, Australia), the birds are a real tourist attraction, some being so tame that they sit on people's shoulders to eat honey-soaked bread.

Most breeding pairs are very prolific as long as they are housed in a long aviary with a roomy night shelter; room temperature must be maintained.

The male's courtship display consists of a weaving, swaying motion accompanied by a rustling sound. He even dances and hops up and down, moving sideways along a thick branch or perch, or hangs upside down. During this display, both sexes blaze their eyes, arch their somewhat fluffed necks and bob, and even hiss, in a manner very characteristic of all *Trichoglossus* species. The birds not only use nest boxes (see dusky lory, page 67), but also dig holes in the ground. It is best to keep the birds in pairs in separate flights to avert quarrelling.

Feeding: as for the green-naped lory (see right).

GREEN-NAPED LORY
Trichoglossus h. haematodus

The green-naped lory belongs to the wedge-tailed lories and has some 20 subspecies. Most can be kept in an aviary that is at least 1.5 m (5 ft) long. In colder climates, they should be kept in an indoor aviary, but as long as room temperature is maintained, there should be no problems. A garden aviary must have a night shelter, with a thick-walled nest/sleep box measuring 25 x 25 x 45 cm (10 x 10 x 18 in), with an entrance diameter of 10 cm (4 in), positioned as high as possible. A 3 cm (1¼ in) layer of wood pulp should be placed on the floor of the nest box; keep an eye on this 'upholstery' and replace it if the copious, fluid droppings make it wet.

The birds become quite pugnacious during the breeding season, and each pair must have its own aviary. Once independent, the young must be moved to separate accommodation as the parents will become aggressive, especially if they want to start a new family. It is essential to shield nervous young birds from the aviary wire by fixing willow or fruit-tree twigs to it to help to prevent injury.

Feeding: provide commercial lory food, along with various soft fruits, but also apples and especially berries and grapes; greens (chickweed, dandelions); carrots cut into small strips; live food (small mealworms, maggots, ant pupae and so on); commercial egg and/or rearing food for soft-billed birds; germinated or milky (grass) seed; buckwheat; millet varieties; millet spray; and some soaked sunflower seeds.

Fact file

DISTRIBUTION:
western New Guinea, in 20 (or 21) subspecies

HABITAT:
widespread, especially in higher levels of its altitudinal range, up to 2,000 m/6,600 ft; also in casuarina groves, rainforests and open areas, often near villages

CLUTCH:
2, occasionally 3, oval, white eggs

INCUBATION:
22 to 24 days, sometimes 25 days, by the female

FLEDGING:
70 days

AVERAGE LIFESPAN:
28 years

SEXING:
the male and female are similar in appearance

JUVENILES:
duller than the adults; brown iris; brownish-black beak; becomes orange by about 4½ months of age

SIZE:
28 cm (22 in)

Fact file

DISTRIBUTION:
in the main, central, mountain area of New Guinea (Weyland mountains)

HABITAT:
up to 2,600 m (8,500 ft), in flowering eucalyptus and silky oaks; also in casuarinas (open country); often nomadic and in groups of 30 or more birds

CLUTCH:
2 almost spherical, white eggs

INCUBATION:
23 days by the female

FLEDGING:
22 to 24 days

AVERAGE LIFESPAN:
30 years

SEXING:
the female is similar to the male; the male's head and bill are slightly larger

JUVENILES:
duller than the adults, with less pronounced streaking; some blue below the eye and dull-bluish or green hind-crown; greyish-brown iris; brownish beak

SIZE:
19 cm (7 in)

GOLDIE'S LORIKEET
Trichoglossus goldiei

This species first arrived in the United States (at Chicago Zoo) in 1949, and has been available in Europe since 1950. It does well on the normal lory diet (see below). Various commercial hummingbird menus can also be offered as a treat, and are especially popular with smaller-sized lorikeets. Although members of this species are a little shy at first, and will typically spend hours in the nest/sleep box, once settled, they will become reasonably tame and trusting.

We have several pairs, and none of them seems to mind when we look into the nest box, even when the hen is sitting on her eggs or caring for her young. The cock often keeps his brooding mate company or sits close to the nest. Due to their very fluid droppings, it is recommended that the nest bedding is renewed at least twice a week – that is, after the young are at least 10 to 12 days old. Both adults and young soon get used to this activity, and we have never lost any young due to it.

These colourful lorikeets are often bred in indoor aviaries and large cages. It is necessary to bring them indoors for the winter unless they have a lightly heated (room-temperature) night shelter.

Feeding: as for the green-naped lory, see page 69. Lories and lorikeets that are given regular supplies of willow or fruit-tree twigs (but not cherry) will leave the aviary or cage frameworks pretty much undamaged.

BLACK-CAPPED or TRI-COLOURED LORY
Lorius lory

This fascinating bird is not a noisy lory, which may be one reason for its popularity. These lories are fairly willing breeders, and hand-reared chicks prove excellent mimics. A pair should never be kept together with the same, or another parrot-like, species; the cock especially can be very aggressive, and would make short work of any other hookbill that got in his way. During the winter, the birds are best kept in heated accommodation at a temperature of 15°C (59°F), but should still have the use of a thick-walled sleep/nest box measuring 30 x 30 x 45 cm (12 x 12 x 18 in), with an entrance-hole diameter of 8 cm (3¼ in).

This species was first described in 1751, at a time when its members were already popular pet birds with their native islands' human inhabitants. The adults' talent for mimicry is not great, but some individuals will learn a few words or repeat sounds, especially the songs of other birds in the area.

These beautiful, generally slow and heavy, flying birds need a lot of space, and cages are not ideal homes for them. The concrete floor of the aviary is best covered with corn-on-the-cob bedding or similar as the birds' droppings are loose, copious and strong-smelling. In the interests of hygiene, a natural floor is considered unsuitable. Provide a selection of thick perches, such as the twigs of fruit trees (but not cherry) and willow trees, with a diameter of 5 to 7 cm (2 to 2¾ in), but note that the birds will continually reduce these to splinters, so that they will have to be regularly replaced.

Feeding: as for the green-naped lory, see page 69. Extra fruit and various insects are eagerly accepted; this species is known for its habit of catching and eating cockroaches.

Fact file

DISTRIBUTION:
Waigeu, Batanta, Salawati and Misool (New Guinea, western Papuan islands); 6 subspecies from various islands in the Geelvink Bay

HABITAT:
lowland forest

CLUTCH:
2 elliptical, white eggs

INCUBATION:
25 to 26 days by the female

FLEDGING:
63 to 70 days

AVERAGE LIFESPAN:
30 years

SEXING:
the female is similar to the male; the bill often appears rounder and less elongated since the male's upper mandible is broader and more protruding

JUVENILES:
duller than the adults; blue upper breast often extending to the throat; dark-brown iris and bill

SIZE:
31 cm (12¼ in)

The Handbook of Cage and Aviary Birds

Fact file

DISTRIBUTION:
northern Molucca islands,
Indonesia (Halmahera and Wedi);
in 3 subspecies

HABITAT:
canopy and forests; sometimes
in coconut trees along the coast
and in coconut plantations

CLUTCH:
2 elliptical, white eggs

INCUBATION:
26 to 27 days; the male sleeps
in the nest at night

FLEDGING:
70 to 76 days; the male can
become hostile towards his young

AVERAGE LIFESPAN:
22 years

SEXING:
the female is similar to the male

JUVENILES:
the red colours are slightly
subdued; dark-brown iris,
orange-brown in 2 to 3 months;
dark-brown beak

SIZE:
30 cm (11¾ in)

CHATTERING LORY
Lorius garrulus

This playful species is
one of the best-known
lories in aviculture,
and an ideal bird
for the beginner.
It is easily managed,
hardy, will quickly
become extremely tame
and will breed
frequently. The parents
are often aggressive when
their young are present,
however. In the wild, they
travel about in pairs and
can be quite quarrelsome
with other members of their
own species, especially when
feeding in trees where the
food supply is limited and the
birds have to rely on their
strength to get the most food.
Each pair has its own territory,
which it defends vigorously, especially
if it contains good feeding areas. In captivity,
these birds are best kept in single pairs, but can be placed with other
birds in aviaries as long as there are no other parrot-like birds.
Lories may occasionally be aggressive towards all other birds, and
very much so when they are protecting young or eggs in the nest.
Wear gloves and carry a net to keep them at bay when entering the
aviary to inspect the nest.

These birds often look scruffy in pet shops because they are given
neither the opportunity to bathe nor a spray of lukewarm water.
They must have an opportunity to bathe daily if their plumage is to
stay in top condition. Watch out when buying these birds from
unreputable stores because imported ones may have been pinioned
by both wings, forever robbing them of their power of flight and
restricting them to a life of running about on the floor of an aviary
or cage.

Feeding: as for the green-naped lory, see page 69. Also offer them
some willow and fruit twigs, a little bird seed and unripe weed seed
every day, and a few fresh endive leaves every other day.

STELLA LORIKEET
Charmosyna papou goliathina

These so-called 'ornamental' or 'honey' lories are small- to medium-sized birds. Elegantly built, they are instantly recognised by their pointed, long tails and are the only lorikeets with such a trailing tail. There is also an easily recognisable sexual dimorphism (the *Charmosyna papou goliathina* hen has a conspicuous yellow patch on its flanks and rump), and the tongue is somewhat longer than in other lories and lorikeets. (Stella lorikeets can lick their eyes with their tongue, which they do when they are wet with fruit juices.) These birds are susceptible to aspergillosis and candidiasis, and must be acclimatised with the greatest of care.

This bird occurs in two subspecies: *C. p. stella* and *C. p. goliathina*; each subspecies also occurs in a melanistic form (black or brownish black) that is dominant over red; *C. p. goliathina* differs from *C. p. stella* primarily in having yellow towards the tip of the head, upper breast and tail feathers.

Tip: melanistic birds cannot tolerate temperatures over 40°C (104°F), and start breathing with open mouths at 37°C (100°F). Normal room temperatures seem best for them, but under no circumstances expose them to temperatures below 10°C (50°F).

Both subspecies have been known in aviculture since about 1900, and the first reported breeding was in Scotland in 1910. At the end of 1970, a number of *C. p. golianthinas* became available in Europe and the USA. They are ideal aviary subjects that mix well with the larger softbills (tanagers, pittas and so on). These lorikeets must have fresh bathwater every day, which they will use frequently.

Feeding: as for the green-naped lory, see page 69, along with a rich variety of fresh fruits every day. Newly acquired birds should be offered soft fruits and a honey–glucose solution with an added vitamin preparation. As these birds feed with their tongues more than most lories and lorikeets, it is important that their diet is quite fluid so that they can easily take it up.

Normal-coloured stella lorikeet.

Fact file

DISTRIBUTION:
New Guinea; in 4 subspecies

HABITAT:
mountainous areas; not in open country

CLUTCH:
2 white eggs

INCUBATION:
25 to 26 days, sometimes 28 to 32 days, by both sexes

FLEDGING:
59 to 60 days

AVERAGE LIFESPAN:
30 years

SEXING:
the female has a yellow spot above the thighs; both sexes have a yellow-tipped, long, trailing tail

JUVENILES:
duller than the adults, with a reddish neck and breast feathers, usually edged in black; brownish iris, brownish-orange beak

SIZE:
body size with full tail: 42 cm (16½ in); tail: 25 cm (10 in)

Fact file

DISTRIBUTION:
New Guinea; in 2 (or 3)
subspecies: *N. m. musschenbroekii*
in Vogelkop and *N. major* (or
N. medius, a disputed race) in
the highlands of Papua New
Guinea (also the Sepik region and
Huon peninsula); *N. medius* in the
Snow mountains

HABITAT:
forest edges; montane forests;
cultivations; up to 2,600 m
(8,500 ft) in central and
eastern highlands

CLUTCH:
2 rounded, white eggs

INCUBATION:
23 to 25 days by the female

FLEDGING:
47 to 60 days

AVERAGE LIFESPAN:
10 years

SEXING:
the female is similar to the male

JUVENILES:
similar to the parents,
but slightly duller; brown
beak; white cere (yellowish
in adults); brown iris
(after 4 months, orange-brown)

SIZE:
20 cm (8 in)

MUSSCHENBROEK'S LORIKEET
Neopsittacus musschenbroekii

It seems that the first pair of birds of this species was brought to England in 1933 by aviculturist H Whitley. The first captive breeding successes are attributed to Sir Edward Hallstrom in Australia during the 1940s. Musschenbroek's lorikeets are today very popular; successful breedings, usually early in the year, are not uncommon.

This lorikeet belongs to the so-called 'mountain lories', and the species of this genus are known for their well-developed gizzard, which indicates a large intake of seed. Our own birds are given a seed menu of various millets, canary grass seed, hemp, black (oil) sunflower seeds (fed sparingly to prevent the birds from becoming too fat), oat groats, rape seed, wheat and buckwheat (not really a seed, but a fruit).

It is a shame that these birds always remain somewhat shy; as you approach, they quickly disappear into the nest/sleep box (which should measure 20 x 20 x 25 cm/ 8 x 8 x 11 in, with an entrance diameter of 6 cm/2^1/$_4$ in). They sometimes sleep on a high perch at night, or hang from the cage's wire. Timber cages or aviaries are not recommended for these birds as they soon destroy wood with their strong beaks.

Feeding: as for the green-naped lory, see page 69. As well as the seeds listed above, they love millet spray and a rich variety of fresh fruits (especially peeled and diced, sweet apples). Also give them figs (including soaked, dried ones); guavas; thawed, frozen peas; pomegranates; grapes; pine nuts; cracked walnuts; green foods like dandelion leaves, spinach and chickweed; fresh corn; carrot strips; and little willow twigs (daily).

PALM COCKATOO
Prosciger aterrimus

This black cockatoo has an impressive beak, naked cheek-patches, a prominent crest and a black-tipped, red tongue. It is noteworthy that the remarkable, red cheeks become bright when the bird is excited ('blushing'). The cere is covered with small, black feathers, but the thighs are bare.

In the wild, this cockatoo spends the greater part of the day high up in the trees, but also enjoys digging up roots, bulbs, palm-tree seeds and grubs, as well as berries, fruits, leaves, buds and insects and their larvae.

In captivity, these expensive and gentle birds breed regularly. They require a large, hollow log as their nest/sleep box (1.2 to 1.8 m/4 to 6 ft high; entrance diameter: 46 cm/18 in). Place a thin layer of wood chips on the bottom, although the birds will carry some nesting material to the nest as long as they are compatible. In the wild, the birds also ensure that their nest will be porous in the event of heavy rainfall. If a new pair is being introduced, watch the male for aggressive behavior, which can even occur during incubation.

The aviary should be well constructed. The shelter should be constructed of metal framing, concrete slabs and heavy, welded mesh because the birds often prefer to spend the night indoors during severe weather.

Feeding: as for the greater sulphur-crested cockatoo, see page 79.

Fact file

DISTRIBUTION:
Cape York peninsula
(northern Australia); New Guinea
(except the central, mountainous
region); Aru islands (Indonesia);
in 3 subspecies

HABITAT:
tropical and monsoon rainforests,
bordering on dense savannah;
lowlands (up to 762 m/2,500 ft);
in small flocks

CLUTCH:
1 white egg that can be pyriform
to elliptical-ovate to broad-elliptical in
shape (the size can vary substantially)

INCUBATION:
30 to 33 days, occasionally
28 to 34 days, by the female

FLEDGING:
after about 80 days

AVERAGE LIFESPAN:
50 years

SEXING:
the female is similar to the male, but
smaller, with a smaller facial patch

JUVENILES:
similar to the parents, but without
the layer of grey powder
(powder down will be produced
much later); many feathers of the
under-wing coverts and underside
are edged with pale yellow; white
facial area; greyish-white bill

SIZE:
60 cm (24 in)

Fact file

DISTRIBUTION:
Australia and Tasmania;
in 2 (or 3) subspecies

HABITAT:
savannah; open country; eucalyptus
woodland; dry, interior plains;
agricultural areas; watercourses;
gardens and parklands; always
inland; follows civilisation;
sometimes in flocks
of 1,000 individuals

CLUTCH:
3 to 6, but usually 3 to 4, broadly
elliptical to elliptical-ovate,
slightly glossy, white eggs

INCUBATION:
23 to 26 days by both sexes

FLEDGING:
48 to 50 days

AVERAGE LIFESPAN:
40 years

SEXING:
sexual dimorphism: adult males
have a dark-brown iris; in
females, it is red or red-brown

JUVENILES:
duller than the parents; crown and
breast tinged with grey; brown iris
(adult eye colour is not attained
until about 23 to 26 months)

SIZE:
35 cm (14 in)

GALAH or ROSE-BREASTED COCKATOO
Eolophus (Cacatua) roseicapillus

This expensive cockatoo readily adapts to the human presence and to captivity, and makes few demands. Above all, this beautiful bird makes an exceptionally friendly, affectionate and amusing pet; some individuals even learn to mimic a few words without much difficulty. This species is usually best kept in an outdoor aviary, but many Australian aviculturists regard the galah as an excellent house pet. Remember, however, that the galah is considered a noisy cockatoo, a bird whose voice can best be characterised as metallic, disyllabic, grating and high pitched. When it is alarmed, its cries are harsh and shrieking.

The galah is a prolific breeder, and appears to be quite indiscriminate concerning its choice of breeding site, a matter that no doubt accounts in part for its popularity as an avian subject that breeds freely in captivity. In the wild, the galah lines its nest with fresh eucalyptus leaves each day, the only cockatoo species to do so. A hollow log or grandfather-clock-type of nest box seems the most logical way to bring the bird to breeding; a daily supply of fresh willow branches (with the leaves) will be greatly appreciated.

Feeding: give galahs pine nuts, peanuts, almonds and such like, along with safflower, canary grass seed, corn and corn on the cob, oats and groats, bunches of seeding wild grasses and a few stems of oats or wheat daily just prior to harvest time. A commercial seed mixture for large parrots, together with pellets (ratio 60:40), dark-green, leafy vegetables (particularly pea pods), melons and other fruits, including berries, willow branches and oyster grit must be available on a daily basis.

LEADBEATER or MAJOR MITCHELL'S COCKATOO

Cacatua leadbeateri

This outstandingly beautiful cockatoo is hardy and breeds well in captivity. Some males can be bred as early as two years of age, and females as young as four; some pairs have been known to continue breeding successfully into their thirties! Breeding pairs will breed consistently year after year, rarely failing to raise two or three youngsters. The species does have a temperamental and protective trait, however, and if the young are excessively interfered with, the cock has been known to kill his offspring. When left alone, the breeding birds rarely fail to live up to their reputation and their keeper's expectations.

The flight cage provided for breeding pairs should be a minimum of 3.6 x 2.4 x 1.5 m (12 x 8 x 5 ft), and larger accommodation should be offered if possible. Heavy-gauged mesh fencing is required because the species' beaks can soon destroy any lighter-gauged enclosures. A hollow log or grandfather-clock-type of nest box can be provided without fear of rejection, as long as the accommodation is at least 1.8 m (6 ft) long, and the actual nest site is about 60 cm (2 ft) from the entrance, in a hollow of about the same size. The bottom of the nest should be covered with decaying wood.

Feeding: as for the the galah (see left).

Fact file

DISTRIBUTION:
interior and south-western Australia; in 2 subspecies

HABITAT:
in thick brush of eucalyptus varieties, and in arid country, often near water; in pairs or family flocks

CLUTCH:
2 to 4, with an average of 3 elliptical, white eggs, without much gloss

INCUBATION:
24 to 26 days by both sexes

FLEDGING:
55 to 57 days

AVERAGE LIFESPAN:
45 years

SEXING:
the female is less pinkish, but more white, than the male, and has a broader yellow band in the crest; the female has a reddish-brown iris; the male has a dark-brown iris

JUVENILES:
duller than the parents; pale-brown iris, lighter in the females

SIZE:
35 cm (14 in)

Fact file

DISTRIBUTION:
Indonesia, Sulawesi (formerly Celebes) and adjacent islands; islands in the Java Sea, Lombok, Sumba, Sumbawa, Flores and Timor; in 4 subspecies

HABITAT:
forests and forest edges; coconut plantations and farmland; near civilisation and coasts; in large flocks

CLUTCH:
2, occasionally 3, elliptical, white eggs

INCUBATION:
28 days by both sexes

FLEDGING:
70 to 85 days

AVERAGE LIFESPAN:
40 years

SEXING:
the female is similar to the male; the female has a red-brown iris; the male has a black iris

JUVENILES:
the iris changes gradually from grey after the second year; prior to fledging, the beak is pinkish-white

SIZE:
33 cm (13 in)

LESSER SULPHUR-CRESTED COCKATOO
Cacatua s. sulphurea

This cockatoo is an unusually quiet species when compared to others within its family. It is one of the most common cockatoos encountered in the United States, and is therefore less expensive than others. This species breeds well in captivity, as do the various subspecies, especially the popular, orange-crested cockatoo (*C. s. cintrinocristata*), which is originally from the island of Sumba.

The preferred size of the flight cage seems to vary considerably from breeder to breeder. We have employed three different-sized flight cages ranging from as short as 3.6 m (12 ft) to as long as 10.6 m (35 ft), all quite successfully.

Grandfather-clock-type nest boxes and hollow logs are equally acceptable to breeding pairs. The nest boxes should generally be placed within the cage anywhere from about the first week of April to the last week of May (the same period as for the galah). Usually, a pair will show interest in the nest site almost immediately after its introduction. The nest box should usually be situated 90 cm to 1.2 m (3 to 4 ft) above the ground. The first egg is usually laid within two weeks of the introduction of the nest box, the second egg generally following two to five days later. Incubation begins immediately after the first egg has been laid. During the first few days after hatching, the nestlings are somewhat noisy. Both adults often feed the youngsters in the nest site at the same time.

Feeding: as for the galah, see page 76.

GREATER SULPHUR-CRESTED COCKATOO
Cacatua g. galerita

This is a very popular cockatoo, despite its shriek (and it is a poor candidate as a companion bird for flat-dwellers or anyone living in relatively congested areas). This bird is otherwise easily trained and proves to be very gentle, affectionate and long-lived (this species often outlives all other parrots).

The bird needs a large cage measuring 50 cm³ (20 ft³), with 2.5 cm (1 in) spacing between bars. If you keep a pair, note that they are likely to bond with each other instead of with their owner. Indoor birds should be kept at room temperature all year round.

Breeding resembles that of the lesser suphur-crested cockatoo (see left), as does that of the two subspecies, *C. g. fitzroyi* (found in Australia) and *C. g. triton*, or the Triton cockatoo (which is native to Papua New Guinea, the Moluccas and the Palau Islands); the latter is well known in aviculture.

All of these cockatoos are very affectionate, but also very demanding; they need a lot of attention every day.

Feeding: a reputable commercial seed mixture mixed with pellets (60:40 ratio) makes a good staple food. Avoid seed mixtures that are high in sunflower seeds because these often lead to obesity and irritability in companion birds. Every day, provide oyster grit in a separate dish; corn on the cob; melons and other fruits, including berries; dark-green, leafy vegetables and other vegetables (pea pods are a favourite); lots of willow branches; various unshelled nuts (especially almonds); some cheese; and mineral blocks.

Fact file

DISTRIBUTION:
eastern, south-eastern and southern Australia and Tasmania; introduced to western Australia and to New Zealand; in 4 subspecies

HABITAT:
a variety of habitats (see galah, page 76), but mostly in open country, with some trees that are used for resting and roosting

CLUTCH:
2 to 3 elliptical-ovate, white eggs, without any gloss

INCUBATION:
26 days by both sexes

FLEDGING:
about 77 days

AVERAGE LIFESPAN:
45 years

SEXING:
the female is similar to the male; in some males, the iris is reddish-brown

JUVENILES:
pale-blue, naked eye-ring; the iris is initially grey, and later brown

SIZE:
51 cm (20 in)

Fact file

DISTRIBUTION:
southern Moluccas and
Indonesia (Seram; formerly
present on Sapurua and Haruki);
introduced to Amboina, but
extinct since the 1980s

HABITAT:
along the coast; in coconut
plantations and forests; on slopes
below 1,000 m (3,280 ft);
once abundant, now (2004)
critically endangered

CLUTCH:
2 elliptical, white eggs

INCUBATION:
28 days by both sexes

FLEDGING:
105 to 110 days

AVERAGE LIFESPAN:
45 years

SEXING:
the female is a bit smaller than
the male, especially the beak and
head; the male's iris is black; the
female's iris is dark brown

JUVENILES:
similar to the parents;
black-grey iris

SIZE:
55 cm (21½ in)

MOLUCCAN or SALMON-CRESTED COCKATOO
Cacatua moluccensis

This impressive cockatoo displays a personality that can be characterised as intelligent, affectionate, trustworthy, dependable, gentle and at times even mischievous. It is an exceedingly rare individual that cannot be tamed and that will not develop a close bond with its owner. At times, these birds can be very demanding. We have yet to acquire an individual that shows a propensity to talk, but some do, softly mimicking words and whistles. Such birds are the exception, however, and are not often encountered. In general, most Moluccans have piercingly loud cries. Moluccan cockatoos do best in an outdoor aviary at least 2.4 m (8 ft) wide, and with plenty of opportunities for play and games; indoors, a climbing tree, firmly anchored in a cement pot filled with sand, is essential.

Breeding in captivity is rather difficult and similar to that of the lesser sulphur-crested cocktoo (see page 78). Provide a large aviary, measuring a miniumum of 4.8 x 1.5 x 1.5 m (16 x 5 x 5 ft), and a nest box measuring 51 x 38 x 25 cm (20 x 15 x 10 in); cover the bottom with a 5 cm (2 in) layer of sawdust, peat moss and rotting wood. After copulation, both adults will spend most of their daytime hours in the nest itself, although at dusk the cock generally leaves the hen to roost outside by himself. An adult is always in attendance at the nest site, and the female, even when considered fully tamed, becomes defensive, threatening and aggressive when the aviary is approached.

Note: nestlings are very nervous birds that are prone to being easily startled by the slightest unusual sound. When startled, youngsters tend to regurgitate their food.

Feeding: as for the galah, see page 76.

UMBRELLA or WHITE-CRESTED COCKATOO
Cacatua alba

This cockatoo makes an excellent companion bird, although the males can be unpredictable, loud and destructive. While not as flamboyant in behaviour as the Moluccan or sulphur-crested cockatoos, the umbrella cockatoo is an extremely intelligent bird that not only learns quickly, but can master a variety of tricks without much effort, and does so in a dignified manner.

Breeding successes seem to be achieved in roomy and (especially) sturdy aviaries (see the Moluccan, left). Pairs do not appear to be too finicky concerning nest-box accommodation, and a Moluccan-sized box will do nicely. The bottom of the box should be covered with humus and a layer of rotting wood. Pairs that are interested in breeding will immediately take to the nest site upon its introduction to the aviary and will begin excavating the substrate. Introduce nest boxes during April as it takes a pair a month or so to prepare the interior of the nest. The completion of the clutch can be expected in May or June. The parents appear to be exceptionally dutiful towards their clutch and nestlings. A young family is never left without a parent in attendance, and the young are not left entirely by themselves until they are seven weeks old.

Feeding: as for the galah, see page 76. Breeding pairs rely heavily on fresh fruits (notably peeled oranges and apples).

Fact file

DISTRIBUTION:
central and northern Moluccas and Indonesia (Obi, Batjan, Halmahera, Ternate and Tidore)

HABITAT:
primary and secondary forests; along the coast; in cultivation (coconut plantations); gardens and parks

CLUTCH:
1 to 2 elliptical, white eggs

INCUBATION:
28 days by both sexes

FLEDGING:
70 to 105 days

AVERAGE LIFESPAN:
40 years

SEXING:
the female usually has a smaller beak and a reddish-brown iris; the male has a dark-brown to black iris

JUVENILES:
similar to the parents; brownish-grey iris

SIZE:
45 cm (17½ in)

Goffin's cockatoo
Cacatua goffini

Fact file

The Handbook of Cage and Aviary Birds

DISTRIBUTION:
Indonesia (Tanimbar islands:
Jamdena, Foradate, Seluru and
so on); also on Tual in the Kay
islands); introduced to Singapore

HABITAT:
forests and forest edges on
the coast and inland; the
birds' sleeping quarters are
near watercourses

CLUTCH:
2 rounded, white eggs

INCUBATION:
28 days by both sexes

FLEDGING:
80 to 85 days

AVERAGE LIFESPAN:
40 years

SEXING:
the female has a somewhat
smaller eye-ring; the female's iris is
brown; the male's iris is black

JUVENILES:
similar to the parents, but with
pink in the head-feathers and
lore; pale-blue eye-ring;
greyish iris

SIZE:
32 cm (12½ in)

The Goffin's cockatoo, or goffin, is one of the smaller cockatoo species. Undemanding, it presents no maintenance problems. It is mainly white, with a salmon-pink lore. A faint-yellow patch tinges the ear coverts. Males have distinctly dark-brown eyes, whereas the hens' are reddish brown. Nestlings have primrose-coloured down.

Once quite rare in aviculture, these cockatoos became vulnerable to capture and exportation, with the near-total destruction of the birds' forest habitat in 1972. Many were sent to Europe and the USA just as the USA opened quarantine stations to deal with animal imports. The rapidly diminishing numbers of goffins in Indonesia are somewhat compensated for by the many breeding successes in captivity. The first breeding success was achieved by E G B Schulte in The Netherlands in 1975, the second (and Britain's first) being achieved by Neil O'Connor in 1977.

The goffin's inconspicuous courtship behaviour is accompanied in both sexes by chattering of the beak. These birds prefer nest boxes measuring 50 x 40 x 30 cm (20 x 15 x 12 in) or 25 x 25 x 40 cm (10 x 10 x 15 in). Breeding birds usually display nervousness in the presence of humans.

Note: this species often screams, even in the dark. Like other cockatoos, goffins that are allowed to roam on the floor may develop a habit of attacking people's toes.

Feeding: as for the galah, see page 76.

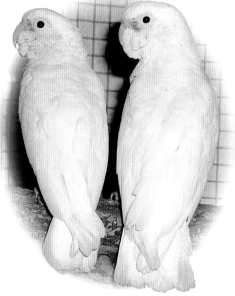

BARE-EYED COCKATOO or LITTLE CORELLA
Cacatua s. sanguinea

Although this small cockatoo can be extremely loud, it has numerous admirable qualities as a pet or companion bird. It is more docile and tractable than most cockatoo species. It is easily tamed, proves quite hardy and has a legendary propensity to talk and acquire a large vocabulary. It is also a most affectionate bird, and has a reputation for mischief.

In the wild, the little corella has followed humankind into cultivation and often inflicts great damage on agricultural areas. In some regions of Australia, this lovely bird has nevertheless received public protection quite consistently over the past century. In Western Australia in particular, it has been protected since at least 1911 in the Gascoyne- and Minilya-river districts because of its fondness for the seeds of the double-gees plant, a noxious creeping vine that is said to lame sheep.

Breeding is relatively easy and reasonably successful. At the San Diego Zoo in California, for example, the first young were reared in 1927, and by 1970 no less than 103 young had hatched from a single pair, most of them then being successfully hand-reared.

Note: this species played an important role in the exploration and settlement of the Australian continent. When crossing any of its many arid and desert regions, early travellers were often aided in locating water sources simply by following flocks of little corellas during their morning and evening flights to and from water holes and roosting sites.

Feeding: as for the galah, see page 76.

Fact file

DISTRIBUTION:
eastern, north-western and northern Australia; in 2 subspecies; *C. s. normantoni* in parts of southern New Guinea

HABITAT:
dry, inland areas; open country; along river courses; cultivation; gardens and parks

CLUTCH:
2 to 3 ovate, white eggs

INCUBATION:
21 to 24 days by both sexes

FLEDGING:
45 to 50 days

AVERAGE LIFESPAN:
40 years

SEXING:
the female is similar to the male, but somewhat smaller

JUVENILES:
similar to the parents, but with a shorter upper mandible; pale-blue eye-ring, greyish skin under the eyes

SIZE:
40 cm (15½ in)

The Handbook of Cage and Aviary Birds

COCKATIEL
Nymphicus hollandicus

Fact file

DISTRIBUTION:
Australia (rarer along the coast);
introduced to Tasmania

HABITAT:
savannah; grassland; parkland;
cultivation; usually near water; in
pairs or large flocks; nomadic in
Queensland, migratory
in southern Australia

CLUTCH:
4 to 8 or more broadly
elliptical, white eggs, with a
slight gloss; average 5 eggs

INCUBATION:
18 to 21 days by both sexes
(the male during the day,
the female at night)

FLEDGING:
30 to 35 days

AVERAGE LIFESPAN:
20 years

SEXING:
the female has duller facial markings
and a grey crest and wing coverts;
the underside of her tail is barred
with grey and yellow; the male has
a yellow face and crest; the
underside of his tail is black

JUVENILES:
similar to the female, but with a
shorter tail and pinkish cere

SIZE:
30 to 35 cm (12 to 14 in)

This charming bird is one of the best-loved cage and aviary birds; it is a great companion bird and an excellent breeder. Always form pairs by placing an inexperienced bird with a bird that knows its way around and has already raised a family. Try using a nest box measuring 35 x 20 x 45 cm (13 x 8 x 18 in), with an entrance hole 6 cm ($2^1/_4$ in) in diameter. (Cockatiels are not that fussy about the form of their nursery, however.) Just below the nest entrance, fix a perch 18 cm (7 in) long and about 1.5 cm ($^1/_2$ in) in diameter so that it protrudes both inside and outside the nest box. Cover the floor of the box with a layer of damp peat mixed with a few wood shavings 4 to 5 cm ($1^1/_2$ to 2 in) deep. In the middle of this layer, form a hollow with your fist to create a place where the hen can later place her eggs. This depression will prevent the eggs from rolling about too much. The youngsters, which initially resemble the hen, often stick their little heads out of the nest and make a peeping, 'sissing' noise. It is a good idea to construct the nest box so that the bird sitting on the eggs has its head at entrance height; do not make the opening too high up. Don't use a nest box whose opening is too low, either, because cockatiels tend to leave the nest when startled. Place a breeding pair in a roomy aviary by themselves. Cockatiels often make outstanding foster parents for *Platycercus* and other Australian parakeet species.

Feeding: provide a commercial seed mixture mixed with pellets (60:40 ratio), lots of greens (particularly when there are young in the nest), privet leaves, willow branches, germinated seeds and a few mealworms and ant pupae every day, along with some slices of apple and carrot.

Cockatiel varieties
Cinnamon (fawn or Isabel) is a sex-linked recessive. Cinnamons, like the autosomal, recessive fallows, are born with red eyes, which become dark within a week, whereas the fallows' eyes remain red. Pied (harlequin or variegated) is an autosomal recessive, as are silver, white face (charcoal) and fallow. The pearl (laced or opaline) is a sex-linked recessive, but the males moult into normal (wild-colour), grey, adult plumage after 6 to 12 months, while the females retain their pearl markings. Lutino and albino are both sex-linked recessives with red eyes (the normal yellows have dark eyes). Lutinos and albinos differ from one another in that the former has its carotenoid and will therefore show some yellow, orange and/or red, while the albino has lost these colours, as well as its melanin colours, leaving a pure-white bird with red eyes.

Normal male cockatiel.

Lutino cockatiel.

Yellow-cheeked cockatiel.

White-masked pearl cockatiel.

The Handbook of Cage and Aviary Birds

Fact file

DISTRIBUTION:
the Moluccas, including Buru, Seram, Ambon, Saparua and Haruku; in 9 (or 10) subspecies in the Moluccas, Sumba (endangered), Tanimbar Islands, New Guinea and the western Papua Islands, Biak, Aru Islands, northern Australia (Cape York peninsula), the Bismarck archipelago and the Solomon Islands

HABITAT:
a broad range of habitats, from lowland forests to open woodland, coconut plantations, savannah, coastal regions and mangroves to high altitudes (up to 2,000 m/6,500 ft)

CLUTCH:
2 broadly ovate, slightly glossy, white eggs

INCUBATION:
26 to 30 days by the female

FLEDGING:
75 to 77 days

AVERAGE LIFESPAN:
30 years

SEXING:
the female is red, with purple underparts and under-wing coverts, a black beak and yellowish iris; the male is green, with red flanks and under-wing coverts, a blue bend of the wing, dark-blue flight feathers, a red upper mandible with yellow tips and an orange iris

JUVENILES:
similar to the parents; a brownish beak in both sexes

SIZE:
35 cm (14 in)

ECLECTUS PARROT
Eclectus r. roratus

Because the sexes are totally different in colour, it was thought for a very long time that they were two species. In 1874, Dr A B Meyer, of the National Museum of Natural History in Munich, Germany, discovered that the males were predominantly green and the females, red (youngsters can be sexed at $3^1/_2$ weeks of age). The female often stirs up trouble in the aviary, and may fight for weeks before settling down with her partner. Provide a conventional nest box measuring 30 x 30 x 50 cm (12 x 12 x 20 in), with an entrance 15 cm (6 in) in diameter. This species is generally willing to raise a family, especially when housed indoors.

Female eclectus parrot.

Imported or very nervous birds require an indoor aviary, with a temperature of about 22°C (71°F). Always place one pair of birds in an aviary. Don't be too surprised if the birds refuse all food at first. Provide a variety of fresh fruits, vegetables and sprouted beans (pulses) and lots of greens. If deprived of vitamin A, the birds will contract candidiasis; extra carrots and sliced tomatoes are excellent sources of this vitamin, and should therefore be offered daily. A dominant female may try to keep her mate away from food sources, which is why it is essential to have at least two different feeding areas in the aviary.

Their natural inability to bond closely and moodiness can make eclectus parrots rather poor companion birds. Hand-reared birds can become tame, however, although they will avoid excessive contact with their owners. Some will learn to speak a few words and mimic sounds. Males make better pets than females as the latter are often bad-tempered and noisy.

Feeding: provide white millet, canary grass seed, hemp and other small seeds, some safflower and sunflower seeds, peanuts, pine nuts, millet spray, celery, cubes of cheese, fresh corn on the cob, cooked rice, green peas, water-soaked brown bread, raisins, bananas, plums, apples, pears, kiwi fruits, flower buds, dandelion, spinach and chickweed.

Right: Male eclectus parrot.

AUSTRALIAN KING PARROT
Alisterus s. scapulari

The Handbook of Cage and Aviary Birds

Fact file

DISTRIBUTION:
eastern Australia and Queensland; in 2 subspecies; *A. s. minor* from eastern Queensland to Townsville and the Eungella district

HABITAT:
open forests and savannah with eucalyptus; also in coastal plains, in the mountains (up to 609m/2,000 ft), in cultivation and in plantations

CLUTCH:
3 to 6 rounded, white eggs

INCUBATION:
20 days by the female

FLEDGING:
35 days

AVERAGE LIFESPAN:
18 years

SEXING:
the female has a green head, breast, upper-tail coverts and tail, a light-blue rump, green under-tail coverts with red ends and a black upper mandible (the male's is pinkish-red)

JUVENILES:
similar to the female, but with a lighter beak and less red; final adult plumage after about 2 years

SIZE:
43 cm (17 in)

Male Australian king parrot.

The song of these robust birds is not unpleasant, but during flight (in the wild), they often let out a rather raw, 'eek-eek-eek-eek'; when sitting alone and undisturbed, they may whistle a soft and musical tune that can sound quite enchanting.

Captive birds are very fussy in their choice of nest site, and this has often led to eggs being dropped from a perch or laid directly on the ground. They prefer a deep nest box, about 1.8 to 2 m (6 to 6^1/$_2$ ft) high and with a floor area measuring 25 x 25 cm (10 x 10 in). The hen prefers to be at ground level, so the nest box can be placed on the floor of the aviary. However, youngsters have been raised in suspended boxes 60 to 100 cm (2 to 3 ft) in height. While the hen is incubating, the cock stays close and feeds her regularly. When the young are a few days old, he helps to feed them.

At fledging time, the youngsters are very similar in colour to the hen. However, the young hen's beak is usually darker in colour than that of the young male. The young cock may show the beginnings of a light wing stripe, and the red on his belly will usually be higher; the rump of the cock is dark blue, while that of the hen is much lighter blue. The young male begins to change colour within a year. There have been cases of adult cocks changing their red colour to orange. The reason for this is unknown. The offspring are normal in colour. A yellow mutation is known, but this is very rare and is autosomal recessive.

Feeding: provide a good commercial seed mixture for large parakeets mixed with pellets (ratio 60: 40) and supplemented by a variety of fruits, berries and green food. The birds need a regular supply of vitamin A. Smallseeds (some hemp, canary, millet and millet spray) are welcome, as are berries, grapes (mainly on account of the seeds), dandelion, chickweed and groundsel.

Right: Female Australian King Parrot

Fact file

DISTRIBUTION:
Australia: New South Wales
and northern Victoria

HABITAT:
blossoming eucalyptus
trees; cultivation; breeding
season outside in pairs;
somewhat nomadic

CLUTCH:
4 to 6 rounded, white eggs

INCUBATION:
20 days by the female

FLEDGING:
35 days

AVERAGE LIFESPAN:
15 years

SEXING:
the female is dull green, often
with some red on the breast,
thighs and tail tips; she is
somewhat heavier than the male

JUVENILES:
similar to the female; brown iris

SIZE:
40 cm (15 in)

BARRABAND'S PARAKEET
Polytelis swainsonii

The Barraband's, or superb, parakeet is known for its long-held whistle, which is quite similar to that of the cockatiel, but is deeper and more abrupt. The birds emit this call almost continually, even when they are flying. In the wild, they live in pairs or small groups and frequently seek eucalyptus seeds on the ground; they also take blossoms, pollen, nectar, fruits, nuts, grains and so on. They can raise their crown feathers in a mini-crest, which the male demonstrates when he approaches his partner perched on a branch, chattering away and trying to impress her. A receptive hen will sink to her knees, raise a mini-crest of her own, spread her wings and emit a soft warbling tone (like that emitted by the young). The cock will then feed her with food that he has brought.

A large nest box of the grandfather-clock-type or a deep, hollow log should be provided; it is best to offer a choice for optimum results. These birds must have a roomy aviary as they are very active on the wing. They also like to bathe and must be offered daily facilities for this.

Feeding: apart from the above-mentioned food, these birds need sunflower seeds, oats, wheat, crushed corn, canary grass seed, sorghum, millet varieties, fruits and berries, raisins and willow branches. Water-soaked, stale brown bread may also be given, especially during the breeding season.

Female Barraband's parakeet.

ROCK PEBBLER
Polytelis anthopeplus

The scientific name says it all: *Polytelis* means 'very fine, noble, aristocratic', while *anthopeplus* means 'feminine attire with flowers'. The hen is somewhat duller in colour than the male, being generally olive-green, with a lighter-coloured rump and head feathers. The red in the wings is less obvious, and there is almost no yellow. The lateral tail feathers have pinkish margins and tips.

In the wild, rock pebblers use a hollow trunk or tree limb during the breeding season; the nest hole is sometimes more than 5 m (16 ft) down within a tree. We have also found nests in rock crevices close to the Murray river. These birds avoid humans wherever possible, and are rarely seen in inhabited areas. In captivity, they are a challenge for the more experienced aviculturist, especially when housed in long aviaries with breeding facilities. This species is fast on the wing and the birds should be kept in pairs. Observed in the wild, they are an unforgettable sight as they fly around in pairs or small groups, resting in the early hours of the morning in the tops of trees, where, against the blue background of the sky and highlighted by the rays of the rising sun, they resemble golden jewels.

Feeding: as for the Barraband's parakeet, see left.

Female rock pebbler.

Fact file

DISTRIBUTION:
north-western Australia; in 2 subspecies; *P. a. monarchoides* is rarer and is found in south-eastern Australia

HABITAT:
open forests; near rivers and water courses; cultivations

CLUTCH:
3 to 6 rounded, white eggs

INCUBATION:
20 days by the female

FLEDGING:
35 days

AVERAGE LIFESPAN:
18 years

SEXING:
the female is duller than the male; she is generally olive-green, with a lighter rump and thighs; the red in the wings is less obvious and there is much less yellow

JUVENILES:
similar to the female, but on fledging, the young males already show more yellow than the females; after 14 to 18 months, the young have their full adult plumage

SIZE:
40 cm (15½ in)

The Handbook of Cage and Aviary Birds

Fact file

HABITAT:
arid desert areas; nomadic

CLUTCH:
4 to 6 rounded, glossy,
white eggs

INCUBATION:
19 to 20 days by the female

FLEDGING:
35 to 42 days

AVERAGE LIFESPAN:
15 years

SEXING:
the female has a greyish-mauve
crown and a greyish-blue back
and rump; her central tail feathers
are shorter than the male's

JUVENILES:
similar to the female, but duller

SIZE:
45 cm (18 in)

PRINCESS OF WALES PARAKEET
Polytelis alexandrae

This species occasionally displays the strange, reptilian habit of lying or sitting along, rather than across, tree branches or thick perches. It has a somewhat rattling call, rather like that of an Australian kingfisher. When resting in trees, these birds emit an almost continuous chattering; the alarm call is a quick 'queen-queen' sound. In 1863, the English ornithologist John Gould named this species for Princess Alexandra, the daughter of the King of Denmark who had recently married the Prince of Wales.

In the wild, this species is very scarce (according to the *Atlas of Australian Birds*, it was last seen in 1981) and nomadic.

These really stunning birds are regularly bred in captivity. Like the Barraband's parakeet and rock pebbler, they require a spacious aviary (with a minimum length of 3.5 m/12 ft) in which to fly about. Because the cock can be somewhat argumentative, it is best to keep each pair separately. These birds are usually most active in the mornings and evenings, when they forage on the ground in search of seeds and insects and their larvae. For the rest of the day, most sit with their heads tucked under their wings.

A nest box measuring 60 x 20 x 20 cm (23^1/$_2$ x 8 x 8 in), with an entrance hole measuring 7 cm (2^3/$_4$ in) in diameter, is ideal. It can be fixed in a slanted position so that the hen can walk to the eggs and not fall on them. The males are prone to kicking the eggs and should be removed for a time if they exhibit this behaviour. Otherwise, make the entrance hole smaller using a piece of bark, for example. The hen will then gnaw the bark to make the hole her own size, keeping the more robust cock outside. You can also replace the eggs with artificial ones, returning the real eggs when the hen begins to incubate seriously. Unlike the other two members of this genus, this species is susceptible to eye infections.

Feeding: as for the Barraband's parakeet, see page 90.

Varieties
Besides the fallow, lutino and blue, there is an albino mutation. All are autosomal recessive in character. Albinos can be produced by crossing a lutino and a blue.

Princess of Wales parakeet.

Fallow Princess of Wales parakeet.

Albino Princess of Wales parakeet.

Blue Princess of Wales parakeet.

PORT LINCOLN PARAKEET
Barnardius zonarius

Fact file

DISTRIBUTION:
central and western Australia; in 3 subspecies: *B. z. semitorquatus* (known as the 'twenty-eight parakeet'), from south-western Australia, *B. z. occidentalis*, from western Australia

HABITAT:
eucalyptus trees along water courses

CLUTCH:
4 to 7 rounded, white eggs

INCUBATION:
20 days by the female

FLEDGING:
35 days

AVERAGE LIFESPAN:
18 years

SEXING:
the female is similar to the male, although she sometimes has a slightly brown head; her beak is smaller than the male's

JUVENILES:
similar to the female, with stripes on the wings; adult plumage has emerged by 18 months

SIZE:
38 cm (15 in)

In both the wild and in captivity, the adaptable Port Lincoln parakeet is primarily a ground-dweller and very active, even after sunset and on moonlight nights. The subspecies *B. z. semitorquatus* is the well-known twenty-eight parakeet (its call is said to resemble the words 'twenty-eight'); this bird is a little larger and has a red forehead band. It is found only in south-western Australia (south of Perth and west of Albany). It is also a rather noisy bird that forages mainly on the ground for food, as well as among the twigs of trees and shrubs.

In order to breed both species of *B. zonarius* successfully, each pair requires a roomy aviary. Young birds develop adult plumage at 17 to 18 months and are sexually mature at two years. Nesting behaviour is similar to that of the Barnard's parakeet (see page 136), but at 7.5 cm (3 in), the nest entrance should be somewhat larger. Most pairs tend to start breeding early; we have seen birds start to breed as early as January and as late as March, which is why the nest boxes should be installed early in the year.

The Port Lincoln parakeet has no mutations. The twenty-eight parakeet has the autosomal recessive blue, but this is very scarce. The twenty-eight parakeet is also more difficult to breed, is rather aggressive and a renowned gnawer of woodwork; even thin mesh is seldom spared and is quickly bitten to pieces!

Feeding: as for the Pennant's parakeet, see page 96.

WESTERN or STANLEY ROSELLA
Platycercus icterotis

This beautiful bird is an ideal aviary bird and the smallest representative of its genus. The hen is somewhat smaller than the cock and is also a little duller in colour. Experienced breeders are able to sex the young by looking at their forehead feathers: those of the hen are light in colour, whereas cocks have dark, reddish-brown feathers.

The western rosella is a fairly peaceful bird, but we would still recommend that each pair has a separate aviary during the breeding season. The nest box, which should either be horizontal and measure 60 x 15 x 15 cm (23$^{1}/_{2}$ x 6 x 6 in) or vertical, measuring 50 cm (19$^{1}/_{2}$ in) in height, with a floor area measuring 20 x 20 cm (8 x 8 in), should be provided with a layer of peat dust or sawdust. In order to increase the humidity when the weather is dry, it is also recommended that the box is lightly sprayed with water from a garden hose.

Like other rosellas, this species is fond of bathing. These birds are quite hardy, but require a minimum of 3 m (10 ft) of flying space. During the autumn and winter, place the birds in a roomy, indoor aviary, but don't provide nest boxes lest unhealthy winter breeding results.

Feeding: as for the Pennant's parakeet, see page 96.

Fact file

DISTRIBUTION:
south-western Australia;
in 2 subspecies

HABITAT:
open eucalyptus forests;
savannah; cleared country;
homesteads, parks and gardens

CLUTCH:
3 to 7, sometimes up to 9,
rounded, white eggs

INCUBATION:
19 days by the female

FLEDGING:
35 days

AVERAGE LIFESPAN:
15 years

SEXING:
the female is green, with red-suffused underparts, a green head with a red forehead and dull-yellow cheeks that are less extensive than the male's

JUVENILES:
less red than the adults; a wing strip is present; a green head with a red forehead; full adult plumage in about 15 months

SIZE:
26 to 28 cm (10 to 11 in)

Fact file

PENNANT'S PARAKEET
Platycercus elegans

The hardy, but sensitive, Pennant's, or crimson, parakeet is unsuitable for a mixed collection, and each breeding pair should be housed in its own aviary. For proper breeding results, limit nest inspections to a minimum. The nest box should measure about 22 x 22 cm (9 x 9 in), with a height of 55 cm (21 in) and an entrance hole 7 cm (2¾ in) in diameter. Members of this species – undoubtedly among the most beautiful Australian parakeets – are fairly easy captive breeders for large cages and aviaries. Although it is not easy to distinguish the cock from the hen, the male's head is larger and more flattened than that of the female. The male's beak is also larger than the female's. Even immature youngsters can be sexed fairly easily by comparing head and beak sizes.

These birds destroy timber, so construct a metal-framed aviary or cover exposed timber with sheet metal. Adult birds are frequently aggressive towards each other. They are hardy and can withstand low temperatures. Members of this attractive species will spend much time rummaging around on the aviary floor.

Mainly green or red chicks sometimes emerge from the nest boxes, and probably also occur in the wild. Experiments have led to interesting results: one fancier removed some of the youngsters from the nest for a few hours each day so that they received less food. Those left in the nest received food from their parents, plus extra food from the fancier. This was done with several broods, and in every case, the poorly fed young became red, whereas the well-fed birds became green. The quantity of food consumed thus seems to affect the feather colour.

Blue Pennant's parakeet.

Cinnamon Pennant's parakeet.

Cinnamon orange Pennant's parakeet.

Albino Pennant's parakeet.

Feeding: provide a commercial parakeet seed mixture with canary grass seed, various millet varieties, small, black, sunflower seeds, some hemp, small nuts, buds, shoots, germinated seeds, fruits (berries, apple slices and so on), seeding grasses, grit and cuttlefish bone.

Varieties

Blue mutations are rather common. Other mutations are cinnamon, yellow and white; there are also lutinos. Blue is well established, but the others are still rare. The blue Pennant cannot strictly be called blue, even though this colour results from a deficiency of carotenoids. The red is replaced by a greyish colour.

The white can be bred from a blue and a yellow, and an albino, from a blue and a lutino. Yellow, blue and white are autosomal-recessive inheritances, while the lutino is probably a sex-linked recessive, although this is not definite as we usually regard lutinos as autosomal recessives. The lutinos keep their red heads, back and breast, whereas the blue and black parts become white; the eyes are always red. Cinnamon is sex-linked recessive.

Relatively recent colour mutations are: orange (autosomal recessive), ino-sex-linked (sex-linked and recessive), ino-non-sex-linked (most likely autosomal recessive), pastel (the same), dominant pied (inheritance still unknown) and yellow black-eyed (the same).

Fact file

DISTRIBUTION:
southern Queensland through New South Wales into Victoria, south-eastern South Australia and Tasmania (*P. e. diemenensis*); introduced to New Zealand; in 2 subspecies

HABITAT:
lightly timbered country with water courses; agricultural areas; cultivation

CLUTCH:
4 to 9, but usually 5, rounded, white eggs

INCUBATION:
18 to 21 days by the female

FLEDGING:
32 to 35 days

AVERAGE LIFESPAN:
15 years

SEXING:
the female is duller red than the male, has a smaller beak, greyish-white cheek patches and small, greyish-brown feathers around the eyes

JUVENILES:
similar to the female, with a very green neck region; adult plumage emerges from 10 to 15 months

SIZE:
30 cm (11$^3/_4$ in)

EASTERN ROSELLA
Platycercus eximius

Members of the eastern-rosella species, which is also called the red or golden-mantle rosella, among other names, are often kept in cages as pets. Once these birds lose their fear of humans, they often become rather aggressive. Some ornithologists recognise a subspecies, *P. e. cecilae* (also known as the golden-mantle rosella), which has a deeper-red head and breast, back and wing feathers edged with yellow and a bluish-green rump (see below).

The eastern rosellas are renowned as good breeders, although the cocks can sometimes become rather aggressive; the best results are obtained from birds over 12 months of age. They require a nest box measuring 50 cm high x 20 x 20 cm (20 in high x 8 x 8 in) and with an entrance hole 6 cm (2$^1/_3$ in) in diameter. The cock will feed the hen during incubation, but will not brood himself.

Female eastern rosella.

Rubino eastern rosella.

Red eastern rosella.

The golden-mantle rosella, a variety of the nominate, is not so readily available in the trade, which is unfortunate as it is an ideal aviary bird that is always ready to breed, given the right conditions. These birds become very tame and will even learn to feed from the hand quite quickly; they also make excellent foster parents. For breeding, the birds should be kept in a roomy aviary. The golden-mantle rosella can even be kept with small finches, but not with other psittacines.

Feeding: as for the Pennant's parakeet, see page 96.

Varieties

Red is an especially beautiful mutation; in fact, this variety is an opaline mutation that is genetically sex-linked recessive. Other mutations are lutino, white wing, pastel, rubino and Isabel. The lutino appeared some years ago in Australia, but now seems to have disappeared. The white wing was first bred in Belgium; it has a yellow tail, light-coloured feet and a golden-yellow back, with hardly any black, while the head is more yellow than red and there is a yellow stripe above the eye. It is genetically dominant. The pastel and Isabel are very similar. The Isabel is more tinted, especially in the wing feathers. In the pastel, this brown leans more towards grey. The Isabel is genetically sex-linked recessive; the pastel is autosomal recessive.

Lutino eastern rosella.

The Handbook of Cage and Aviary Birds

Fact file

DISTRIBUTION:
Australia: south-western Queensland to Victoria (sometimes near the coast), and southern and north-eastern South Australia; in 2 subspecies

HABITAT:
sparsely timbered grassland; riverine woodland; parks, farmland and cultivation; more on the ground than in trees; in pairs or flocks

CLUTCH:
4 to 7 rounded, white eggs

INCUBATION:
19 days by the female

FLEDGING:
32 to 34 days

AVERAGE LIFESPAN:
15 years

SEXING:
the female is duller than the male, is greyish-green above and yellowish-grey below, and has a green rump and pale wing-bar

JUVENILES:
similar to the parents, but duller; males may have red on the rump; females have a pale-yellow bill, males, a grey one; adult plumage arrives in about 1 year

SIZE:
27 cm (10½ in)

RED-RUMPED PARAKEET
Psephotus haematonotus

This hardy species is almost the ideal aviary bird: always ready to breed, a caring foster parent, intelligent, long-lived and very pretty! The hen is mainly olive-greenish-brown, with a little orange in her neck and belly; she has a pale-blue shoulder patch and a grey beak.

The species' voice is a two-noted whistle, with a soft, not unpleasant, chattering and a louder chattering when tussling.

Provide a roomy nest box measuring 35 cm high x 12 x 25 cm (13 in high x 4 x 10 in), with an entrance hole 6 cm (2⅓ in) in diameter. As soon as they are feeding independently, the young should be separated from their parents as the cock can behave aggressively towards them. We personally prefer to give each pair of red rumps a large aviary (at least 4 m/13 ft long) to themselves. They may also be used as foster parents, sometimes even for non-Australian parakeets.

Varieties
There are various mutations available, including lutino, cinnamon, fallow, blue and pastel-blue. The yellow mutation is by far the best known, but is really a cinnamon mutation. Another reasonably common mutation is the olive (pied), in which the red rump of the male is lost. Also gaining in popularity is the white mutation, a product of yellow (cinnamon) and blue (pastel); the white is really more silver, but this will be improved in time; the mutation can only be produced by split-offspring. The yellow mutation with red eyes is not silver-yellow as in the lutino, but more pastel coloured. The fallow and cinnamon are sex-linked recessive, whereas the blue (pastel), lutino and olive (pied) are autosomal recessive.

Feeding: as for the Pennant's parakeet, see page 96.

Elegant grass Parakeet
Neophema elegans

In 1925, an aviculturist wrote that this species needed to be saved from extinction. Recently, however, the elegant grass parakeet has appeared to be the most plentiful of all *Neophema* species in the wild. These birds follow human habitation and show up wherever woodland has been cleared; they have even occurred as far north as the Pilbara district (in Western Australia), in the tropics. They are also common along the coast; we have often seen them early in the morning, flying high in the sky like larks. Groups of 20 to 100 birds are not at all uncommon, and only in the breeding season do they disperse into pairs or small groups. In captivity, their care is similar to that described for Bourke's parakeet (see page 102).

Lutino elegant grass parakeet.

Varieties
Yellow-pied, pastel-green, cinnamon and lutino mutations occur. The yellow pied is dominant in character, so that pied young can arise from a pairing with a normal bird. There are no 'split' birds, but it is an uncommon mutation, as are pastel green and cinnamon, which are respectively autosomal recessive and sex-linked. The lutino is silver-yellow, with red eyes and white feathers where they are blue in the normal. Contrary to most lutinos, this form of the elegant is not sex-linked, but autosomal recessive in character. Both sexes can thus be split for lutino.

Feeding: as for the blue-winged grass parakeet, see page 104.

Fact file

DISTRIBUTION:
southern New South Wales, western Victoria, South Australia and south-western Australia

HABITAT:
sparsely wooded grassland; agricultural areas and other cultivations; the birds follow human habitation

CLUTCH:
4 to 5 round, white eggs

INCUBATION:
18 to 19 days by the female

FLEDGING:
28 to 35 days

AVERAGE LIFESPAN:
12 years

SEXING:
the female is duller than the male, with less yellow and no orange on the belly; the flight feathers are brown, with lighter borders

JUVENILES:
similar to, but duller than, the female, and without or with only a very small frontal band; the bill is lighter than an adult female's

SIZE:
23 cm (9 in)

The Handbook of Cage and Aviary Birds

Fact file

DISTRIBUTION:
south-western Queensland and western New South Wales through central Australia to the far north of South Australia and the inland of Western Australia

HABITAT:
often close to watering facilities for cattle in mainly arid and semi-arid scrublands (especially mulga)

CLUTCH:
4 to 6 white, rounded eggs

INCUBATION:
18 to 19 days by the female; the male feeds her on the nest

FLEDGING:
28 to 30 days

AVERAGE LIFESPAN:
12 years

SEXING:
most of the blue above the bill is lacking in the female, and there is less pink on the underside, which is marked in buff

JUVENILES:
similar to the female, but with less pink on the abdomen; the frontal blue band is missing and the bill is also lighter than the adult female's

SIZE:
19 cm (7½ in)

BOURKE'S PARAKEET
Neophema bourkii

In the wild, this little parakeet is active at dusk and flies about on moonlit nights. Due to the clearing of many water holes, these birds are decreasing alarmingly in number. Being nomadic, they are probably more abundant than is apparent; we have often observed them at water holes very late in the evening.

These birds start breeding early in the year, so one must beware of egg-binding. A pair can rear two or three broods per season. During this time, feed the birds with ant pupae, small mealworms, rolled oats, a little hemp, crushed corn (maize), small sunflower seeds and a little fruit (if they will eat it; many individuals will not). As the birds are very peaceful, they can be kept in a communal aviary with finches, doves and other small-parakeet species, but one pair per aviary is recommended. They must have a roomy flight as they like to fly a lot. Many fanciers seed the floor of the flight so that the birds can forage in the grass. The nest box should measure 15 x 15 x 30 cm (6 x 6 x 12 in), with an entrance 5 cm (2 in) in diameter; place a layer of turf on the bottom of the box. Always give the birds a choice of two or three nest boxes.

Red or opalin
Bourke's parakeet.

Rubino Bourke's parakeet.

*Dilute Isabel
Bourke's parakeet.*

Bourke's parakeet.

*Fallow
Bourke's parakeet.*

Feeding: as for the Pennant's parakeet,
see page 96, and see also the previous page.
Also offer hard-boiled eggs (or commercial rearing
food) daily, as well as biscuits, a variety of green food,
fresh twigs (willow) and buds.

Varieties

Yellow is autosomal recessive; this mutation shows a soft-yellow
back and wings; the head and breast are dull pink and the nails are
very light, as though illuminated. The cocks are usually somewhat
darker than the hens, the latter appearing more yellow. The Isabel
is similar to the yellow, but shows more pink and less yellow,
tending more towards brown; the feet and claws are more greyish,
but the eyes are red, like those of the yellow. The genetic character
is sex-linked recessive.

The fallow also belongs to the 'yellow series'. It is similar to the
Isabel, but somewhat duller in colour. The eyes are also red. The
fallow has an off-white beak, whereas the Isabel's is more horn-
coloured. The fallow is an autosomal recessive mutation. The rose
Bourke is, in fact, an opaline mutation. It shows much variation in
the pink and is sex-linked recessive in character.

Fact file

DISTRIBUTION:
Australia: western New South
Wales, Victoria, southern South
Australia, King Island and
Tasmania (winter migrants)

HABITAT:
various; mainly open forests,
woodlands, grasslands, coastal
heathlands and salt marshes

CLUTCH:
4 to 6, sometimes up to 10,
white, almost spherical eggs

INCUBATION:
18 to 19 days by both sexes

FLEDGING:
25 to 30 days

AVERAGE LIFESPAN:
10 years

SEXING:
the female is duller than the male,
the blue is diluted with
yellowish-green and the flight
feathers are brown (the male's
are black); during the breeding
season, the plumage of both
sexes becomes brighter

JUVENILES:
no, or a faint, blue forehead
stripe; barely apparent blue in
the wings; duller than the adult
female; horn-coloured bill

SIZE:
21 cm (8¹/₄ in)

BLUE-WINGED GRASS PARAKEET
Neophema chrysostoma

This beautiful species (*chrysostoma* means 'golden beak') responds well to good husbandry, soon becoming tame and trusting. It is suitable for a community aviary at least 3 m (10 ft) in length. In the wild, these birds live in pairs or small groups, often accompanying other species, such as the swift parakeet and yellow-bellied rosella. We once found eight separate blue-wing nests in abandoned owl nests! At other times, they are found in the abandoned nests of starlings or swallows. Nevertheless, these birds seem to do better in captivity if given a nest box that is not too small. The minimum size should be 40 cm (15³/₄ in) deep and 20 x 20 cm (8 x 8 in) in area, with an entrance hole 5 to 7 cm (2 to 2³/₄ in) in diameter. A piece of rope, bark or cork should be fixed just below the nest opening so that the hen can spend time hanging on to the box (as she is apt to), inspecting the interior.

Feeding: as for the Bourke's parakeet, see page 102; also provide sweet, soft apples; grass and herb seeds; water-soaked, brown bread (especially in the breeding season); millet spray; crushed, small sunflower seeds; small insects and small invertebrates (spiders and such like).

Splendid grass parakeet
Neophema splendida

The splendid, or scarlet-chested, grass parakeet is unfortunately a rare species in the wild, possibly due to its quiet and secretive habits. If approached in the wild, it stands stock-still in the undergrowth and becomes virtually invisible. The bird is not too fearful of humans, however, and those that live near habitations will show themselves. Its soft chatter is pleasant to listen to, and not as raucous as the voices of many other psittacines.

Although not common in captivity, once one has a true pair, they will breed readily; their care and management are similar to that described for other *Neophema* species. In the wild, the hens line their nest hollows with leaves and other soft material; they bite the leaves from the twigs and tuck them under their rump feathers for transportation.

Varieties
The mutations include yellow-pied, sea-green, pastel-blue, blue, Isabel, cinnamon, fallow and red-bellied birds. The pied version has a number of green feathers replaced by yellow and a number of blue feathers replaced by white; in both cases, the blue is missing. The pied mutation is dominant in character. Fledglings are not pied; this arises with the first moult. Sea-green, pastel-blue and blue are autosomal recessive; Isabel and cinnamon are sex-linked. The fallow can be described as a somewhat paler version of the wild colour, with dark-red eyes; the genetic make-up is autosomal recessive. The red-bellied mutation in both the splendid and turquoisine is developed through selective breeding. Further colours can be developed by breeding combinations of the above mutations; examples include silver (from cinnamon x blue) and sky-blue (from Isabel x blue).

Feeding: as for the blue-winged grass parakeet, see left.

DISTRIBUTION:
southern and south-west Australia and the interior

HABITAT:
this species is fairly nomadic, and can be seen in varied habitats, including acacia scrub

CLUTCH:
2 to 6 round, white eggs

INCUBATION:
18 to 19 days; the male feeds the female, both outside and inside the nest

FLEDGING:
28 to 30 days; the young are very nervous in the first few days

AVERAGE LIFESPAN:
12 years

SEXING:
the female has a yellow-greenish underside; her breast has an olive-green tinge and no scarlet; she has some blue on her head

JUVENILES:
similar to the adult female, but duller; young males often have blue on their heads; the inside of the wing is darker and the little outer feathers are ultramarine, but lighter and blue in females; the bill is lighter than an adult female's

SIZE:
20 cm (8 in)

The Handbook of Cage and Aviary Birds

Fact file

DISTRIBUTION:
Australia: central Queensland, south through New South Wales to the border with Victoria

HABITAT:
open woodland; close to water; grassland; mountain slopes

CLUTCH:
4 to 7 rounded, white eggs

INCUBATION:
18 to 19 days by the female

FLEDGING:
26 to 28 days

AVERAGE LIFESPAN:
12 years

SEXING:
the female is duller and lacks the male's red wing patch; she has less blue on her face and head, a greener breast and her lower underside and beneath her tail are pale green

JUVENILES:
young males develop red shoulder patches early in life, and are in full colour by 8 to 10 months; the bill is greyish-white

SIZE:
20 cm (8 in)

Male and female turquoise grass parakeet.

TURQUOISE GRASS PARAKEET
Neophema pulchella

The turquoise (or turquoisine) grass parakeet is a friendly species that can be housed in a roomy aviary with finches, doves and various Australian parakeets that don't belong to the *Neophema* genus. The hen lacks the male's red shoulder patches and has less blue on her head; her eyes are surrounded by yellow and her breast is greener. In the wild, these birds are partly crepuscular and appear to drink just once per day, often before the first light.

Breeding pairs should be provided with a nest box 40 cm (15³/4 in) deep and 20 cm (8 in) square, with a layer of damp woodchips and mulch in the base. The entrance hole should be about 6 cm (2¹/3 in) in diameter. During the breeding season, like all *Neophema* species, these birds must have a supply of water-soaked, stale, brown bread, germinated seeds and commercial rearing food. The aviary should be roomy and ideally planted with a few low shrubs. The shelter must be well protected from dampness and draughts. During long spells of dry weather, it is wise lightly to mist-spray the nest boxes on a daily basis so that the eggs do not become desiccated. Turquoises are somewhat aggressive during the breeding season, and each pair requires its own aviary. On reaching independence, juveniles must also be separated from their parents as their father may attack them.

A number of mutations are well established: the yellow-pied, olive-green, yellow, fallow, blue, opaline and lutino; the yellow-pied, lutino and opaline are sex-linked in character, while the yellow, fallow and blue (to date more pastel blue than blue) are autosomal recessive. The olive-green appeared in Denmark in 1980.

Feeding: as for the blue-winged grass parakeet, see page 104

RED-FRONTED KAKARIKI
Cyanoramphus novaezelandiae

These easy-to-breed birds have become enormously popular. Very nimble in movement, they clatter comfortably about the aviary wire with their long toes and scratch on the floor like little chickens in search of titbits. Unfortunately, this means that they are susceptible to worm infections. This scratching habit may also be performed in the seed dish, which is why it should be constructed in such a way that makes scratching impossible (use hoppers with small openings, for example). This species is fond of a daily water bath; ensure that the water is not more than 5 cm (2 in) deep because newly fledged youngsters (also enthusiastic bathers) could otherwise easily drown.

The chances of breeding success are increased by providing a reasonably sized flight: a length of at least 4 m (13 ft) is recommended for a pair of these birds. The best breeding results occur with a nest box 32 cm (13 in) high and 20 cm (8 in) square. Two or three nest boxes (installed no earlier than the end of March) should be given to each pair to allow them a choice. The hatchlings are at first covered in white down, but this changes to grey in a few days and their eyes open after about eight days. The cock will feed the hen through the entrance hole of the nest box. As soon as the young have hatched, he will reach right inside the box to assist the hen in feeding them. Kakarikis are outstanding foster parents.

There is a yellow-pied and a cinnamon mutation, both being sex-linked recessive in character. The young are born with red eyes.

Feeding: provide a good parakeet mixture without too many sunflower seeds. These birds are fond of the leaves and roots of various grasses, and a daily upside-down sod of grass will keep them occupied for hours. They will also eat the small insects that they find in the soil. Some individuals will eat apples, pears, grapes, peanuts, raisins, berries, mealworms and aphids. During the breeding season, it is essential to give them germinated seeds, as well as a commercial rearing food suitable for budgies or canaries.

Fact file

DISTRIBUTION:
New Zealand and adjacent and outlying islands; in 8 subspecies, one of which is extinct

HABITAT:
forest; open scrub; grassland

CLUTCH:
5 to 12 broadly elliptical, white eggs

INCUBATION:
19 days by the female

FLEDGING:
35 to 43 days

AVERAGE LIFESPAN:
8 years

SEXING:
the female has a clear wing-bar that is sometimes present in the male

JUVENILES:
fewer red head markings than the adults; when leaving the nest, the base of the beak is pinkish; brown iris

SIZE:
26 cm (10¼ in)

Red-fronted kakariki

Fact file

DISTRIBUTION:
central and western Africa in 3 subspecies. *P. e. timneh* (Timneh grey parrot) is several inches smaller and from western Africa (southern Guinea, Sierra Leone, Liberia and western Ivory Coast)

HABITAT:
primary lowland and secondary rainforests; forest edges; gallery forests; coastal mangroves; wooded savannah; cultivation; large gardens and parks

CLUTCH:
2 to 5 rounded-ovate, somewhat glossy, white eggs

INCUBATION:
28 to 30 days by the female

FLEDGING:
10 to 13 weeks

AVERAGE LIFESPAN:
50 years

SEXING:
the female is somewhat smaller and lighter in colouration than the male; her eye-ring is rounded instead of pointed obtusely backwards; her head is less flat and more rounded

JUVENILES:
similar to the adult hen; the upper-tail is darker red, the under-tail shows grey; the black iris turns grey in about 1 year, and then finally light yellow

SIZE:
36 cm (14 in)

AFRICAN GREY PARROT
Psittacus e. erithacus

This parrot makes an excellent, intelligent, companion bird. Members of this species are known to be good talkers (although they are not noisy) and great mimics, but may have an unreliable temperament. If neglected or left alone for hours at a time, they become easily stressed and can turn into feather-pluckers. Agitated birds oscillate their pupils and raise their nape feathers. Like most cockatoos, the African grey parrot is a one-person bird. With sufficient care and management, captive birds can reach a ripe old age (40 to 60 years), and can end up being even older than they would be in the wild. This is something to consider before buying any large parrot species!

Indoors, the African grey should be housed in a spacious cage, measuring 150 x 150 x 160 cm (59 x 59 x 63 in), in which the bird can move about freely; avoid round cages as these can (and usually will) make the bird nervous and stressed. When housed in an aviary, the recommended mesh size is 12.5 x 25 mm ($^1/_2$ x 1 in), the wire gauge being 16G. When housed in an aviary, these birds love to take showers in the rain; companion birds should be misted daily, preferably in the morning.

The Timneh grey parrot (*P. e. timneh*) is also very popular. Darker than the nominate, its under-tail and upper-tail coverts are maroon, not scarlet, and the upper mandible is pinkish-red, with a black tip. Both species will breed in captivity. Provide a nest box measuring 40 x 45 x 65 cm (16 x 18 x 26 in), with an entrance measuring 15 cm (6 in) in diameter. Although these birds engage in courtship behavior in their second or third year, the females don't start breeding until they are in their sixth year.

Feeding: provide a good commercial seed mix, without too many sunflower seeds; during the winter, give extra hemp. Also provide soaked and sprouted seeds, corn on the cob and boiled corn (maize), sprouted mung beans, pine nuts, some peanuts, millet spray (ensure that this is always available) and a rich variety of fruits and vegetables offered in two separate dishes. Cooked vegetables, lean meat, pasta, cooked rice, yogurt and, in moderation, cheese can also be given. Before and during the breeding season, also give whole-wheat bread soaked in water (not milk), grated carrots, endives and diced, cooked egg. It is essential to provide oyster grit, cuttlebone and fresh drinking water throughout the year.

CAPE PARROT
Poicephalus robustus

Fact file

DISTRIBUTION:
south-eastern Africa (Cape, Mpumalanga and KwaZulu-Natal; the provinces of South Africa to western Swaziland) (for nominate); Tanzania, south to Mozambique (*P. r. suahelicus*); Gambia and southern Senegal to northern Ghana and Togo (*P. r. fuscicollis*)

HABITAT:
evergreen mist forests dominated by yellowwood (*Podocarpus*); cultivation; farmland and exotic plantations; declining in many areas

CLUTCH:
2 to 4 glossy, rounded, white eggs

INCUBATION:
28 to 32 days by both sexes

FLEDGING:
70 to 77 days

AVERAGE LIFESPAN:
25 years

SEXING:
the female is similar to the male, but with a deep-red forehead and crown and a smaller bill; the female is more colourful than the male

JUVENILES:
lack the adults' red shoulders and thighs; a greenish-black tail; females acquire orange-red head colouration by 6 or 7 months (nominate race only); the male's beak is larger

SIZE:
32 cm (12½ in)

The nine species of the genus *Poicephalus* can be described as the African counterparts of members of the *Pionus* genus. Together with its cousin, Jardine's parrot (right), the Cape parrot is the largest, and its robust beak stands out clearly. Imported Cape parrots are rare, and the ones that do come to Europe, the USA and Canada remain nervous; even captive-bred birds are easily stressed or remain shy for a very long time. The most common subspecies in aviculture is undoubtedly *P. r. suahelicus*. This bird is very similar to the nominate, but has a beautiful, silver-grey head, often displaying pink, brown, rose and tan speckles. The reddish frontal band, absent in the nominate, is rarely displayed.

All *Poicephalus* representatives are winter-breeders, meaning that they generally start a family in October and breed through February and into the first week or so of March. As a result, the majority of the young have to be hand-reared. These parrots require either a nest box about 28 cm (11 in) square, placed in a quiet, roomy aviary, or else a large, cubical, suspended cage measuring at least 2 x 1.5 m (6 x 3 ft); a larger cage is even better. These birds also like grandfather-clock-style, 'L'- or boot-shaped nest boxes. To help them to overcome their shyness and fear, provide a deep nest box. Don't forget to attach an internal ladder so that the birds do not become trapped inside. To promote better breeding, let outdoor birds enjoy a mild rain shower and give them privacy from other birds especially. Indoor birds can be sprayed with a plant-mister, preferably mid-morning. Do not breed from birds that are younger than 2 years; even better, wait until they reach 4 to 5 years of age.

P. r. fuscicollis, which has a brown band in the neck, has been regarded as a new subspecies since 2001. There is little difference between it and *P. r. suahelicus*, and in our view, it is more like a geographical race.

Feeding: as for Jardine's parrot, see right.

JARDINE'S PARROT
Poicephalus gulielmi

In behaviour and breeding requirements, this species is similar to the Cape parrot (see left). As far as housing is concerned, these parrots like a roomy flight in which they can fly from front to back; birds housed in small cages, or birds that are bored or extremely bonded, may start plucking out each other's feathers to the point of total baldness (although this doesn't seem to interfere with their willingness to raise a family). Mature four-year-old pairs are very fertile, and incubation usually commences with the first egg. The newly hatched chicks are remarkably small and resemble the youngsters of the African grey parrot, with the exception of their light-coloured beaks. Do not disturb the breeding female, especially during the first few days after the youngsters have hatched. When hand-feeding is necessary, don't start until the chicks are 4 to 5 days old; always feed a formula that is high in electrolytes and keep the young comfortably warm at all times. This species may suffer from yolk-sac retention (when the internal yolk sac is retained and becomes infected, causing death at around the fourth or fifth day after hatching). This problem can be compounded by feeding the chicks a formula that is too thick; for the first 4 to 5 days, the formula should have the consistency of milk.

Regardless of their sex, Jardine's parrots are rather quiet, and are known for their soft whistle. Their mimicking ability is average, and we have had birds that could speak only about 20 different words.

Feeding: give a reliable commercial seed mixture enriched with various fruit kernels (the birds crack open the kernels and eat only the pips), nuts (walnuts, pecan nuts, hazelnuts, palm nuts and peanuts in their shells), hawthorn berries, vegetables, fruits (apples, wild plums, melon and figs), and extruded pellets, sometimes called nuggets. Supply calcium with vitamin D_3, phosphor and a multivitamin supplement throughout the year, especially during the breeding season.

Fact file

DISTRIBUTION:
southern Camaroon and the Central African Republic, south to northern Angola (nominate); Liberia, Ivory Coast and Ghana (*P. g. fantiensis*); southern Kenya and northern Tanzania (*P. g. massaicus*); central Kenya (*P. g. permistus*)

HABITAT:
forests with primarily yellowwoods (*Podocarpus*) and in tall trees adjacent to coffee plantations; up to 3,500 m (11,500 ft) in the mountains

CLUTCH:
2 to 4 glossy, rounded, white eggs

INCUBATION:
26 to 27 days by both sexes

FLEDGING:
70 to 77 days

AVERAGE LIFESPAN:
25 years

SEXING:
the female is similar to the male

JUVENILES:
paler than the parents; the red on the forehead, bend of the wings and thighs is lacking; dark-grey wing markings; greyish iris; the upper mandible has a horn-coloured base and grey tip

SIZE:
28 cm (10⅓ in)

Fact file

DISTRIBUTION:
Senegal to Guiana and southern Mali (nominate); Ivory Coast, Ghana to Nigeria (*P. s. versteri*); eastern and north-eastern Nigeria, south-western Chad and northern Cameroon (*P. s. mesotypus*)

HABITAT:
open forest; savannah; woodland (primarily with baobab trees, locust beans and palms, *Borassus* sp.)

CLUTCH:
2 to 4 rounded, white eggs

INCUBATION:
22 to 29 days by the female

FLEDGING:
63 to 77 days

AVERAGE LIFESPAN:
25 years

SEXING:
the female is similar to the male

JUVENILES:
duller than the parents, with a brownish head and light-grey ear coverts; the yellow in the breast is lacking; dark-brown iris; a greyish-brown bill that is pink at the base

SIZE:
22 to 25 cm (8^1/$_2$ to 9^3/$_4$ in)

SENEGAL PARROT
Poicephalus senegalus

This popular, readily available species occurs in the wild in three subspecies. The birds are known for their call: a series of rather unattractive, whistling notes. They are also notorious for their powerful beak, which is capable of destroying thin, aviary mesh, so use 16G wire and protect all wooden posts and frameworks with metal strips or mesh.

Their breeding season usually starts in mid-October and runs through February or later. Provide a well-sheltered nest box (see Cape parrot, page 110), positioning it in a secluded, and relatively dark, corner, and house only one pair per aviary. Use an 'L'-shaped or grandfather-clock-style nest box; 4 cm (1^1/$_2$ in) plywood is recommended, and join the panels with screws, rather than nails, so that the box can be dismantled for easy cleaning or repair. All *Poicephalus* species like to use the nest box as a night shelter. Clean and disinfect it regularly.

There is a subtle dimorphism: the hens have a larger area of green on the upper chest, which gives the impression of a sharp 'V' shape; the termination point ends between the legs. They usually have a smaller bill, with a sharper, more rounded curve towards the chest. The beaks of the males tend to be wider and longer.

Senegal parrots are very amiable birds, especially hand-reared ones. They are also rather lively, and form a deep attachment to humans. They do learn to speak a few words and to whistle tunes, although their voice sounds a bit thin. Companion birds should be obtained at an early age; wild-caught ones are extremely nervous, quickly stressed, wild and unruly, and often become terrible screamers. Turning such a wild parrot into a loving, pleasant companion involves a lot of hard work, as well as much time, dedication and love.

Feeding: as for Jardine's parrot, see page 111.

MEYER'S PARROT
Poicephalus meyeri

This species is always reasonably priced and generally quieter than most of its cousins, although it may resort to attacking the woodwork in the aviary. It is remarkable for the bright-yellow colour on the bend of its wings and the yellow crown patch, thighs and under-wing coverts; this colour may occur in a variety of shades, from bright to pale yellow, depending on the subspecies.

There are six subspecies: *P. m. meyeri* has a yellow band across its crown; *P. m. saturatus* has a yellow band on its forehead; *P. m. matschiei* has an extensive yellow area running from its forehead to its crown; *P. m. reichenowi* and *P. m. damarensis* lack any yellow on their heads, however; and, finally, *P. m. transvaalensis* has a yellow band across the top of its head. *P. m. damarensis* and *P. m. transvaalensis* are regularly imported from South Africa, and are popular birds, especially in Europe. *P. m. meyeri* and *P. m. saturatus* are almost identical in appearance; the latter has a green-coloured rump washed in a little light blue, while the former has a clean blue rump. Immature birds are not only much duller than their parents, but also lack their yellow markings. Mature birds are difficult to sex. The only way to ascertain their sex is by DNA blood analysis or by surgically sexing. We prefer the first method as it eliminates the need to invade the bird surgically: all that is required is a small blood sample.

Meyer's parrot and its subspecies are mediocre mimics, but have a pleasant nature. Their care, management and breeding methods are similar to those used for the Senegal parrot (see left).

Feeding: as for Jardine's parrot, see page 111.

Fact file

DISTRIBUTION:
central and southern Africa (southern Chad and north-eastern Cameroon to western Ethiopia); in 6 subspecies, of which 2 lack yellow on the crown

HABITAT:
broad-leaved woodland and savannah; flocks congregate regularly at waterholes

CLUTCH:
2 to 4 glossy, slightly ovate, white eggs

INCUBATION:
29 to 30 days by the female

FLEDGING:
56 to 63 days

AVERAGE LIFESPAN:
25 years

SEXING:
the female is similar to the male

JUVENILES:
similar to the parents, but duller; they lack the yellow bar across the crown; greyish iris; fully coloured at about 1 year

SIZE:
21 cm (8⅓ in)

Fact file

DISTRIBUTION:
northern Namibia and southern Angola (south-western Africa)

HABITAT:
dry woodland; thornveld and dry river courses; in the north, a preference for stands of baobab trees

CLUTCH:
3 to 4 ivory-white eggs

INCUBATION:
28 to 30 days by the female

FLEDGING:
56 to 63 days

AVERAGE LIFESPAN:
25 years

SEXING:
the female is brighter than the male, with a more intensive blue on the vent and a blue rump

JUVENILES:
similar to the female, but with a duller blue on the abdomen and only a faint tinge of yellow on the bend of the wings; yellowish-white under-wing coverts; brownish iris; black bill, legs and feet

SIZE:
22 cm (8½ in)

RÜPPELL'S PARROT
Poicephalus rueppellii

This popular and much-loved little parrot is the quietest representative of its genus. The male is mainly dark grey, with a small, yellow bend of wing and yellow thighs and under-wing coverts; the female is very pretty, with her blue back, rump, under-tail coverts, lower abdomen, and part of her thighs.

Rüppell's parrot is not particularly well established, except in South Africa, where various breeders are doing very well. However, interest in this beautiful bird is growing rapidly in Europe (especially in The Netherlands, England, Germany and Denmark).

Its care, breeding and management are similar to those of other species of the *Poicephalus* genus. The Rüppell's is a mediocre mimic that, when kept indoors as a companion bird, likes to have a variety of toys, which should be regularly cleaned and replaced.

Feeding: as for Jardine's parrot, see page 111.

BROWN-HEADED PARROT
Poicephalus cryptoxanthus

This energetic little parrot knows how to raise its voice! Once it is accustomed to its owner and surroundings, however, it quickly settles down and becomes extremely friendly. Young, hand-reared birds make excellent pets and are very highly recommended for the novice fancier.

The brown-headed parrot does not need a large nest box: one measuring 25 x 25 x 38 cm (10 x 10 x 15 in) is sufficiently large. Like all other *Poicephalus* species, this parrot likes its nest box to be positioned out of the sun's glare. With a compatible mate and a roomy cage or small aviary, this species can be prolific. Hens will often start breeding quite young (aged between 1½ and 2 years); 2- to 3-year-old females make much better, more reliable breeders, however.

This parrot and its subspecies (of which the *P. c. zanzibaricus* is virtually unknown in aviculture) are not great mimics. We have, however, heard birds with a small vocabulary of between 10 and 22 words. This species is nevertheless very sweet and definitely exceptionally lovable.

Supply these birds with plenty of toys to keep them occupied and prevent feather-plucking. Their care, management and breeding parallel those of other *Poicephalus* species.

Feeding: similar to that of Jardine's parrot, see page 111. Before and during the breeding season, add a dependable, commercial rearing food for soft-billed birds (one that contains a large percentage of animal protein), which they will enthusiastically offer their offspring as well.

Fact file

DISTRIBUTION:
south-eastern Africa (nominate); Mozambique; southern Malawi, eastern Tanzania and coastal Kenya, Zanzibar and Pemba Islands (*P. c. tanganyikae*)

HABITAT:
dry thornveld; riverine forests; open woodland; sparsely timbered grassland

CLUTCH:
3 to 4 glossy, rounded, white eggs

INCUBATION:
26 to 30 days by the female; the male feeds her on the nest

FLEDGING:
77 to 85 days

AVERAGE LIFESPAN:
25 years

SEXING:
the female is similar to the male

JUVENILES:
resemble their parents, but are generally paler, with less vivid yellow under-wings and upper breast; pink cere; greyish iris

SIZE:
22 cm (8½ in)

The Handbook of Cage and Aviary Birds

Fact file

DISTRIBUTION:
central Ethiopia to north-eastern Tanzania (nominate); Somalia and eastern Ethiopia (*P. r. pallidus*)

HABITAT:
dry woodland with flat-topped acacia and thornbush with baobab trees

CLUTCH:
1 to 3 rounded, ivory-white eggs

INCUBATION:
27 to 28 days by the female

FLEDGING:
84 to 86 days

AVERAGE LIFESPAN:
25 years

SEXING:
the female's lower breast and underparts are green; her under-wing coverts are greyish

JUVENILES:
duller than the female; the males have orange under-wing coverts and orange markings on the upper belly; blackish iris; fully coloured at about 1 year

SIZE:
25 cm (10 in)

RED-BELLIED PARROT
Poicephalus rufiventris

This parrot shows a dramatic sexual dimorphism: mature males sport a breathtaking soft-red lower abdominal area, whereas the hen is bluish-green. When still in the nest, the chicks resemble their mother, but it doesn't take long before one is able to distinguish the young males from the females as the former quickly develop some orange on their wing coverts, with little orange feathers scattered over their abdomens.

Wild-caught pairs remain nervous; always try to avoid stressing them. It's best to house individual pairs separately to avert skirmishes near the nest box. The nest box should be placed in a secluded and relatively dark area where it is impossible for the sun to shine on the bottom of the box. The nest box can be 'L'-shaped or of the grandfather-clock type. We have also had breeding successes in nest boxes measuring 30 x 30 x 60 cm (12 x 12 x 23 in), with an entrance hole 10 cm (4 in) in diameter.

This parrot became rather popular after the mid-1980s. Two subspecies (*P. rufiventris* and *P. pallidus*) are now recognised by most ornithologists, but a debate as to whether there are genetic differences between the two continues. DNA studies will eventually provide the answer.

Care, management and breeding run parallel with those for other *Poicephalus* species. This parrot is a very intelligent and friendly companion bird, although it often becomes a one-person friend.

Feeding: as for Jardine's parrot, see page 111.

MADAGASCAR LOVEBIRD
Agapornis c. cana

Together with the hen Abyssinian lovebird (see page 118), the female Madagascar, or grey-headed, lovebird is clearly the dominant sex as she selects the nest site and defends it against other birds. She will even snap at her mate. Rather than mutual, the preening of both species is rather one-sided. Nevertheless, lovebirds are in general delightful birds, whether kept in a roomy cage, a large aviary or observed in the wild. The Madagascar has one subspecies (*A. c. ablectanea*), which is found only in the south-west of the island, and is identified by the lighter-grey of its head, neck and chest, and the sharper green of its wings and underside.

A. c. cana is primarily a season-breeder: November and December. During autumn and winter, it is best kept indoors. The hen will often use a budgerigar's nest box and will make a little cushion of various materials (dried leaves chewed into the desired shape and size) in the cavity of the nest. Grass, straw, strips of newspaper, the bark of willow and fruit trees (except cherry), larch needles and other materials are also accepted.

Feeding: provide a good commercial seed mixture for lovebirds (or budgerigars); a variety of grass seeds; millet spray (daily!); sweet berries (such as mountain ash and hawthorn); fruit (apples, pears, bananas, strawberries, raspberries, rosehips, pitted cherries, sweet oranges, grapes, tangerines and kiwis); a selection of small grains, pellets and greens (such as fresh peas in the pod, spinach, endive, mango leaves, strips of carrot and kohlrabi, fresh corn, radish, red beet, parsley, dandelion, clover, chickweed – excellent for all birds – watercress and various garden herbs, including milk thistle and foxtail).

Fact file

DISTRIBUTION:
Malagasy Republic (formerly Madagascar); introduced to Rodriguez Island, Mauritius and Comore Islands; Seychelles, Zanzibar and Mafia Island; in 2 subspecies; *A. c. ablectanea* is found only in the south-western region of Malagasy

HABITAT:
coastal areas near forest edges and cultivations; usually in, or near, trees that shed their leaves; in small groups

CLUTCH:
5 to 7 rounded, white eggs

INCUBATION:
20 to 23 days by the female

FLEDGING:
42 to 47 days

AVERAGE LIFESPAN:
8 years

SEXING:
the female's head is green instead of grey; her under-wing coverts are green instead of black

JUVENILES:
young females are a more intense green on the back and wings, and the grey can be seen quite early in life, sometimes while they are still in the nest; dark marks at the base of the upper mandible

SIZE:
14 cm (5½ in)

Fact file

DISTRIBUTION:
southern Eritrea and the south-west
highlands of Ethiopia (formerly
Abyssinia); in 2 subspecies;
A. t. nana is from northern Ethiopia

HABITAT:
woods in highlands; *Juniperus*
or *Podocarpus* forests; savannah
grasslands with acacia; sometimes at
a height of 3,050 m (10,000 ft);
in small flocks

CLUTCH:
5 to 6 rounded, white eggs

INCUBATION:
23 to 26 days by the female

FLEDGING:
45 to 50 days

AVERAGE LIFESPAN:
10 years

SEXING:
the female lacks the male's red
facial adornment; her eye-ring is
green and her under-wing coverts
are greenish or sometimes have
brownish-black markings (the male
has black under-wing coverts)

JUVENILES:
similar to the female, except for the
beak, which remains brownish-
yellow, with black markings on the
base of the upper mandible, for a
few weeks, when the whole beak
turns red; young males have black
under-wing coverts; the birds are
fully coloured at 4 months

SIZE:
15 to 16.5 cm (6 to 6½ in)

ABYSSINIAN or BLACK-WINGED LOVEBIRD
Agapornis t. taranta

In the wild, this robust bird, the largest representative of its genus, generally lives in small groups of some 20 individuals. The nest is used as a year-round resting place, making the population stationary. The subspecies *A. t. nana* has shorter wings and a smaller beak and is seldom seen in aviculture.

In captivity, *A. t. taranta* rarely builds a nest, so provide a thick layer of moist wood shavings, pressing them down firmly, otherwise the hen will quickly remove them. Don't be surprised to see females breeding their clutch on the bare floor of the nest box. Some hens, however, will line the nest chamber with a few of their own breast and belly feathers; in some cases, they may even completely denude their front area for this purpose! The nest box should measure 25 cm (10 in) long x 15 cm (6 in) deep x 18 cm (7 in) high, with an entrance diameter of 5 cm (2 in) (these measurements are interior dimensions), and should be placed off-centre so that the birds do not damage their eggs or young while entering the box. It is advisable to separate the young from their parents once they have become adults to avoid accidents.

Hand-reared youngsters make excellent companion birds, although the females tend to remain shy for a long time. Their voices are far from annoying. Even while breeding, the hens will usually cower in one corner of the nest box if one inspects their eggs or young. Nevertheless, during the breeding season, they often become rather aggressive, and will pluck out each other's feathers, which is why colony breeding is not always recommended.

Varieties
There are a few interesting mutations, and the dominant dark and olive green are well established (the nominate is considered to be light green). The fallow is sometimes available, and has red eyes, rose-coloured legs and all-black becomes grey; this mutation is autosomal recessive. Cinnamons and lutinos are still extremely rare, as are blues; the latter is likely to be autosomal recessive; the first two are sex-linked recessive.

Feeding: as for the Madagascar lovebird, see page 117.

PEACH-FACED LOVEBIRD
Agapornis r. roseicollis

Fact file

DISTRIBUTION:
south-west Africa; in 2
subspecies; *A. r. catumbella* is
from south-western Angola

HABITAT:
near water in savannah and
dry woodland; up to 1,500 m
(5,200 ft) in mountainous areas in
Namibia and south-west Africa;
in small groups (20 to 30) or flocks
(up to 200 birds)

CLUTCH:
3 to 7 rounded, white eggs

INCUBATION:
22 to 23 days by the female;
breeding starts after the second egg

FLEDGING:
43 to 45 days; mature in
4 to 5 months

AVERAGE LIFESPAN:
10 years

SEXING:
the female is similar to the male,
although her green and blue colours,
and particularly the orange in her tail,
are considerably less sharp than
the male's colours; her beak is darker

JUVENILES:
similar to the female, but generally
greyish green; the red colouring on
the forehead is lacking, or very pale
red; a yellowish beak and black
streaking on the upper mandible

SIZE:
15 cm (6 in)

This species is by far the best-known and most prolific lovebird. Although it was initially identified as being a subspecies of the red-faced lovebird (see page 123) in 1793, it was recognised as being a distinct species in 1817. The hens are solely responsible for the construction of the nest, which they build using strips of bark and grass about 10 cm (4 in) in length, which they then bend in half and tuck between the feathers of their rump and back. We have seen birds transferring six to eight strips at a time. Strips that are dropped while flying to the nest are never picked up again.

In captivity, these lovebirds present no problems regarding their care, management and breeding, and the numerous colour mutations (over 30 at the time of writing) are proof of this. Supply a roomy nest box measuring 25 x 20 x 20 cm ((10 x 8 x 8 in), with an entrance hole 6 cm (2½ in) in diameter, as the female uses a large amount of building materials. After laying the second egg, the female alone starts to incubate the eggs, while the male faithfully and regularly comes to the nest to feed her. The young birds are at first covered with orange-red down that quickly changes to grey, usually within ten days.

Feeding: as for the Madagascar lovebird, see page 117.

Varieties
Lutino: the first peach-faced lovebird lutinos (also called inos or creaminos, which are sex-linked recessive) were exported from North America in around 1973. It is not known exactly when this mutation first occurred in the United States. No inbreeding is necessary to perpetuate the lutino, so it can be steadily outcrossed unless the breeder wants a lutino male. The main advantage of this mutation is that once males become available, the strain will provide self-sexing peach-faced lovebirds.

Par-blue: this recessive mutation is sea-green in appearance, with the red and peach of the face being quite dilute.

Pied peach-faced
lovebird.

Olive peach-faced
lovebird.

Red morph
peach-faced lovebird.

Cinnamon
peach-faced lovebird.

Pied: this is a dominant mutation, which, in its original form, shows a stunning colour contrast between yellow and green. This mutation was first bred in California during the 1960s. The amount of pied in a single bird depends on chance. A pair that is not very well marked can produce offspring with colouring that is as perfect as though the young were from two correctly marked pieds.

Par-yellow or golden cherry: this mutation was bred in 1954 in Japan by Masuru Iwata. Since then, intensive breeding seems to have damaged the birds genetically. A stronger stock has been produced by crossing imported birds with European and American stock. This mutation is autosomal recessive.

Olive: this dominant mutation is delineated in the following manner: if two olive genes are present in a peach-faced lovebird, the bird is olive; if there is only one olive gene, the bird is dark green; if there are no olive genes, the normal green of the wild peach-faced is called light green. The history of the olive dominant is largely unrecorded, but we do know that it is an Australian bird. It is probable that the first examples of the olive mutation introduced into Europe were those bred by Dr Romauld Burkard in 1972.

In addition to the primary colour mutations of the peach-faced lovebird, there are also new mixtures formed from combinations of the mutant colours.

RED-FACED or ANGOLA LOVEBIRD
Agapornis p. pullaria or *pullarius*

This beautiful lovebird belongs to the sexually dimorphic group as the hen differs in colour from the male: her face is orange rather than tomato red, and this coloured area is usually smaller than the male's. The covering feathers under her wings are green (black in males).

The red-faced lovebird is difficult to breed. The best method is to provide a big drum or nest block measuring 25 x 25 x 20 cm (10 x 10 x 8 in), with an entrance-hole diameter of 8 cm (3 in), filled with moistened moss and/or cork sheets and peat moss that are then left to dry. Our nest boxes have a double bottom incorporating a heating element; drilling a few holes in the false bottom allows the heat to enter the nest chamber, and we maintain a temperature of 35˚C (95˚F). Branches and twigs should be arranged on top and around the nesting place. In the wild, red-faced lovebirds carve their nests in large, still inhabited, arboreal termitaria, as well as in termite hills, a job that is primarily performed by the female. The lodging should resemble a small tunnel with a widened, fairly round, cavity (called the 'kettle').

Feeding: as for the Madagascar lovebird, see page 117. This species will eat ant eggs and decapitated mealworms, especially during the breeding season. A commercial rearing food for soft-billed birds (one that is rich in animal protein) is also welcome.

Fact file

DISTRIBUTION:
Africa: southern Ethiopia and southern Sudan to north-western Tanzania; in 3 subspecies; *A. p. ugandae*, from south-western Ethiopia to north-western Tanzania and eastern Zaire; *A. p. guineensis*, from Guinea to northern Zaire and south to Angola

HABITAT:
secondary forests; lightly timbered grassland; cultivation; often in large flocks

CLUTCH:
4 to 7 rounded, white eggs; nest in arboreal termitaria

INCUBATION:
23 to 25 days by the female

FLEDGING:
40 to 47 days

AVERAGE LIFESPAN:
10 years

SEXING:
the female's face is orange, rather than tomato red, and less extensive; her under-wing coverts are green instead of black

JUVENILES:
similar to the female, although the male's under-wing coverts quickly become black; yellow chin; orange-red bill with a yellow tip; black near the base of the upper mandible

SIZE:
15 cm (6 in)

Fact file

DISTRIBUTION:
central Africa: northern and central Tanzania; introduced into south-east Kenya, Mombassa, Nairobi and Naivasha; Dar es Salaam and Tanga in Tanzania

HABITAT:
well-timbered, grassy prairies (with baobabs and acacias); nomadic; often hybridises when occurring in the habitat of the Fischer's lovebird, which is less than 80.5 km (50 miles) from the masked's

CLUTCH:
3 to 6 rounded, white eggs

INCUBATION:
21 to 24 days by the female

FLEDGING:
42 to 46 days

AVERAGE LIFESPAN:
10 years

SEXING:
the female is similar to the male, but weighs more (which is normal in lovebirds): 56 versus 50 g (2 versus 1¾ oz)

JUVENILES:
similar to the parents, but duller, and with small, black markings at the base of the upper mandible

SIZE:
15 to 15.5 cm (6 to 6½ in)

MASKED LOVEBIRD
Agapornis p. personata or *personatus*

The masked, black-masked or yellow-collared lovebird is slightly larger than the Fischer's lovebird (see page 127). Natural hybridisation will occur wherever both species live in close proximity, although this is quite rare. It is likely that these two species have evolved from the same ancestor.

The masked lovebird is nomadic by nature, survives on the seeds of available trees and roosts in the crevices and crannies of baobab trees. This bird, which is considered to be the nominate race of all of the birds with a pronounced, white, periophthalmic ring (eye-ring), will nest in swifts' nests and will breed in the approximately 7 cm (3 in) of space between the tiles of a roof and the boards underneath. They often also nest under iron roofs that retain much of the heat radiated by the sun. They brood in colonies and can be kept with three or more pairs in a large aviary. The hen constructs the nest alone. We kept three pairs together in an aviary, provided them with 10 nesting boxes to avert quarrelling, and were rewarded with success.

If it is a warm and sunny spring, hose off the nest boxes each morning, but take care that none of the water seeps inside. Males often scratch their heads with their feet prior to mating. Females line the nests, so provide a good supply of willow twigs and such like. Always offer more nest boxes than there are pairs.

In breeding cages, one nest will suffice.

Feeding: as for the Madagascar lovebird, see page 117.

Masked lovebird.

Blue masked lovebird.

Pied violet masked lovebird.

Olive-green masked lovebird.

Violet masked lovebird.

Varieties

Blue: a very attractive mutation. The collar, chest and belly are off-white, the head is black and the beak is horn-coloured.

In late 1927, Chapman received a blue male, which was then sold to the Zoological Society of London. At first, it was shown as a cage bird, but was later placed in an aviary to breed. By late 1929, ten birds split for blue had been produced. The blue male was then mated with one of his own split-blue daughters, who unfortunately died of egg-binding after another split-blue was produced. By December 1930, the splits were paired, and they raised one blue and three greens.

By the end of World War II, very few blues were left in Europe, but there was hope for the blue mutation. Although no one knew it at the time, Chapman had sent some split-blue lovebirds (*A. p. personata*) to France in 1927. There, in 1935, Monsieur Morin bred several blues, the descendants of which were still available at the end of 1945.

In the United States, there appear to have been a few split-blues in the original importation. The first report of them was from California in 1932. In 1935, F H Rudkin raised four blues from three pairs. When four male blues were paired with the wild, green or normal *A. p. personata*, one of the hens appeared to be split-blue, thus making it possible to produce another generation of blues. By 1945, the blues in California were flourishing.

Mauve masked lovebird.

Lutino masked lovebird.

Par-yellow: this mutation is, like the blue, autosomal recessive, and is usually called 'yellow'. It appears to have retained, in a very dilute form, the blues and melanins of the original. The first par-yellows were apparently bred by Mr Scheu of Upland, California, in 1935. Many of the present par-yellows come from his stock. Another par-yellow was raised in Japan.

Acquired yellow: acquiring yellow is not a hereditary trait. In 1932, at the San Diego Zoo in California, there was a normal masked lovebird that turned yellow for the most part, but nothing more was heard about this mutation.

Other colours can be obtained by combining the primary colour mutations: par-white, for example, is produced by combining blue and par-yellow. The par-yellow mutation does not completely reduce melanin production, so the par-white still has black in its mask, while the body is a very pale shade of blue. This mutation was apparently produced in Japan about a year after the end of World War II. The first Japanese exportation to Europe was in 1955 (H van Dijk, Animali-Zoo, Eindhoven, The Netherlands, presented the senior author's father with three birds).

A white *A. p. personata* was bred in Denmark from a blue/par-yellow mated to a green/par-yellow/blue. The white bird had no trace of a mask whatsoever.

FISCHER'S LOVEBIRD
Agapornis personata fischeri

This is a hardy and very sociable lovebird, especially in an outdoor aviary. The flight of these birds is straight and fast, and the rustling of their wings can clearly be heard, as can their high-pitched chirping. In captivity, this species is best bred in roomy and separate breeding cages (these are commercially available). House pairs in separate cages, especially if you are breeding specific colours. Their care, management and breeding parallels those of other lovebird species.

Varieties

The well-known blue mutation is autosomal recessive and originates from South Africa. The first breeder, Ronald Horsham (in 1957), used a blue masked lovebird; the blue Fischer is smaller in build and has a rather pale-grey head rather than a black one, while the blue is somewhat lighter. The black-eyed yellow is also widely available. An autosomal recessive that first appeared in France in 1944, this bird has a red beak and an orange forehead. The par-yellow, an autosomal recessive, has a red head and looks very similar to the par-yellow masked lovebird. It is most likely the result of a cross between a par-yellow masked and a green Fischer's lovebird. The rather striking lutino and albino were established by crossing the Nyasa (see page 129) with the Fischer's lovebird. The inofactor, dominant, comes from *linianae*, cinnamon or Isabelle, white and par-blue were bred by Dr R Burkard (Switzerland) and are autosomal recessive. The spangled and long feather (autosomal recessive) are the latest mutations, along with the pied, which is recognised in three forms: recessive pied, dominant pied and mottled.

Extra care should be taken to ensure that breeding stock is not tainted with hybrid genes. The young may sometimes show a dull, and somewhat greyish, tone in their masks, which will disappear in about 3 months in proper mutants. Older birds that show this tone are definitely hybrids, however, and should therefore be excluded from all serious colour-breeding programmes.

Feeding: as for the Madagascar lovebird, see page 117.

Fact file

DISTRIBUTION:
south and south-east of Lake Victoria; introduced into east Africa, north of Tanzania (Tange district)

HABITAT:
savannah at elevations of 975 to 9,144 m (3,200 to 30,000 ft); cultivation; usually in small, but sometimes large, flocks

CLUTCH:
3 to 8 rounded, white eggs

INCUBATION:
21 to 24 days by the female

FLEDGING:
35 to 40 days; after another 10 to 12 days, the youngsters are totally independent of their parents

AVERAGE LIFESPAN:
10 years

SEXING:
the female is similar to the male

JUVENILES:
similar to their parents, but duller, especially on the head; the base of the upper mandible has blackish markings that disappear after about 3 months

SIZE:
15 cm (6 in)

Fact file

DISTRIBUTION:
Africa: a small region in northern
Zimbabwe, around the Zambezi
river and Victoria Falls, all in all, a
relatively limited area, less than
129 km (80 miles) in diameter

HABITAT:
various woodlands
(without evergreens), including
acacia savannah; river valleys;
between 600 and 1,005 m
(2,000 and 3,300 ft)

CLUTCH:
3 to 6, sometimes 2 to 8, slightly
elliptical, white eggs

INCUBATION:
16 to 24 days by both sexes

FLEDGING:
30 to 44 days

AVERAGE LIFESPAN:
10 years

SEXING:
the female is similar to the male,
but somewhat duller

JUVENILES:
similar to their parents, but duller;
some young have black
markings on the base of
the upper mandible

SIZE:
11 cm (4¹/₈ in)

BLACK-CHEEKED LOVEBIRD
Agapornis personata nigrigenis

In the wild, the black-cheeked lovebird lives in all types of forest except evergreen forests. These birds are cheerful and fast, and not particularly timid. We have often observed them taking baths early in the morning and late in the afternoon in little streams and small waterfalls. The species is endangered, but well-established in captivity since its introduction to aviculture in 1907. Pairs can be very prolific, as long as they are cared for properly. They especially like to take a daily bath, even during the breeding season.

Outside Europe, the species is becoming rather rare, and there is too much hybridisation for this reason, especially in the USA. Unions between black-cheeked and Fischer's lovebirds result in offspring with a blue rump area. The pure black-cheeked lovebird has no blue on its rump, making it easy to spot hybrids.

In captivity, the hen constructs an elaborate nest in late autumn and winter; most breedings therefore take place inside, in breeding cages or small aviaries. These birds are excellent breeders and care well for their young.

As pets, they are sweet and peaceful, even when housed with fellow lovebirds or other exotic birds. When well-housed and comfortable, pairs may breed more than five times per season. Breeding should be limited to three times at the most to protect the hen from egg-binding, however. The male does not feed the female while she is incubating the eggs.

At the time of writing, at least two melanin mutations have been recognised. The first is a black melanin reduction of 80 to 90 per cent; this mutant has a rather light mask and body; the green appears to be mixed with yellow. The second mutation has a melanin reduction of 15 to 20 per cent, and looks very similar in colour to the normal or wild black-cheeked lovebird.

Feeding: as for the Madagascar lovebird, see page 117.

NYASA LOVEBIRD
Agapornis personata lilianae

The Nyasa lovebird is very sociable in an aviary and friendly towards birds of a similar size. In the wild, it prefers building free nests to using tree holes and crevices. The nest is typically somewhat bulky, dome-shaped, with a tubular entrance. It is constructed of stalks and bark strips exclusively by the hen, the material being carried in her beak rather than being held between her rump feathers.

In captivity, these birds prefer nest boxes, ideally 22 x 22 x 25 cm (8½ x 8½ x 9¾ in) in size, with an entrance-hole diameter of 6 cm (2¼ in). Although these birds breed in colonies, and results have been achieved with multiple broods in the aviary, it's best to separate the various couples and to house them in adjoining breeding cages or small aviaries.

The Nyasa lovebird has a beautiful, lutino mutation, the physical characteristics being a red head and yellow body; it is rather small in size. The first recorded breeding of this particular mutation was in 1933, by Prendergast, in Adelaide, South Australia. It is quite possible that the mutation was unwittingly imported from the wild in the 'split' form.

The first lutinos to arrive in England were exported from Australia in 1937. It is evident that split-lutinos were in the United States many years before their presence was discovered because lutinos were bred in California in 1940.

Feeding: as for the Madagascar lovebird, see page 117.

Fact file

DISTRIBUTION:
Africa: southern Tanzania, north-eastern Zimbabwe, eastern Malawi and central and northern Mozambique

HABITAT:
near water and in acacia and mopane woodlands; various elevations ranging from 488 to 1,494 m (1,600 to 4,900 ft); their habitat borders that of *A. p. nigrigenis* (no crossbreeding seems to occur); in small groups or quite large colonies

CLUTCH:
4 to 6 slightly elliptical, white eggs

INCUBATION:
21 to 28 days by the female

FLEDGING:
35 to 44 days; after another 10 days, the youngsters are totally independent

AVERAGE LIFESPAN:
10 years

SEXING:
the female is similar to the male, although the red on her head may be a little less bright; the female weighs 43 g (1½ oz), and the male, 38 g (1⅓ oz)

JUVENILES:
similar to their parents, but duller, with the green and red colours being somewhat darker; the colour of the cheeks is still a little unclear; a reddish-yellow beak, with black markings at the base of the upper mandible

SIZE:
13 to 14 cm (5 to 5½ in)

The Handbook of Cage and Aviary Birds

Fact file

DISTRIBUTION:
southeast Asia, especially
Malaysia, Borneo, Sumatra
and Singapore

HABITAT:
lowland to 1,130 m (3,700 ft);
farmland, riverine growth, forests
and forest edges, mangroves,
bamboo clumps, orchards,
coconut groves and so on

CLUTCH:
3 to 4, sometimes 5,
rounded-oval, white eggs

INCUBATION:
20 days by the female

FLEDGING:
35 to 37 days

AVERAGE LIFESPAN:
8 years

SEXING:
the female usually lacks the
male's red bib and has a smaller
blue patch on the crown;
her under-tail is blue

JUVENILES:
duller green than the
adults; lacking a blue crown;
a yellow bill; adult plumage
in about 1 year

SIZE:
13 cm (5 in)

BLUE-CROWNED HANGING PARROT
Loriculus galgulus

The blue-crowned hanging parrot, which has been regarded as the prototype of all hanging parrots, has been familiar to Westerners for centuries (Linnaeus described it in the late 18th century). Geographically, this bird displays colour differences. In young, imported birds, the adult plumage appears only in the second year, probably due to the stress involved in being caught, confined and transported. After leaving the nest, it takes about three months for its colour to develop so that the sex can be determined.

The captive breeding of this species poses few problems. Provide the bark of willow, birch, hazel and fruit trees (except for cherry), plus grass, hay and green leaves (especially privet) as nest material, which the hen will carry between her breast and rump feathers. The youngsters develop rather slowly, and are first sexually mature after two years. If they are kept in indoor cages (which is recommended), the floor must be cleaned frequently because of the fluid consistency of their droppings. In outdoor aviaries, the birds regularly take a shower in the rain, spreading their wings with obvious pleasure. Caged birds can be given a regular spray, in addition to their normal bath in a dish or similar type of container.

The male's courtship behaviour begins with strutting. The throat feathers are fluffed out and the tail is spread to show the red rump; the wings are drooped so that the yellow and crimson colours are displayed. In this position, the male runs up and down the perch on his long, strong legs, nods his head and chews at the white, frothy paste that he regurgitates, like a child with bubblegum. He then feeds the hen with this paste, after which he lets out a 'yeat-yeat' call.

This species usually sleeps (and roosts) like a bat, generally hanging by one foot, the other foot being tucked into the plumage. As it sleeps, the bird holds its head close to its body, with its feathers puffed out (the head is therefore not tucked beneath a wing or rested on the back).

Feeding: provide a commercial rearing food for soft-billed birds (with animal protein), enriched with small mealworms, pupae, enchytrae and so on, small seeds (such as grass seeds and millet spray), soft fruits, flowers (and their nectar and pollen) and greens.

Fact file

DISTRIBUTION:
northern India, Nepal, Pakistan,
Bangladesh, Bhutan, Assam,
Sri Lanka, northern Thailand,
northern Kampuchea, Laos, central
and southern Vietnam, Andaman
and Cocos Islands; in 5 subspecies

HABITAT:
lowland forests and woodland;
cultivation; mangroves and
coconut plantations

CLUTCH:
2 to 5 broad-oval, slightly
glossy, white eggs

INCUBATION:
21 to 24 days by the female

FLEDGING:
49 days

AVERAGE LIFESPAN:
35 years

SEXING:
the female is duller than
the male and lacks his pink
and black collar 'rings'

JUVENILES:
similar to the female, but
with a shorter tail

SIZE:
body: 45 to 50 cm ($17^3/_4$ to $19^1/_2$
in); tail: 27 to 28 cm ($10^1/_2$ to 11 in)

ALEXANDRINE PARAKEET
Psittacula e. eupatria

The female Alexandrine parakeet is very similar to the male, although she lacks the black and pink bands on the collar and cheeks. This species can have a top-heavy appearance, and does not look its best when it has just arrived after a long trip: too often housed in a cage that is much too small, it may have damaged tail feathers as a result. These birds are best kept in pairs in long aviaries with night shelters. Mature adults (with undamaged tails) are beautiful birds that will enhance any aviary. Provided that they have a good shelter, with thick perches (to prevent their toes from freezing), these intelligent birds can remain outdoors during the winter. Only when kept in a large cage can a young bird be taught to speak.

These birds are tolerant of their own species, except during the breeding period, but are a nuisance to, and may even endanger, small and large, exotic birds.

In contrast to, for example, the rose-ringed or Indian ringneck parakeet (see page 134), Alexandrines gnaw their own nests in trees. In captivity, they can quite easily be led to breed as long as they are housed by themselves in a lengthy aviary. The nesting box should measure about 45 x 40 cm (18 x 16 in), and the entrance hole should have a diameter of at least 11 to 12 cm ($4^1/_4$ x $4^3/_4$ in). There are various colour mutations, of which the most popular are: lutino (sex-linked recessive), blue (autosomal recessive), bronze fallow (the most recent name for cinnamon or Isabelle; inherited autosomal recessive) and par-blue (autosomal recessive).

Feeding: indiscriminate feeders, these birds will accept medium-sized pellets, flowers, foliage, fruits and berries, a commercial parrot-seed mixture, corn on the cob, vegetables, willow branches (they will attack woodwork) and grit. See also the Indian ringneck parakeet, page 134.

PLUM-HEADED PARAKEET
Psittacula c. cyanocephala

The female plum-headed parakeet's head band is consistently lighter than that of the male, and she lacks his red shoulder marking, while her head is greyish-purple. Young birds attain their adult markings and colours after two years. Since young males look like females before the age of two, be very careful when purchasing these wonderful, intelligent birds. They have a pleasant nature and are tolerant of their own kind, but may be aggressive towards small, exotic birds. In the wild, they live on fruits, especially bananas, flowers, buds, seeds and rice; in captivity, however, they sometimes have problems becoming accustomed to a seed menu (of oats, hemp, canary grass seed and grains, for example).

Before the birds commence breeding, cover the bottom of the nest box, which should measure 20 x 25 x 30 cm (8 x 10 x 12 in), with an entrance opening 8 cm (3 in) in diameter, with woodchips and sawdust. The male will feed the hen from his crop during the breeding period.

Their not unpleasant song has contributed to these birds' popularity. Breeding results are obtained only when a pair has an aviary to itself; the aviary should measure at least 4 x 3 m (12 x 9 ft). Rest is very important for the birds during their breeding period, as well as for the success of the clutch; these parakeets are particularly timid and are quickly frightened during this time. A plentiful number of shrubs, both inside and in front of the aviary, will help to alleviate their jumpiness. The birds can be kept all year round in an outdoor aviary with a frost- and draught-free shelter; furnish this area with thick perches (to avoid their toes freezing).

Various colour mutations are available: lutino (autosomal recessive), par-yellow (autosomal recessive) and cinnamon or Isabelle (now named bronze fallow in Europe).

Feeding: as for the Indian ringneck parakeet, see page 134.

Male plum-headed parakeet.

Fact file

DISTRIBUTION:
India, Pakistan, Nepal and Bhutan; also in Sri Lanka, but declining; in 2 subspecies

HABITAT:
lowland; woodland; farmland; foothills

CLUTCH:
4 to 5 spherical, white eggs

INCUBATION:
23 to 25 days by the female

FLEDGING:
49 to 50 days

AVERAGE LIFESPAN:
25 years

SEXING:
the female is green, with a bluish-grey head and pale-yellow bill; she lacks the male's plum-coloured wing patch and her tail is shorter

JUVENILES:
similar to the female; young males have a greenish head tinged with grey, and show a hint of salmon on the lore and forehead; the central tail feathers are shorter

SIZE:
35 to 37.5 cm (13³/₄ to 14³/₄ in)

Fact file

DISTRIBUTION:
peninsular India, south of about
20°N latitude, and Sri Lanka; feral
populations in the USA,
Singapore, England and Europe;
nominate (African ringneck
parakeet/*P. k. krameri*) from
southern Sudan to Senegal

HABITAT:
a variety of woodlands
and forests; savannah; riparian
forest and cultivation; nominate
up to 2,000 m (6,500 ft)

CLUTCH:
4 to 5, sometimes 6,
broad-oval, white eggs

INCUBATION:
23 to 24 days by the female

FLEDGING:
49 to 55 days

AVERAGE LIFESPAN:
25 years

SEXING:
the female is similar to the male,
except that she lacks the male's
markings on the head and neck

JUVENILES:
similar to the female, but with
shorter tails; dark-pink beak; brown
iris; adult plumage in about 3 years

SIZE:
41 cm (16 in)

INDIAN RINGNECK PARAKEET
Psittacula krameri malillensis

This species, also known as the rose-necked parakeet, is extremely popular, and many mutations are known. Young birds take their time in achieving their true colours, however, and are sometimes 2 to 3 years old before their sex can be determined.

These intelligent birds were introduced to Europe hundreds of years ago. The ancient Greeks were familiar with them, and they were mentioned by Archimedes (287–212 BC).

In captivity, the hen starts her nest inspections very early in the year, in around January, and will build up the nest by chewing wood shavings and woodchips into the required shape. The nesting box should measure 25 x 25 cm (10 x 10 in) and 45 to 60 cm (18 in 24 in) in height, with an entrance-hole diameter of 8 cm (3 1/2 in). The female will take about three days to build up the nest. When all is in order, she will start to lay the eggs. Only the hen sits on them. The male feeds both the female and the offspring. After about a week, the female will help in feeding the young.

This species is reasonably hardy and can remain outside during the winter, as long as part of the aviary is covered and draught-free. Young birds can learn to speak quite well, although a certain amount of isolation will be necessary. In India, some young birds are even reared by hand; such birds make excellent cage birds once they are independent, and generally have a remarkable repertoire of words and melodies. These are performed amid whistles and other tricks that will delight owners. A pet ringneck should have a large cage; breeding pairs are best housed in an aviary of generous proportions, measuring at least 4 to 5 m (12 to 16 ft). Males housed in areas that are too small may become sterile. Do not start breeding too early in the year. The best time is the middle of May, and if nesting boxes are hung up towards the end of March, the female has ample opportunity to gnaw the nesting materials into the right shape.

The courtship ritual is very interesting: the male will hop around his mate in short little paces, making various little bows; he will also feed her with regurgitated food.

Fallow par-blue Indian
ringneck parakeet.

Lutino Indian
ringneck parakeet.

Blue ringneck
parakeet.

Male Indian
ringneck parakeet.

Varieties

Various mutations are presently available: bronze fallow (sex-linked),
turquoise (autosomal recessive), clearhead fallow (autosomal
recessive), grey (autosomal dominant), fallow (or dominant-edged
dilution; sex-linked) and lacewing (sex-linked).

Feeding: provide a commercial budgerigar seed mix, flowers, buds,
ripe and unripe fruits, sown seeds, greens, sprouted seeds, rearing
food for soft-billed birds and grit.

The Handbook of Cage and Aviary Birds

Fact file

DISTRIBUTION:
eastern and south-eastern Australia;
in 3 subspecies: *B. b. whitei*
(a hybrid of *B. b. zonarius* x *B. b.
barnardi*), from Flinders Ranges
(South Australia); *B. b macgillivrayi*
(known as Cloncurry parakeet),
from north-eastern Queensland

HABITAT:
in arid areas with eucalyptus
(mallee) trees and scrub

CLUTCH:
4 to 6, usually 5, rounded,
white eggs

INCUBATION:
20 to 22 days by the female

FLEDGING:
35 to 37 days

AVERAGE LIFESPAN:
18 years

SEXING:
the female has a dark-grey-green
nape and back, dark-brown eyes
and a pale-grey beak

JUVENILES:
similar to the female, but the
crown is mainly brown; the adult
plumage is in place between
12 and 18 months, when the
males lose the wing stripe

SIZE:
35 cm (13¾ in)

BARNARD'S or MALLEE RINGNECK PARAKEET
Barnardius barnardi

The rather temperamental Barnard's parakeet needs a large aviary and also prefers a grandfather-clock-type nest box, which should be placed on the aviary floor. We use nest boxes measuring approximately 60 x 20 x 20 cm (24 x 8 x 8 in), with an entrance hole measuring 6 cm (2¼ in) in diameter.

There are three subspecies: *B. b. whitei*, *B. b. macgillivrayi* and *B. b. cloncurry*, all rather popular in aviculture. The common name 'mallee' refers to several species of low-growing, shrubby eucalyptus that thrive in the drier parts of the Australian bush. They have no main trunk, but rather a number of trunklets emerging from the ground. The mallee ringneck obviously inhabits the mallee areas of Australia.

'*Whitei*' refers to Samuel Albert White (1870–1954), who was born in Adelaide and undertook several expeditions into the Australian outback in search of birds. '*Macgillivrayi*' commemorates Alexander Sykes Macgillivray (1853–1907), an Australian farmer and amateur ornithologist who discovered the Cloncurry parakeet, named after a town in Queensland, the area in which the Cloncurry parakeets occurs. This species lacks a red frontal band above the beak. Care and management are similar to those of the rosellas. Note that the brooding hen leaves the nest to feed only in the early morning and late afternoon, while her mate stays near the nest and warns her of any possible danger. During the breeding season, this species can be very aggressive, and should be left in peace once breeding has begun.

Feeding: as for the Pennant's parakeet, see page 96.

BLUE AND GOLD (or YELLOW) MACAW
Ara ararauna

These highly intelligent birds are very popular as pets and avicultural subjects; they have been kept in captivity since the eighteenth century. Successful breeding results are regularly obtained in large aviaries, and the first successful breeding occurred in 1818. A pair in Germany's Magdeburg Zoo bred in a small aviary measuring
4 x 2 x 3.5 m (13 x 6$^{1/2}$ x 11$^{1/2}$ ft), using a nest box measuring 50 x 50 x 60 cm (19$^{1/2}$ x 19$^{1/2}$ x 23$^{1/2}$ in), with an entrance-hole diameter of 14 cm (5$^{1/2}$ in). The box was constructed from boards
4 cm (1$^{1/2}$ in) thick. Breeder E Kjelland (of Chicago, the USA) had a pair housed in a cage measuring 60 x 120 x 120 cm (23$^{1/2}$ x 47$^{1/4}$ x 47$^{1/4}$ in) that stood in his shop. They bred in a metal box containing a layer of cedar shavings and woodchips. The first time, the female laid two eggs, one of which was fertile. The second clutch consisted of three eggs. All of the eggs hatched, but one youngster died when it was only a couple of days old; the two surviving chicks were brought up by hand, as soon as they were completely feathered.

Blue and golds are adaptable, as the above examples prove. They are also prolific. In warm areas, such as Spain, Hawaii and southern California, the hen incubates the eggs up to three days less than birds that are incubating their clutches in cooler climates, such as Scandinavia and parts of Canada. Well-established couples may produce three, or even four, clutches per season. Many youngsters are hand-reared for the pet industry. However, we strongly advise breeders to give all macaw species the opportunity to rear at least one clutch per season. It is also important to realise that hand-raised chicks take much longer to become independent. Note that breeding birds may become extremely protective of their young, and therefore aggressive towards their owners, during the breeding season. Provide all pairs with nest boxes all year round.

Feeding: as for the hyacinth macaw, see page 138.

Fact file

DISTRIBUTION:
central and South America:
Panama, northern Colombia, the Amazonian region, southern Venezuela, the Guianas, northern Bolivia, central and south-eastern Brazil, south-western Ecuador and Peru; reintroduced to Trinidad (in December 1999)

HABITAT:
wooded countryside and lowland forests, usually close to water; gallery forests; savannah; swamp forests; regularly seen near human habitation

CLUTCH:
2 to 4 elliptical, white eggs

INCUBATION:
24 to 28 days by the female

FLEDGING:
90 to 100 days

AVERAGE LIFESPAN:
50 years

SEXING:
the female may have a somewhat narrower head, but is in general similar to the male

JUVENILES:
very similar to their parents, but with a shorter tail (full grown in about 5 months); brownish iris

SIZE:
90 cm (35$^{1/2}$ in)

Hyacinthine or Hyacinth Macaw
Anodorhynchus hyacinthinus

Fact file

DISTRIBUTION:
central South America: Brazil, south of the Amazon, Santa Cruz (eastern Bolivia) and north-eastern Paraguay (where it is almost extinct); CITES Appendix I, vulnerable

HABITAT:
semi-open areas; deciduous woodland; swamps (with buriti and other nut-bearing palms)

CLUTCH:
2, occasionally 1 or 3, white eggs

INCUBATION:
28 to 29 days by the female

FLEDGING:
14 to 14½ weeks

AVERAGE LIFESPAN:
50 years

SEXING:
the female is similar to the male

JUVENILES:
pale-yellow skin around the eyes and lappets around the lower mandible; a whitish tongue; a shorter tail than their parents'

SIZE:
100 cm (39¼ in)

The giants of the macaws are undoubtedly the hyacinths. These birds are justifiably renowned for their great beauty, and are friendly with those whom they know, but tend to distrust strangers. In spite of their almost human, smiling expression, hyacinths tend not to rate highly in their speaking capability. These intelligent, predominantly violet-blue, birds have a rather long, graduated tail, a yellow, bare, periophthalmic ring (eye-ring) and a small, thin strip of yellow skin bordering the lower mandible. The hyacinth is the largest, and probably the most expensive, parrot in existence, with the exception of the Spixs macaw (*Cyanopsitta spixii*) from north-eastern Brazil, as well as the world's most endangered parrot, which is why it cannot be considered an avicultural species. In the wild, hyacinths live in pairs or small families along rivers, and feed primarily on palm nuts. The population of hyacinths in the wild is currently below 3,000; this species has been placed on the Convention on International Trade in Endangered Species (CITES) Appendix I, classified as vulnerable.

Captive-bred birds are inquisitive and will, in time, breed freely and with confidence. Breeding successes seem very promising. The first youngster was raised at Bratislava Zoo, in Czechoslovakia, in 1969; it died after three weeks, however. Ralph Small, of Brookfield, Illinois, in the USA, is probably the only person who had great success in the early years of hyacinth-breeding. He purchased his first pair from Brookfield Zoo and housed them in his basement, in an enclosure measuring approximately 2 x 4.25 x 1.5 m (7 x 14 x 5 ft). He used a 227.25 l (50-gallon) steel drum half-filled with bark as a nest box and maintained a temperature of 25 to 26°C (77 to 79°F) around it.

Wooden nest boxes measuring 1.5 x 1.5 x 1.8 m (3½ x 3½ x 4 ft) are also used. From the age of 5 years onwards, these birds must be given the opportunity to mate and breed.

Feeding: provide a commercial parrot-seed and pellet mixture, plenty of fruits, greens, vegetables, carrots, corn on the cob and apples. Also give them pine nuts, Brazil nuts, hazelnuts and other small nuts, fresh stems of wheat and oats just before harvest time and bunches of seeding grasses and weeds (like thistles), grit and willow branches.

MILITARY MACAW
Ara m. militaris

The Handbook of Cage and Aviary Birds

Fact file

DISTRIBUTION:
Colombia, western Venezuela, Narino, northern Peru, parts of Ecuador, north-west Argentina, Mexico; 4 proposed subspecies: *A. m. sheffleri* (Mexico), *A. m. mexicana* (Mexico) and *A. m. boliviana* (Bolivia and north-western Argentina), but all are questionable due to plumage and biometric similarities

HABITAT:
foothills in wooded areas up to 1,500 m (4,900 ft)

CLUTCH:
2 to 3 elliptical, white eggs

INCUBATION:
26 to 27 days by the female

FLEDGING:
81 to 91 days

AVERAGE LIFESPAN:
50 years

SEXING:
the female is similar to the male

JUVENILES:
similar to their parents, but with a shorter tail; greyish iris

SIZE:
70 to 75 cm (27 to 29 in)

This impressive, but rather monotonously coloured, macaw lives in groups of approximately 40 birds in the wild, in arid and semi-arid regions and pine and oak country, with lots of open areas. Like all macaw species, these birds leave their resting places in the early morning to forage, and return to the same roosting spots in the evening. They live on nuts, berries, fruits, buds, greens and seeds.

The military macaw has an active lifestyle and requires a large cage when kept as pet in captivity, or else an aviary measuring at least 9 m (15 ft) in length. Although it presents no problems, breeding is seldom realised as the birds are not very popular in aviculture. They are nevertheless easily tamed, though often moody and not always trustworthy, with a moderate talking ability.

Pairs like to use barrels or drums filled with woodchips (they will remove any surplus) as roosting and nesting places. During incubation, the male will usually rest on top of the barrel.

Feeding: as for the hyacinth macaw, see page 138.

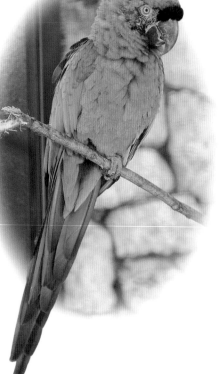

Scarlet Macaw
Ara m. macao

In the wild, these magnificent, predominantly red, birds, with their yellow wings and shoulders, can often be observed flying in pairs, their wings nearly touching. They are extremely sociable, and there is a deep bond between couples. They are very affectionate towards their keeper, but remain noisy (especially when frustrated or bored), and their earth-shattering screeches are a real drawback. Like all macaw species, the scarlet loves to bathe. It is interesting to watch a bird sitting in a rain shower, slapping itself with its wings.

Provide a large nest box measuring 60 x 60 x 65 cm ($23^1/_2$ x $23^1/_2$ x $25^1/_2$ in) all year round as they will also use it as their roosting place. Only the hen incubates, although the male sits beside her. Once feathered, many youngsters are hand-raised for the pet industry. Scarlet macaws are in general fine pets, but demand much time and affection from their owner as they can often become boisterous and aggressive as they mature. It is advisable to pair up such birds; experience has shown that they are never completely trustworthy as pets.

Feeding: as for the hyacinth macaw, see page 138. The keeper is also advised to offer oranges, bananas, various nuts, berries, carrots, calcium (in the form of cuttlefish bone), wheat bread, tomatoes and a daily supply of fresh twigs (from willow and fruit trees).

Fact file

DISTRIBUTION:
South America: Mexico, central and tropical South America; in 2 subspecies; seriously endangered, especially in Mexico, Costa Rica and Panama; extinct in El Salvador; CITES Appendix I

HABITAT:
tropical gallery forests; pine forests; savannah; cultivation; usually close to water in pairs or small flocks (of up to 30 individuals)

CLUTCH:
2 to 4 elliptical, white eggs

INCUBATION:
24 to 25 days by the female

FLEDGING:
100 to 106 days

AVERAGE LIFESPAN:
50 years

SEXING:
the female is similar to the male

JUVENILES:
similar to their parents, but with a shorter tail; on fledging, greyish lower mandible; grey iris

SIZE:
85 cm (33 in)

The Handbook of Cage and Aviary Birds

Fact file

DISTRIBUTION:
central South America:
north-western Argentina,
eastern and northern Bolivia,
northern Paraguay, south-western
and north-eastern Mato
Grosso do Sol in Brazil

HABITAT:
forests; forest edges; woodland;
savannah; gallery forests; up
to 1,700 m (5,577 ft) in
north-western Argentina

CLUTCH:
3 to 4 rounded, white eggs

INCUBATION:
24 to 26 days by the female

FLEDGING:
70 days

AVERAGE LIFESPAN:
30 years

SEXING:
the female is similar to the male

JUVENILES:
whitish ridge of the upper
mandible (culmen); reddish
nuchal collar; greyish iris and feet

SIZE:
38 cm (15 in)

YELLOW-COLLARED MACAW
Ara (Propyrrhura) auricollis

This dwarf macaw, which is also known as the yellow-naped or Cassin's macaw, has reddish eyes and a yellow collar on the back of its neck; it is also known for its sharp, high-pitched screeching. These birds are becoming popular in the USA and, to a lesser extent, in Europe, perhaps because they are very affectionate pets that exhibit clownish behaviour. They can be kept in a large cage, although they should be allowed to 'stretch their legs' daily for several hours. In an aviary, breeding successes are possible. Provide a few nest boxes measuring 45 cm² (17³/₄ in²) and cover the bottom with a layer of damp soil, peat and some moss.

Note that all dwarf macaws are very sensitive to draughts and cold.

Feeding: provide a commercial seed mixture and pellets; they especially like canary grass seeds and millet varieties (millet spray); also provide small nuts, berries, greens, fresh branches and corn on the cob (the latter must be on the menu when the young are being reared).

RED-SHOULDERED or HAHN'S MACAW
Diopsittaca [Ara] n. nobilis

This macaw is very well established in aviculture the world over, and strongly resembles the yellow-collared macaw (see left). The Hahn's has less white, bare skin around the eyes (which extends to the beak) than the yellow-collared macaw, however. The Hahn's is the smallest of the macaw species, and, like the yellow-collared macaw, is more reminiscent of conures than macaws.

Pairs need a nest box throughout the year as they prefer spending the night 'indoors' rather than on a perch; they like to roost in a sturdy box even outside the breeding season. They are quite sociable birds, and it is possible to house three pairs in a large aviary. Watch out for any signs of aggression, however, especially during introduction, and never place new couples in the aviary during the breeding season.

The subspecies *D. [A.] n. cumanensis* is somewhat larger, at 34 cm (13¼ in), and has a pale-cream-coloured upper mandible as opposed to the black beak of the nominate. This subspecies has recently been imported from Guyana in large numbers, and is also widely kept, bred and loved. Hand-raised youngsters make very nice pets, and become surprisingly tame.

Breeding and care for both species parallels those for the yellow-collared macaw.

Feeding: as for the yellow-collared macaw, see left.

Fact file

DISTRIBUTION:
northern South America: eastern Venezuela, the Guianas, north-eastern Brazil, central and south-eastern Bolivia, south-eastern Peru; in 3 subspecies

HABITAT:
semi-open, wooded habitats, including savannah and groves (in Surinam); sand-belt forests; coastal plantations (in Guyana); near human habitations; in Venezuela, up to 1,400 m (4,593 ft); often in large flocks

CLUTCH:
2 to 5, generally 4, rounded, white eggs

INCUBATION:
24 days by the female, but the male joins her during the night

FLEDGING:
55 to 58 days

AVERAGE LIFESPAN:
45 years

SEXING:
the female is similar to the male, but sometimes somewhat smaller

JUVENILES:
similar to their parents, but the head is all green; the red bend of the wing and carpal edge are lacking; red under-wing coverts; the feathers on the forehead are margined with dark grey; dark-grey iris

SIZE:
30 cm (12 in)

The Handbook of Cage and Aviary Birds

Fact file

DISTRIBUTION:
eastern Bolivia (at about 2,000
m/6,562 ft in the mountains);
Brazil (western Mato Grosso);
northern Venezuela; western
Uruguay; north-western
Argentina south to
La Pampa and Buenos Aires;
in 4 subspecies

HABITAT:
open forests; cultivation
(fruit trees); grass steppes
(northern Colombia);
nomadic, in large flocks

CLUTCH:
3 rounded, white eggs

INCUBATION:
24 to 25 days by the female

FLEDGING:
56 to 58 days; fed by the male

AVERAGE LIFESPAN:
24 years

SEXING:
the female is similar to the male

JUVENILES:
the blue on the head
is subdued; white lower
mandible; greyish iris

SIZE:
37 cm (14½ in)

BLUE-CROWNED or SHARP-TAILED CONURE
Aratinga a. acudicaudata

This species is somewhat noisy, although not as bad as the Jenday, sun, or Nanday conures. But when the birds have eggs or young, they are very quiet.

The nominate form was probably bred for the first time in captivity on the Isle of Wight by the Englishman K Bastien in 1971. The captive-bred young quickly became tame and affectionate and were extremely intelligent, but unfortunately had very loud voices. Remarkably, some possessed red feathers on their shoulders and wings, something that did not occur in the parents. They also lacked the blue on their parents' head.

In 1987, we obtained a number of sexed pairs. Five pairs became sexually mature after 2 years; two pairs reached maturity after 2½ years. Each pair has its own flight 6 m (19½ ft) long, and a choice of three nest boxes 20 cm (7¾ in) long, 50 cm (19½ in) deep and 20 cm (7¾ in) high, with an entrance hole 8 cm (3 in) in diameter. After laying the first egg, the hen seldom leaves the nest and is fed by the cock.

Feeding: conures are not particularly fussy about their food. Provide a good mixture of seeds (including only a few sunflower seeds as conures can become addicted to them to the exclusion of other seeds), plus greens (spinach, watercress, field lettuce, chickweed and dandelions), willow twigs and twigs from elder, hawthorn, poplar and fruit trees (but not cherry!), fruits (berries, apples, pears, cherries, grapes, bananas and pieces of coconut), insects (small mealworms, aphids and white worms), mineral and vitamin supplements. Ensure that fresh drinking water is always available.

WHITE-EYED CONURE
Aratinga e. leucophthalmus

This species is extremely active and quite abundant in the wild, especially in agricultural areas. These birds seem to prefer cultivated areas interspersed with natural woodland, but inhabit only the woodland edges. They like to rest in low vegetation. They seem to pair up for life.

At the authors' aviary, these birds have bred in a nest log measuring 60 cm (23½ in) deep and 20 cm (7¾ in) in diameter, with an entrance hole 9 cm (3½ in) in diameter positioned 30 cm (11¾ in) above the base of the log. The birds barely gnawed at the log. They would probably also accept a nest box measuring 40 to 50 cm (15¾ in to 19¾ in) high, with a floor area measuring 20 x 20 cm (7¾ x 7¾ in); an entrance hole 7 cm (2¾ in) in diameter would seem to be adequate.

Like some parrots, these birds frequently hang upside down from a twig, often using only one foot. Pairs, or even various couples, will feed, drink and sleep together. In the wild, there may be some 300 birds roosting together, making an ear-splitting noise as they squabble over the best roosting sites.

Feeding: as for the blue-crowned conure, see left. Like most aratingas and other conures, they like the occasional small nut, as well as wheat, corn or other grains, but only when other food supplies are insufficient.

Fact file

DISTRIBUTION:
throughout South America east of the Andes; in 2 subspecies

HABITAT:
lowland forests and woodlands

CLUTCH:
3 to 4 rounded, white eggs

INCUBATION:
23 to 24 days by the female

FLEDGING:
64 to 66 days

AVERAGE LIFESPAN:
25 years

SEXING:
the female is similar to the male

JUVENILES:
in comparison to the adults, less or no red on the bend of the wing and the forehead; no yellow in the under-wing coverts; brownish iris

SIZE:
32 cm (12½ in)

Fact file

DISTRIBUTION:
South America: the Andes, from
Venezuela to north-western Peru

HABITAT:
evergreen and deciduous forests;
desert; dry, thorny scrub; farm
areas; mountain woodlands, at
an altitude between 1,006 and
2,530 m (3,300 and 8,300 ft)

CLUTCH:
3 to 4 rounded, white eggs

INCUBATION:
23 to 24 days by the female

FLEDGING:
57 to 58 days

AVERAGE LIFESPAN:
27 years

SEXING:
the female and male are similar

JUVENILES:
often have no red feathers
on the side of the head;
yellowish eye-ring;
dark-brown iris

SIZE:
33 cm (13 in)

RED-MASKED CONURE
Aratinga erythrogenys

This is a very abundant species. Unfortunately, the birds have a nerve-grating call, which even hand-tamed specimens retain. They can learn to repeat a few words.

A Dutch fancier reported a successful breeding in a cubic nest box measuring 30 cm³ (11¾ in³). But it is better to use a box 40 to 50 cm (15¾ to 19½ in) deep, with a floor area of 15 to 20 cm² (6 to 7¾ in²), or a hollow log with an inner diameter of 20 cm (7¾ in); the entrance hole should be 7 to 8 cm (2¾ to 3 in) in diameter.

A pair of birds was bred in captivity in Germany in 1982. Three eggs, each weighing 14 g (½ oz) and measuring 28 x 34 mm (1 x 1¼ in), were laid. The hen started to incubate as soon as the first egg was laid, and the incubation time was about 24 days. Only one of the eggs hatched, however, and it is not known if it was the first one. The young bird, weighing 220 g (7¾ oz), left the nest at 58 days and was independent 22 days later.

An English fancier hatched red-masked conure eggs in an incubator. The newly hatched young weighed 8.27 and 8.38 g (around ¼ oz). Their eyes opened after about 2 weeks, and the birds were leg-banded (ringed) at 23 days. They had red feathers here and there on their heads, and were independent after 8 weeks.

Like all conures, these birds bathe frequently in the aviary. In general, they remain shy for a relatively long time. They are very hardy and can withstand quite low temperatures. Although they are not totally unknown in aviculture, they are not frequently available.

Feeding: as for the blue-crowned conure, see page 144.

GOLDEN-CAPPED CONURE
Aratinga a. auricapilla

This intelligent and beautiful bird is also known as the golden-headed conure. It is a very popular cage and aviary bird in the United States and Canada. This bird is sometimes confused with the Jenday conure, and requires similar care.

The subspecies *A. a. aurifrons*, or the golden-fronted conure, from south-eastern Brazil, is also very popular in England and Europe. This bird has a somewhat larger head and the wide, orange-red band extends to the crown. The rump feathers are green (these have a reddish-brown border in the nominate form).

The golden-capped conure is a hardy bird that can tolerate northern climates well, even in the winter in an outdoor aviary, provided that it has adequate shelter from the elements.

A two-year-old hen usually lays just two eggs, but the clutches get bigger as she ages. The best breeding results have usually occurred in deep nest boxes measuring 103 x 23 x 16 cm (40$^{1/2}$ x 9 x 6$^{1/4}$ in). It is quite easy to breed young in a roomy aviary.

Feeding:
as for the blue-crowned conure, see page 144.

Fact file

DISTRIBUTION:
north-eastern Brazil; northern and central Bahia; in 2 subspecies

HABITAT:
open woodlands; forests (population declining in southern Rio de Janeiro due to deforestation); and savannah

CLUTCH:
3 to 5 broadly elliptical, white eggs

INCUBATION:
25 to 26 days by the female

FLEDGING:
49 to 56 days

AVERAGE LIFESPAN:
25 years

SEXING:
the female is similar to the male

JUVENILES:
a little yellow and red in the plumage; brownish-red on the flanks and lower belly; red head markings duller than the adults'; no yellowish tinge on the cheeks or under-wing coverts; blackish eye-ring; brownish iris

SIZE:
30 cm (11$^{3/4}$ in)

Fact file

DISTRIBUTION:
southern Guiana, southern
Venezuela and north-eastern
Brazil (in Roraima, northern
Amazonas and Para)

HABITAT:
open savannah and woods;
palm groves; in flocks

CLUTCH:
3 to 4 rounded, white eggs

INCUBATION:
24 to 25 days by the female

FLEDGING:
49 to 55 days

AVERAGE LIFESPAN:
25 years

SEXING:
the female is similar to the male,
however, many males are more
red-orange (especially around
the eyes and on the forehead,
cheeks and abdomen)

JUVENILES:
variable; generally washed-out
greenish-yellow; white eye-rings;
adult colouration after 18 months;
sexually mature at 24 months

SIZE:
30 cm (11¾ in)

SUN CONURE
Aratinga (auricapillus) solstitialis

This species is similar in colour to the Jenday conure, but is more yellow and has more gold-orange tints, which frequently glint orange, especially below the wings and in the area around the eyes.

Breeding is frequently achieved with single pairs in roomy aviaries. A German fancier gave one pair a choice of a nest box measuring 45 x 30 x 30 cm (17¾ x 11¾ x 11¾ in) and a natural log 40 cm (15¾ in) in diameter and 80 cm (31½ in) high. The birds preferred the first until the natural log was replaced with another box measuring 120 cm (47¼ in) high, and with a diameter of 45 cm (17¾ in), which they used to rear a family.

This species is infamous for its loud, grating voice, but because it is not difficult to breed, it is now commonly found in Europe, the United States and elsewhere.

During the winter, the birds should be kept in a lightly heated shelter to avoid their toes becoming frostbitten. At night, they like to retire to a tree hole or nest box. After the young have left the nest, but while they are still being fed by both parents, they like to spend the night in the original nesting box.

Feeding: corn on the cob and various ears of grain can be given as extra rearing food, as well as grass seeds, fruits, green food, wholewheat bread soaked in water and squeezed out, hard-boiled eggs, boiled rice, oats, dried shrimps, mealworms and canary- or parakeet-rearing food. See also the blue-crowned conure, page 144.

PETZ or ORANGE-FRONTED CONURE

Aratinga c. canicularis

The Petz conure is one of the most popular parakeets in United States' aviculture; in Europe, somewhat less so. Many fanciers keep this bird as a cage pet, and it seems to do very well, often becoming tame and affectionate and learning to speak a few words. Since little seems to have been done to promote the captive breeding of this species, reports of successes are not common. Perhaps this will change with the introduction of import restrictions by the Convention on International Trade in Endangered Species (CITES). In order to maintain this, and all other species of conures, in captivity, aviculturists must put their efforts into saving these birds, for they are in danger of becoming extinct.

In Walsrode, Germany, the well-known subspecies *A. c. eburnirostrum*, or half-moon conure, a native of south-western Mexico, was bred in the parrot house in 1988. The pair shared an aviary measuring 2 x 3 x 2 m (7 x 10 x 7 ft) with a pair of Leadbeater cockatoos (see page 77). Each of the three eggs was laid at a two-day interval. Incubation started with the first egg and lasted for 23 days.

In the wild, these two conure species breed in termite mounds (of the species *Nasutitermes nigriceps*), where they dig out a tunnel and chamber with their beaks. Although these conures have been known to use artificial nest boxes, better results would probably be obtained if some attempt were made to provide captive birds with the kind of nest that they would accept in nature. In Walsrode, successful breeding with the Petz took place in a box 60 cm (23$\frac{1}{2}$ in) high and 30 cm (11$\frac{3}{4}$ in) in diameter, with an entrance tunnel 30 cm (11$\frac{3}{4}$ in) long.

Feeding: as for the blue-crowned conure, see page 144.

Fact file

DISTRIBUTION:
south-west Mexico (Chiapas) and south to Costa Rica; in 3 subspecies

HABITAT:
deciduous woods and sparsely wooded open savannah; cultivation, but always near termite mounds (of the species *Nasutitermes nigriceps*), in which the birds nest after digging out a tunnel and breeding chamber

CLUTCH:
3 to 5 round, white eggs

INCUBATION:
25 to 30 days by the female; the male spends the night inside the nest

FLEDGING:
49 to 50 days

AVERAGE LIFESPAN:
25 years

SEXING:
the female is similar to the male

JUVENILES:
the orange band on the forehead is narrower than in the parents; dark-brown iris

SIZE:
24 cm (9$\frac{1}{2}$ in)

The Handbook of Cage and Aviary Birds

Fact file

DISTRIBUTION:
north-eastern Brazil (Bahia to
south of the Rio Sao Francisco
and to the state of Minas
Gerais); in 2 subspecies

HABITAT:
open forests; caatinga
scrubland and semi-desert areas
with cacti and succulents

CLUTCH:
4 to 6 broadly elliptical,
white eggs

INCUBATION:
24 to 25 days by the female

FLEDGING:
49 to 50 days

AVERAGE LIFESPAN:
25 years

SEXING:
the female is similar to the
male, although many males
have paler plumage

JUVENILES:
paler than the female; white cere;
yellowish-green abdomen,
frequently edged with orange;
dark-brown iris

SIZE:
25 cm (9³⁄₄ in)

CACTUS CONURE
Aratinga cactorum cactorum

The cactus
conure derives its
name from the fact that
the main part of its diet
consists of cactus fruits.

The subspecies *A. c. caixana*, which occurs in eastern
Brazil, is difficult to distinguish from the nominate form.
It is somewhat paler, and the brown colour on the throat and
breast is a little deeper. These subspecies are often confused.

Both subspecies require a large aviary for successful breeding. We
bred from a pair of cactus conures in a nest box whose dimensions
were 25 x 50 x 30 cm (9³⁄₄ x 19¹⁄₂ x 11³⁄₄ in), with an entrance
hole 6 cm (2¹⁄₄ in) in diameter.

These birds can become tame and affectionate pets. They are not
particularly destructive, and are relatively quiet when compared
with other members of their genus.

Feeding: as for the blue-crowned conure, see page 144. As extra
food, the birds can be given pieces of fresh, sweet apple; millet
spray; pieces of melon; figs; berries; soaked and germinated seeds
(especially during the breeding season); and a rich variety of green
food and vegetables.

GOLDEN-CROWNED or PEACH-FRONTED CONURE
Aratinga a. aurea

This bird is very similar in appearance to the Petz conure (see page 149). It has a light-grey-greenish back, with lighter green beneath, and is sometimes olive-green, especially on the upper breast. *A. a. major* occurs at two localities about 120 km (75 miles) apart, on the banks of the Paraguay river in northern Paraguay to southern Bolivia, south-western Mato Grosso and north-western Argentina.

Both subspecies breed fairly readily if given an aviary of sufficient length. We have had many successes using a nest box measuring 35 cm (13¾ in) long, about 25 cm (9¾ in) wide and 25 cm (9¾ in) high, with an entrance hole about 8 cm (3¼ in) in diameter. Note that these birds are aggressive during the breeding season and are best kept in single pairs. If housed next to other parrot-like species, they should be separated by double mesh to prevent possible injuries. A fancier in Brazil possesses a blue and two cinnamon mutations of the peach-fronted conure.

Despite being fairly destructive and very noisy, both species are quite popular. They can rapidly become attached to their keeper, and can even be taught to speak a few words.

Feeding: as for the blue-crowned conure, see page 144.

Fact file

DISTRIBUTION:
most of Brazil (Mato Grosso and Sao Paulo), south of the Amazon and east of the Madeira river to eastern Bolivia; also in the province of Salta (Argentina) and in Surinam; in 2 subspecies

HABITAT:
woodland; scrubby vegetation; savannah; cultivation

CLUTCH:
4 to 6 rounded, white eggs, although clutches of 2 to 6 eggs do occur

INCUBATION:
24 days by the female

FLEDGING:
49 to 56 days

AVERAGE LIFESPAN:
25 years

SEXING:
the female is similar to the male, but more green and less yellowish-green

JUVENILES:
lack the adults' orange feathers around the eyes; have less and duller forehead colouring; both mandibles, or only the upper mandible, pale pinkish-white

SIZE:
25 cm (9¾ in)

Fact file

DISTRIBUTION:
northern Argentina; Paraguay;
south-eastern Bolivia;
southern Mato Grosso;
various feral populations in
the southern states of the USA

HABITAT:
open country; savannah;
forest regions; palm groves;
rice fields; cultivation

CLUTCH:
3 to 5 ovate, white eggs

INCUBATION:
24 to 25 days; the male often
sits on top of the nest box
while the female is incubating

FLEDGING:
56 to 58 days

AVERAGE LIFESPAN:
25 years

SEXING:
the female is similar to the male

JUVENILES:
less blue on the upper breast
and a much shorter tail than in
the adults

SIZE:
30 to 31 cm (11³/₄ to 12¹/₄ in)

NANDAY CONURE
Aratinga (Nandayus) nenday

Extremely popular cage and aviary birds, Nanday conures readily breed in a suitable aviary in captivity. They become sexually mature at three years of age. They quickly acclimatise to their surroundings and can be kept outside all year round. A nest box measuring 40 x 40 x 25 cm (15³/₄ x 15³/₄ x 9³/₄ in), with an entrance hole 7 cm (2³/₄) in diameter, should be provided. Nest inspections are best kept to a minimum. We have had the best breeding successes with a single pair in an aviary measuring 75 cm x 4 m x 2 m (29¹/₂ in x 13 ft x 6¹/₂ ft). Do not hang nest boxes too high because they like sitting on top of them and making very loud comments. While the female is incubating the eggs, the male may sit for hours in silence on the roof of the nest box, and often sleeps on it at night as well.

Nanday conures are fairly sociable birds, even with other species, but have one drawback: they have a very loud, piercing screech that makes them unsuitable as house pets and may annoy neighbours (and owners), even in a town-garden aviary. Once tame and used to their surroundings, they do become a little quieter, but are in general best suited to fanciers who live in the country or have very large gardens. For those who can tolerate the noise, they make reasonable and affectionate pets that will feed from the fingers and can learn to speak various words (they are considered good talkers).

Feeding: as for the blue-crowned conure, see page 144. During the breeding period, they must have a good food, with calcium and mineral supplements.

LESSER PATAGONIAN CONURE
Cyanoliseus p. patagonus

Both the lesser and greater Patagonian conure (*C. p. byroni*) are very hardy birds. They need a daily supply of twigs (from willows and fruit trees) to satisfy their desire to chew. Strong netting and an aviary constructed of metal are therefore essential.

In the wild, both subspecies live together in groups throughout the year and nest close together in holes in inaccessible rock faces and cliffs. In the spring (October to November), the natives climb the cliffs and often successfully remove the young from their nests using long bamboo poles with a hook at the end. The young birds are then hand-reared and tamed, ready to sell to international livestock traders.

In captivity, both subspecies have been bred successfully, usually in a large aviary. The best type of nesting facility is a hollow log with an inner diameter of 30 cm (11¾ in) and about 62 cm (24½ in) deep. The birds will gnaw at the interior walls, forming a bed of woodchips on which eggs are laid. The lesser Patagonian will also accept a wooden nest box 75 cm (11¾ in) long, 25 cm (9¾ in) wide and 25 cm (9¾ in) high, with an entrance-hole diameter of 10 cm (4 in).

In spite of their loud, screeching calls, both subspecies are much sought after as pets.

Feeding: these species do well on a diet that includes safflower and some sunflower seeds, as well as canary grass seeds, various millet varieties, millet spray, some hemp, thistles, raisins, apples, bread softened in water and squeezed out, green food, chickweed and fruits and berries (especially those of *Empetrum rubrum* or Argentinian crowberry).

Fact file

DISTRIBUTION:
central and southern Argentina; during winter migration, Buenos Aires, Mendoza and into Uruguay; in 3 subspecies

HABITAT:
savannah; palm groves; forest edges; open woods; cultivation (rice fields)

CLUTCH:
3 to 5 almost spherical, somewhat glossy, white eggs

INCUBATION:
24 to 25 days by the female

FLEDGING:
53 to 64 days

AVERAGE LIFESPAN:
28 years

SEXING:
the female is similar to the male

JUVENILES:
white upper mandible, which grows dark after about 8 months; greyish iris

SIZE:
45 cm (17¾ in)

154

Fact file

DISTRIBUTION:
south-eastern Brazil; Uruguay; eastern Paraguay; northern Argentina; in 3 subspecies

HABITAT:
all types of forest, especially araucaria along the Atlantic coast; eucalyptus plantations at altitudes of between 822 to 1,300 m (2,697 to 4,265 ft); corn fields; orange plantations, palm groves and other cultivations; in large groups

CLUTCH:
3 to 6 rounded, white eggs

INCUBATION:
22 to 23 days by the female

FLEDGING:
56 to 63 days

AVERAGE LIFESPAN:
25 years

SEXING:
the female is similar to the male

JUVENILES:
all red colours are slightly duller than in the adults, or brown-red

SIZE:
26 cm (10¼ in)

RED-BELLIED or MAROON-BELLIED CONURE
Pyrrhura f. frontalis

This species is irregularly available throughout the year, although it is quite common in worldwide aviculture. A lutino form is also available.

The red-bellied conure breeds readily, sometimes raising several broods per season. Easy to care for, it is an ideal species for the beginner and is ready to breed at 1 year of age. These birds prefer a natural, hollow log about 50 cm (19½ in) deep as a nest box. The inside dimensions should be similar to those recommended for *Neophema* species (see pages 101 to 106). (All birds of the *Pyrrhura* genus prefer a log to a box.) They should be allowed to keep their log outside the breeding season for sleeping in to prevent their toes from becoming frostbitten. A hiding place also helps them to lose their shyness more quickly. Spread partly rotten wood pulp on the floor of the box for the hen to gnaw into a fine bed for the eggs.

Inbreeding is deleterious to the health and viability of future offspring, so do not try to mate the offspring of one pair, but endeavour to obtain fresh blood by exchanging birds with other fanciers.

Once the birds have become accustomed to captivity and their diet, they will become very affectionate and will probably soon come to take a delicious morsel from your hand. They are not very destructive.

These birds do not demand much room and will happily live in a lovebird cage, although this is far from ideal. They can be kept in a group in an aviary, but should be separated into individual pairs for breeding.

Tip: place a number of unrelated individuals together and let them choose their own partners.

Feeding: provide a trusted commercial parakeet seed mixture for budgerigars, plus a variety of fruits and green food, along with cuttlefish bone and fresh water every day. A regular supply of fresh willow- and fruit-tree twigs will occupy their attention.

CRIMSON-BELLIED CONURE
Pyrrhura perlata

This beautiful species does not have any geographical variations. The crimson-bellied conure is often also called the pearly conure, which is incorrect because Dr N J Collar gave this bird a new scientific name in 1997, and the pearly conure is now taxonomically called *Pyrrhura lepida*, a name that was first applied to an immature, crimson-bellied conure. In other words, crimson-bellied and pearly conures are two different species. Both are very sociable, affectionate and curious birds, but the new species is rarely seen in aviculture.

These birds like to sleep in a large nest box measuring 25 x 25 x 30 cm (9³/₄ x 9³/₄ x 11³/₄ in). Because they are adept at escaping, the aviary mesh should be regularly checked. They should be given sufficient twigs and branches to gnaw at, too. During the autumn and winter months, they are best kept indoors in a roomy flight at least 3 m (9³/₄ ft) long. This species is very tolerant of others in a large, communal aviary.

Feeding: as for the red-bellied conure, see left.

The Handbook of Cage and Aviary Birds

Fact file

DISTRIBUTION:
northern Brazil, south of the Amazon between the Rio Madeira and Rio Tapajos, and as far as northern Mato Grosso; in 4 subspecies

HABITAT:
damp forests along rivers; lowlands; in large swarms in the upper foliage of tall trees

CLUTCH:
4 to 6 rounded, white eggs

INCUBATION:
24 to 25 days by the female; the male spends the night inside the nest box

FLEDGING:
55 to 57 days

AVERAGE LIFESPAN:
25 years

SEXING:
the female is similar to the male

JUVENILES:
duller and greener than their parents; green underparts; lighter-greyish beak and legs than those of their parents

SIZE:
24 cm (9¹/₂ in)

Fact file

DISTRIBUTION:
west-central Brazil; southern
Mato Grosso; northern and
eastern Bolivia; north-western
Argentina; in 5 subspecies

HABITAT:
forest regions at altitudes of up
to 2,000 m (6,562 ft)

CLUTCH:
4 to 7, but usually 5, rounded,
white eggs

INCUBATION:
22 to 24 days by the female

FLEDGING:
55 to 57 days

AVERAGE LIFESPAN:
25 years

SEXING:
the female is similar to the male

JUVENILES:
duller than their parents;
the red belly spot is only
faintly visible at first

SIZE:
26 cm (10¼ in)

GREEN-CHEEKED or MOLINA'S CONURE
Pyrrhura m. molinae

The last few years have seen a healthy interest in this species, which is irregularly imported, or in one of its five, possibly six, races. The nominate, the green-cheeked conure, has a maroon tail and a large, maroon patch on its belly. The most striking subspecies, *P. m. autralis*, from north-western Argentina and south-eastern Bolivia, is also becoming rather popular. This subspecies is the only *Pyrrhura* representative with a light-yellow underside marked with some narrow, pale margins on the throat and breast; the latter has an extensive maroon patch. The under-tail coverts show less blue than the nominate's.

The green-cheeked conure was first bred in 1974 by Dr R Burkard of Switzerland. He kept 14 birds in adjoining flights, but several birds gained access to a neighbouring aviary by gnawing under the floorboards in the night shelter. One of the pairs then nested on the floor in a tunnel measuring 1 m (3¼ ft). The well-known British veterinarian and aviculturist Dr George A Smith reared three young in 1979; the authors raised five from two pairs in 1985. We offered our pairs a nest box measuring 28 x 27 cm (11 x 10½ in), with a depth of 18 cm (7 in) and an entrance hole 10 cm (4 in) in diameter.

These rather shy birds take a long time to become accustomed to their keeper. They shriek with alarm at the slightest of disturbances.

Feeding: some of these birds have a rather unfortunate tendency to eat too many sunflower seeds and ignore other food. Coax them to eat other seeds, such as hemp, millet varieties, millet spray and canary grass seed, as well as apples, pears and pieces of banana. For more information, see the red-bellied conure, page 154.

WHITE-EARED CONURE
Pyrrhura l. leucotis

Of the five subspecies, the white-eared and Emma conure
(*P. l. emma*), from Venezuela, have been regularly available. The
Emma is a larger bird, with more blue on its head and a reddish-
brown forehead, the colour running over its crown. It also has
some blue in its cheeks, neck and throat.

There have been some reports of breeding by both species,
although the nominate is still favoured, and has been imported into
Europe since 1871.

This pleasant, easily tamed bird breeds regularly in a medium-
sized aviary at least 4 m (13 ft) long. The nest box dimensions
should be 25 x 35 cm (9¾ x 11¾ in), with an entrance hole 6 cm
(2¼ in) in diameter. During the incubation time, the male stays on
the nest at night and feeds his partner during the day.

Feeding: as for the red-bellied conure, see page 154.

Tip: once the young have
hatched, supplement the
menu with soaked, stale,
wheat bread; cooked
corn; some small, black
sunflower seeds;
boiled potatoes;
a little hemp
and oats; and
sliced carrots.

Fact file

DISTRIBUTION:
northern Venezuela; eastern
Brazil and an established colony
in the Botanic Gardens in
Rio de Janeiro; in 5 subspecies

HABITAT:
Atlantic forests; plateaux;
foothills; bushland

CLUTCH:
4 to 5, or 3 to 8, broadly
elliptical, white eggs

INCUBATION:
21 to 25 days by the female,
but the male offers food
during the day

FLEDGING:
45 to 52 days; mature
at about 15 months

AVERAGE LIFESPAN:
25 years

SEXING:
the female is similar to the male

JUVENILES:
duller, with a less pronounced
barred breast than in their
parents; white eye-rings
(grey in their parents)

SIZE:
21 cm (8¼ in)

Fact file

DISTRIBUTION:
the Guyanas; Surinam; Venezuela; northern Colombia; south-east Peru; northern Bolivia; northern Brazil; in 9 subspecies

HABITAT:
lowlands and forests along rivers; in Surinam, in swamps in the interior and on the sandy banks of the coastal region

CLUTCH:
4 to 8, usually 2 to 3, elliptical, white eggs

INCUBATION:
25 to 27 days by the female; the male supplies food during the day and will remain in the nest box for hours (very rare for *Pyrrhura* species)

FLEDGING:
30 to 38 or 44 days

AVERAGE LIFESPAN:
40 years

SEXING:
the female is similar to the male

JUVENILES:
duller than their parents; green bend of wing, sometimes with a few red feathers; light-grey eye-rings (the parents' are dark grey); initially pinkish legs

SIZE:
22 cm (8½ in)

PAINTED CONURE
Pyrrhura p. picta

Only a few breeding successes have been reported for these birds in captivity, but individual breeders report that they are good breeding birds. They require a thick-walled nest box or, if possible, a natural, hollow log with minimum dimensions of 30 x 30 x 40 cm (11¾ x 11¾ x 15¾ in) and an entrance diameter of 7 cm (2¾ in). In Europe, including England, the birds nest very early, sometimes even in December. A pair is thus best kept in a roomy aviary, with a minimum flight length of 4 m (13 ft) and a dry, draught-free night shelter.

We kept a pair for some time in The Netherlands. They were extremely active and reared one clutch per year, in a bird log of the dimensions specified above. The hen laid 4 to 5 eggs, but usually only 2 or 3 were fertile. The incubation time was 26 to 27 days. The young left the nest 31 to 32 days later, but were still fed by their parents for 2 to 2½ weeks.

Note that the white-eared conure (page 157) is very similar to the painted conure, but about 2 cm (¾ in) shorter. The painted conure has cream-coloured ear patches and the pattern on its neck and head is a closed, accolade-like edge, with a fine network of markings. This is in contrast to other members of the genus, in which each feather is more or less edged. The Latin name *picta* (meaning 'painted') is thus well chosen.

Feeding: as for the red-bellied conure, see page 154.

MAROON or BLACK-TAILED CONURE
Pyrrhura m. melanura

Since 1970, this species has been regularly available in the trade, especially in the United States and Germany. It requires care similar to that for the red-bellied conure (see page 154), but is probably not as interesting.

This conure breeds readily in captivity. The nest box should be 35 cm (13¾ in) deep and 25 cm (9¾ in) square. Place a layer of damp peat moss on the base.

Feeding: as for the red-bellied conure, see page 154.

Fact file

DISTRIBUTION:
central Colombia; southern Venezuela; north-western Brazil; Ecuador; north-eastern Peru; in 5 subspecies

HABITAT:
in mostly forested or partly deforested areas at altitudes of between 1,280 and 2,620 m (4,200 and 8,596 ft)

CLUTCH:
4 to 5 ovate, white eggs

INCUBATION:
22 to 25 days by the female

FLEDGING:
52 to 56 days

AVERAGE LIFESPAN:
25 years

SEXING:
the female is similar to the male

JUVENILES:
identical to their parents, but with less pronounced breast markings and a slightly lighter beak

SIZE:
24 cm (9½ in)

Fact file

DISTRIBUTION:
south-west Argentina; southern Chile; in 2 subspecies

HABITAT:
the Andes, at altitudes of 2,000 m (6,562 ft), from September to March; during the rest of the year, at lower altitudes; in groups of 10 to 100

CLUTCH:
4 to 7 rounded, white eggs; in the absence of natural hollows, a nest of twigs and grass will be constructed

INCUBATION:
26 to 28 days by the female

FLEDGING:
53 to 64 days

AVERAGE LIFESPAN:
25 years

SEXING:
the female is similar to the male

JUVENILES:
darker and duller than their parents; lacking their parents' red forehead band and red abdomen; a shorter bill with a white tip; light-greyish eye-ring

SIZE:
37 cm (14½ in)

AUSTRAL or MAGELLAN CONURE
Enicognathus f. ferrugineus

Austral conures live mainly in woodlands, although we have also seen them in parks and other cultivated areas. The birds were first exported in 1866, but are relatively scarce in aviculture today. The better-known subspecies *E. f. minor* (the Chilean conure) and the full species *E. leptorhynchus* (long-billed or slender conure), from Chile, are respectively 34 cm (13¼ in) and 40 cm (15¾ in) in length. The Chilean conure is somewhat darker than the Austral, including the red forehead band and red belly patch, which can be so dark as to virtually disappear in the darker green. The long-billed conure lives mainly in wooded country, in noisy groups of 50 to 300 birds; it has a crimson streak running from the forehead to just behind the eyes.

In Europe, all three can breed as late as December. A good night shelter is advisable, and a sleeping box (which is used as nest box) measuring 60 x 50 x 45 cm (23½ x 19½ x 17¾ in) is essential throughout the year. During the summer, they appreciate a water bath. All three conures are recognised as excellent birds, with a reasonably pleasant voice, which they like to exercise towards the evening.

All species should be kept in a roomy outdoor aviary with a dry, draught-free night shelter. The flight should be at least 4 to 5 m (13 to 16½ ft) long as all three conures are rather active. They also like to forage on the ground, so occasionally sprinkle seeds on the aviary floor. These conures are not aggressive towards members of their own kind or other *Enicognathus* birds, although pairs are best kept alone for breeding. Thick perches about 56 cm (22 in) in diameter are very much appreciated by these birds.

Feeding: provide millet varieties, canary grass seeds, oats, some hemp, corn, small, black, sunflower seeds, plus fruits (especially apples) and greens, including carrots and root vegetables. Some individuals will eagerly take mealworms and may be given a few each day. The seeds can also be offered germinated or sown on the floor of the aviary.

THICK-BILLED PARROT
Rhynchopsitta pachyrhynchus

This macaw-like parrot, with its big head, impressive, black beak and short tail, was once a casual winter visitor to south-eastern Arizona (the Chiricahua mountains) and, before 1935, also to New Mexico. While in flight, the bright-yellow patch on the under-wing coverts is conspicuous. The bird is rare in both nature and captivity, and has been placed on Appendix I of the Convention on International Trade in Endangered Species (CITES). The thick-billed parrot has the most northerly distribution of any neo-tropical parrot. More recently, it has been seen only in Mexico, although nests with eggs and young have been found in snags (dead pine-tree stumps) within approximately 150 km (93 miles) of the United States' border. Ranching, mining and prospecting in the mountains of Arizona have vanished, and what remains of the human population is no longer a threat to the small groups of parrots there.

Thanks to breeding and release programmes, the thick-billed parrot is now slightly more common in US aviculture, although it is less popular in Europe, including England. In September and October 1986, some 13 wild-caught birds were released. This was a thoughtless act on the part of ornithologists, however, as many birds fell victim to various raptors during their autumm migration. The breeding of this handsome parrot has been relatively successful, and is executed under strict rules and regulations.

The maroon-fronted parrot (*R. terrise*) is closely related to the thick-billed parrot, although it is much larger, at 45 cm (17¾ in), and lives in north-eastern Mexico. It has a maroon-brown forehead and silver-grey under-wing coverts. It is unknown in aviculture, however.

Feeding: as for the blue-crowned conure, see page 144.

Fact file

DISTRIBUTION:
Mexican highlands; in the past (in reports dating from 1935), large numbers occasionally migrated to southern Arizona and south-west New Mexico; there have been active breeding and release programmes since 1986 in order to save the species; in 2 subspecies

HABITAT:
stone-pine forests at altitudes of between 1,500 and 6,400 m (4,921 and 21,000 ft); declining in number due to deforestation (pine forest is the bird's only habitat)

CLUTCH:
2 to 4 ovate to rounded, white eggs

INCUBATION:
28 days by the female

FLEDGING:
62 to 70 days

AVERAGE LIFESPAN:
25 years

SEXING:
the female is similar to the male, but the male has a broader beak

JUVENILES:
the adults' eye-stripe is lacking, as is the red on the bend of the wing and carpal; green shoulders; horn-coloured bill

SIZE:
38 cm (15 in)

The Handbook of Cage and Aviary Birds

Fact file

DISTRIBUTION:
southern Brazil to south of
Rio Negro; introduced to and/or
nests found in New York, New
Jersey, Connecticut, Massachusetts,
Virginia and Florida; also in Puerto
Rico, Rio de Janeiro (Brazil),
Berlin (Germany), Austria
and Mediterranean locations;
in 4 subspecies

HABITAT:
lowland; savannah; farmland,
orchards and cultivated areas;
follows civilisation; damages fields
and gardens (at harvest time, the
birds fly out in noisy flocks of
hundreds or thousands into fields)

CLUTCH:
5 to 8, but usually 4 to 6, white
eggs in a large, bulky nest with
various nesting chambers

INCUBATION:
23 to 25 days by the female; the
male spends the night in the nest

FLEDGING:
40 to 45 days

AVERAGE LIFESPAN:
25 years

SEXING:
the female is similar to the male

JUVENILES:
similar to the female, but the
forehead is tinged with light green

SIZE:
29 cm (11½ in)

QUAKER or MONK PARAKEET
Myiopsitta monachus

This *Myiopsitta* species is well known for its gigantic nests, which are loosely constructed in treetops in the wild, usually in the outermost branches.

Because these parakeets are both easy to keep and hardy, they are popular in captivity, but are frequently set free (probably on account of their loud, screeching calls), the result being that many have now set up home in areas outside their natural territory. Young birds can become exceedingly tame and can learn to repeat a few words.

Compared with many other birds, they are somewhat aggressive, especially during the breeding season, so it is better to keep them either in single pairs or else together in groups of three or more pairs (as colony breeders/nesters). They should be kept in a roomy aviary with well-protected woodwork. Breeding cages with minimum dimensions of 100 x 70 x 50 cm (39¼ x 27½ x 19½ in) can also be used. A few pairs can be extremely entertaining in an outdoor aviary measuring 3 x 2 x 2 m (9¾ x 6½ x 6½ ft). They can spend the winter outdoors, and temperatures as low as 13°C (55°F) do not seem to worry them. Either erect a timber, cross-shaped shelf up in one corner or affix an open platform with dimensions of about 50 x 60 cm (19½ x 23½ in) high up in the aviary. Place large quantities of willow, aspen, birch, oak and fruit-tree twigs measuring from 20 to 100 cm (7¾ to 39¼ in) on the aviary floor as nest material. Both sexes build the next at first, but the hen does most of the initial work. Quakers can be rather destructive when faced with timber and wire, so use 16G-gauge wire (mesh size 15.5 x 25 mm/½ x 1 in) for the latter.

There are various mutations, of which the blue, established in Belgium during the early 1950s by aviculturist M J Bruyneel, is known the world over. This mutation is autosomal recessive.

Feeding: provide a reputable commercial parakeet mixture with white millet, canary grass seeds, some small sunflower seeds and some hemp. Also provide weed seeds, oats and groats, various fruits (for example, apples, bananas and oranges), vegetables and green food. During the breeding season, give the birds sprouted seeds, seeding grass, fresh willow and fruit-tree branches, commercial rearing food for large parakeets, bread soaked in water, adequate grit (free choice) and fresh water.

Fact file

DISTRIBUTION:
from southern Mexico to
western Panama, up to 2,500 m
(8,202 ft); mountains (nominate);
the Andes of Peru and northern
Venezuela, above 2,500 m
(8,202 ft) (subspecies *B. l. tigrinus*)

HABITAT:
mountain forests; subspecies also in
upper tropical vegetation; during the
winter, in lowland rainforests

CLUTCH:
3 to 8, usually 4 to 6, rounded,
white eggs

INCUBATION:
18 days (in the wild); 20 to 24
days by the female; the male
spends the night in the nest

FLEDGING:
32 to 34 days

AVERAGE LIFESPAN:
10 years
(especially domesticated males)

SEXING:
the female is similar to the male

JUVENILES:
less barring than in the adults;
the forehead is more blue
(this applies to the wild colour;
at the time of writing, there
are at least 10 established
colour mutations; see text)

SIZE:
16 cm (6¼ in)

LINEOLATED or BARRED PARAKEET
Bolborhynchus lineola

This species is very popular, especially in Europe, including England, and may be kept in an aviary or large cage with other small, exotic birds since it is peaceful and non-aggressive. These parakeets spend much of their time on the ground, both in the wild and in captivity, seeking seeds and insects. It is recommended that the flight floor be regularly (and deeply) raked to prevent worm infection.

These attractive little hookbills are not at all destructive in their aviary; they slowly climb up branches, which should preferably be 4 cm (1½ in) in diameter, or hang head downwards while performing careful acrobatics. They are sensitive to low temperatures and must be kept in gently heated indoor accommodation during the autumn and winter.

With good husbandry, a pair should go to nest and will accept a lovebird or parakeet nest box. They frequently carry nest material into the box as a lining – sometimes as much as 4 cm (1½ in) deep – for the floor. They prefer strips of willow bark, small, soft feathers and similar materials. Hang the nest box out of the glare of the sun since these birds seem to avoid sunshine as much as they can, a habit that we have also seen in the wild. These birds breed most successfully if kept together in groups of three or more pairs.

There are various mutations, some of which have not yet received a definite name. The well-known and well-established mutations are: (pastel) edge dilute (dominant sex-linked), ino and cinnamon (both recessive sex-linked), dark factor and violet (both autosomal dominant), seagreen and faded (both autosomal recessive), lutino (recessive sex-linked) and pied (which can be both recessive and dominant).

Feeding: provide a reputable parakeet seed mixture with additional pellets, small, black, sunflower seeds and hemp (both sparingly), millet spray and millet varieties and a regular multivitamin and mineral supplement. These birds also love apples and other fruits, chickweed, seeding grasses, the twiggy branches of hazel and hawthorn, insects, germinated seeds and a commercial rearing food for parakeets during the breeding season; provide some grit (free choice) and water, too.

SPECTACLED PARROTLET
Forpus c. conspicillatus

With their graceful shape, soft colours and charming behaviour, these parrotlets are not only suitable for an indoor or outdoor aviary, but also for a roomy cage in a room in the house. The birds are very loving to one another, and some become tame and trusting. However, this species is in no way easy to impress: on the contrary, the birds will stand their ground and are not as timorous as the green-rumped parrotlet (see page 168). It is recommended that pairs be kept singly, in a large cage or aviary. Like all parrotlets, they like plenty of space, but a cage with a minimum length of 100 cm (39¼ in) or 120 cm (47¼ in) is adequate, and breeding will probably then be successful.

Spectacled parrotlets are less aggressive than celestial or Pacific parrotlets, although mature males will fight for the best nesting sites; these squabbles usually take place at the beginning of the breeding season. Our nest boxes are 110 cm (43¼ in) long, 40 cm (15¾ in) wide and 60 cm (23½ in) high; we have also had success with wooden budgerigar nest boxes varying in size from 20 to 25 cm (7¾ to 9¾ in) long, 15 to 25 cm (6 to 9¾ in) wide and 25 to 35 cm (9¾ to 13¾ in) high. Position the nest boxes horizontally and make the entrance hole in the outer corner of one of the long panels; the nest cavity must, of course, be situated at the opposite end of the box so that the birds cannot damage the eggs when they enter it. Rough sawdust or pine bedding can be placed in the nest cavity, although it may not stay there as many parents have a habit of turning everything out. If this happens, try replacing it, but if they turf it out again, let them go without.

It is best to let your birds start breeding in around May. Begin to feed animal protein (in the form of a suitable rearing food and various insects) to the prospective breeding pairs at least three months before the beginning of the breeding season.

Feeding: provide a reputable commercial seed mixture for parakeets, some hemp and black sunflower seeds, millet varieties, spray millet, canary grass seed, corn (softened and crusted), oats, wheat, leguminous plants, fresh and germinated seeds, greens, fruits, fresh twigs, egg food, cottage cheese, yoghurt, pieces of cereal bar, uncooked, dry pasta, grit (free choice) and fresh water.

Fact file

DISTRIBUTION:
Colombia (except the north-east); Gulf of Darien; eastern Panama, connected with the Magdalena river; the western slopes of the eastern Andes; in 3 subspecies

HABITAT:
open forest to an altitude of 1,600 m (5, 249 ft); bushland

CLUTCH:
4 to 6 spherical to elliptical, white eggs without a gloss

INCUBATION:
22 to 24 days by the female; the male checks in regularly and feeds the female from his crop

FLEDGING:
32 to 34 days

AVERAGE LIFESPAN:
20 years

SEXING:
the female is paler green than the male, with an emerald rump; all blue is lacking; she is more yellow on the forehead

JUVENILES:
similar to the female; young males have a blue tinge on the tips of their under-wing coverts (visible only on close examination)

SIZE:
males: 13 cm (5 in); hens somewhat larger, up to 14 cm (5½ in)

The Handbook of Cage and Aviary Birds

Fact file

DISTRIBUTION:
western Ecuador to north-
western Peru; in 2 subspecies

HABITAT:
semi-open lowland, from desert
scrubland through to lighter
woodland and deciduous
forests; locally in humid forests

CLUTCH:
4 to 6 ovate, white eggs,
without a gloss

INCUBATION:
20 to 22 days by the female;
the male will feed the female
on the nest

FLEDGING:
30 to 37 days

AVERAGE LIFESPAN:
20 years

SEXING:
all cobalt colouration is lacking in
the female; her feathers are dull
blue behind the eyes

JUVENILES:
similar to their parents, but paler

SIZE:
13 cm (5 in)

CELESTIAL or PACIFIC PARROTLET
Forpus c. coelestis

This beautiful bird is a rather compact parakeet, with a straight bearing (of 55 to 60 degrees), especially when viewed from a distance, and of contrasting colours. There is one subspecies, the recently rediscovered *F. c. lucida*, from Colombia, whose females have blue rumps.

In the wild, the celestial parrotlet lives in flocks consisting of many different families. These birds are not particularly fussy with regard to their choice of nesting site, and will nest in abandoned woodpecker holes, rotten fence posts, holes in walls and, indeed, in almost any hollow or cavity that is large enough.

In aviculture, this species is one of the easiest to breed and has the largest number of mutations: lutino, blue and fallow, for example; all three are autosomal recessive. These birds make excellent pets if kept in cages or roomy aviaries in a room in the house; they can learn various tricks in a short time and soon master words and short sentences. Singletons are seldom really happy, even if you spend a lot of time with them, so give them partners! Multiple pairs in aviaries do not always get along well with one another, however, and their strong territoriality can lead to jealousy and squabbling, which may develop into more serious fighting, especially during the breeding season. In general, these birds are not cowardly and are well able to hold their own.

For breeding, try square, half-open nesting boxes measuring 30 x 30 x 30 cm (11¾ x 11¾ x 11¾ in) that have been especially designed for parrotlets and other small parrots. The boxes should have a perforated zinc bottom and be placed on a tray containing water so that water vapour can pass through the holes, thus keeping the eggshell membrane moist enough to ensure hatching. Horizontally mounted nest boxes for budgerigars are also popular. The entrance hole should made in a side and a nest hollow with a raised edge should be provided inside the other half of the box to prevent the eggs from rolling around.

Feeding: as for the spectacled parrotlet, see page 165. Additional germinated seeds, vegetables (especially spinach), weeds (particularly dandelion and chickweed) and berries are welcome in conjunction with a reputable parakeet-rearing food.

YELLOW-FACED PARROTLET
Forpus xanthops

In the wild, the birds of this species, the largest member of its genus and very similar to the celestial or Pacific parrotlet in looks, live in small flocks. In captivity, these charming birds do best in a large aviary; one pair per flight is recommended. If kept in a garden aviary, they must be brought indoors during the winter, placed in a breeding cage at least 120 cm (47¼ in) long and kept at a minimum temperature of 15°C (59°F) and at a minimum humidity level of 80 per cent.

For care and breeding, see the celestial or Pacific parrotlet (left).

In the not-too-distant past, many newly imported yellow-faced parrotlets were infected with immature, parasitic worms (microfilariae). These worms occur in the bird's circulatory system and were responsible for the sudden deaths of birds that otherwise appeared healthy. The disease was described as 'avian malaria'. Newly acquired wild birds should be immediately examined by an avian veterinarian. However, prevention is certainly better than cure, and captive-bred birds are a better acquisition. But even these should be inspected if they have been in contact with wild-caught birds.

Feeding: as for the spectacled parrotlet, see page 165.

Fact file

DISTRIBUTION:
north-western Peru, especially in the valley of the Maranon river (a tributary of the Amazon)

HABITAT:
tropical woodland (primarily tree and brush savannah), at an altitude of between 600 and 1,700 m (1,969 and 5,577 ft)

CLUTCH:
3 to 6, but normally 5 to 6, spherical to elliptical, white eggs, without a gloss

INCUBATION:
24 to 25 days by the female

FLEDGING:
35 to 42 days

AVERAGE LIFESPAN:
20 years

SEXING:
the female is similar to the male, but with a pale-blue lower-back and rump area, which is smaller than the male's; her primaries and secondaries are green, tinged with blue; her under-wing coverts are grey

JUVENILES:
similar to the female, but with less yellow on the head

SIZE:
14 to 15 cm (5½ to 6 in)

GREEN-RUMPED PARROTLET
Forpus p. passerinus

Fact file

DISTRIBUTION:
northern Trinidad through
Venezuela, along the Orinoco river
to eastern Colombia, and from the
south-eastern section of the
Rio Branco to eastern Amazonas
and north-eastern Brazil; introduced
into Curaçao, Jamaica and
Barbados; in 4 (or 5) subspecies

HABITAT:
open terrain sparsely dotted with
trees and tall scrub; near rivers; not in
rainforests or densely wooded cover

CLUTCH:
3 to 7 spherical to elliptical, white
eggs without a gloss

INCUBATION:
20 to 21 days by the female

FLEDGING:
30 to 45 days

AVERAGE LIFESPAN:
20 years

SEXING:
the female lacks the male's
blue markings on the wings; she
has a yellowish forehead

JUVENILES:
similar to the female; young
males soon begin to show the
blue in their plumage

SIZE:
12 cm (4³/₄ in)

There are 5 subspecies: *F. p. passerinus*, or the green-rumped parrotlet; *F. p. delicious*, or the delicate green-rumped parrotlet (from northern Brazil and Macapa in Amapa); *F. p. cyanophanes* (from northern Colombia), which is similar to *F. p. viridissimus*, but with a more intensive violet-blue colour on the bend of the wings; *F. p. viridissimus* (from northern Venezuela, and now introduced to Trinidad, Curaçao, Jamaica and Barbados); and *F. p. cyanochlorus* (from the upper Branco river in northernmost Brazil, Venezuela, Curaçao and Surinam), which is similar to the nominate, but with more yellow on its underparts; the beak is smaller, too.

Pairs of these small birds can be housed in parakeet or lovebird breeding cages of a minimum length of 100 cm (39¹/₄ in). The temperature must not drop below 15˚C (59˚F). Newly acquired birds should be handled with care as they are easily frightened when confronted by new situations. One of their first reactions is to refuse to feed (and they rarely take millet spray). Give the birds enough time to become accustomed to their keeper, surroundings and so on. The green-rumped parrotlet is prone to abnormalities of the beak (it may become overgrown or misshapen, for instance), for which there is no explanation, nutritional deficiencies, genetic flaws and environmental and medical problems having been excluded in most cases. Fortunately, their beaks are easy to trim, so correct beak abnormalities as soon as possible.

Because of their comparative nervousness, it is best to place their breeding cages fairly high up: 2 m (6¹/₂ ft) is ideal. If you use battery cages placed in stacks, it is best to reserve the uppermost cages for green-rumped parrotlets. The best breeding results are obtained when each pair is given its own abode. The birds can become quite aggressive toward other birds during the breeding season, and will aim for the little feet of their fellow inmates.

Feeding: as for the spectacled parrotlet, see page 165.

CANARY-WINGED PARAKEET
Brotogeris chiriri

Until 1977, when Brazil stopped its exportation, the canary-winged parakeet was one of the most commonly imported South American psittacines. The species was exhibited at England's London Zoo as early as 1868. Over the years, it has turned out to be an exemplary aviary inmate and an excellent family pet.

It is unfortunate that these beautiful parrots have such nerve shattering voices, which they usually vent when not wholly contented, but they should not be too much trouble if kept in a roomy outdoor aviary. The best kind of nest box is a natural birchwood log. Alternatively, use a homemade box measuring 45 x 25 x 25 cm (17¾ x 9¾ x 9¾ in). A layer of humus or peat about 4 cm (1½ in) thick should be laid on the bottom. The box should be fixed high in the aviary for the best breeding results. The birds can winter in an outdoor aviary provided that they have a dry, draught-free shelter. They love to bathe in a large bowl of water.

The subspecies *B. c. behni*, which is slightly larger, is no longer available and less common in both Europe and the United States.

Feeding: the menu should consist of a variety of fruits (cherries, apples, pears, bananas, bits of pineapple, oranges and soaked raisins and currants), corn, rice, oats, fresh willow branches and buds, various grass seeds and other grains, rearing food for parakeets, small beetles (but no dangerous insects or spiders), small mealworms, ant pupae, grit (free choice), cuttlefish bone and drinking water daily.

Clipped birds still arrive on the market. These must be housed separately for some time and be given extra nutrition in the form of rice, willow bark, fruits, berries, blossoms, a good commercial seed mixture for budgerigars and vegetable matter.

Fact file

DISTRIBUTION:
Amazon drainage basins and eastern, central and southern Brazil into northern and eastern Bolivia, Paraguay, northern Argentina (Chaco, Missiones) and eastern Peru; in 2 subspecies

HABITAT:
forest edges; open woodland; civilization; in small flocks (of up to about 50 individuals and pairs)

CLUTCH:
3 to 5, occasionally 6, rounded, white eggs; breeds in the nests of tree termites

INCUBATION:
23 to 26 days by the female, but the male stays on the nest at night

FLEDGING:
50 to 60 days; the young often return to the nest for the night (the young develop rather slowly)

AVERAGE LIFESPAN:
15 years

SEXING:
the female is similar to the male

JUVENILES:
similar to their parents, but duller; the beak is darker, but this is only for a very short time

SIZE:
21.5 to 22 cm (8½ in)

The Handbook of Cage and Aviary Birds

Fact file

DISTRIBUTION:
central, southern and eastern Brazil;
northern Argentina (Salta),
Tucuman and Latamarca in the
east and Santa Fe in the west;
in 4 subspecies

HABITAT:
lowland forests; gallery woods;
open deciduous and dry forests;
in pairs and small groups

CLUTCH:
4 to 5 broadly elliptical to short
ovate, white eggs

INCUBATION:
24 to 26 days by the female

FLEDGING:
64 to 74 days

AVERAGE LIFESPAN:
25 years

SEXING:
the female is similar to the male

JUVENILES:
have less blue on the upper
breast than adults; most
have a yellow-orange or
orange-red forehead,
sometimes speckled
with 1 or 2 little,
deep-red feathers

SIZE:
29 cm (11½ in)

MAXIMILIAN'S or SCALY-HEADED PARROT
Pionus m. maximiliani

The first breeding successes for the Maximilian's parrot were accomplished in England's London Zoo in 1862. Of all of the *Pionus* representatives, this parrot is by far the most tranquil. When housed in a long aviary, a pair likes to fly back and forth, but may roost for quite some time upon their favorite perch or branch. They are strong fliers and don't make much noise. However, they will screech enthusiastically when there is an opportunity to frolic in the rain! They seldom vocalise during the morning and evening hours, but will utter little chuckling noises and make soft, chatty sounds throughout the rest of the day.

Although these birds prefer roomy, outdoor aviaries, large cages measuring 120 x 80 x 100 cm (47¼ x 31½ x 39¼ in) are accepted. Offer a normal, wooden nest box measuring 35 x 35 x 40 cm (13¾ x 13¾ x 15¾ in), with an entrance-hole diameter of 10 cm (4 in). These birds are not aggressive towards their keeper or other birds during the breeding season. For more details, see the blue-headed parrot (right).

Feeding: this species requires an extensive menu. Besides a good seed mixture for medium-sized parrots, it must have a daily supply of germinated seeds and various fruits, vegetables and berries. Greens (like dandelion, spinach and chickweed), willow branches, millet spray and ground nuts are also important, as is grit. Daily fresh drinking water is essential.

BLUE-HEADED PARROT
Pionus m. menstruus

This species is by far the most popular of the genus *Pionus*, and is reared each year in aviaries the world over. The first breeding successes were established in France in 1890.

Often called the 'poor man's Amazon', this species is relatively inexpensive and makes an ideal companion bird (being quiet, affectionate and, due to the attractive sheen and colours of its plumage, delightful to admire). Hand-reared birds are especially in demand and make exquisitely beautiful and quiet companions.

Since these parrots like to climb, and especially to fly, they are best housed in a good-sized aviary at least 5 m (16½ ft) long, although they will accept large breeding cages (see the Maximilian's parrot, left). Hand-tamed companion birds should be placed in large cages and be given free access to a playpen and a variety of branches, toys and feeding cups. Such a playpen should either be mounted on top of the cage's roof or positioned next to the cage. Commercially manufactured playpens are available, but they are easy to make.

Companion birds are best kept in pairs (or with more birds) as they are colony-breeders by nature. If your companion bird is a singleton, you must devote at least 4 to 6 hours a day to it.

For breeding details, see Maximilian's parrot, left.

Feeding: as for the Maximilian's parrot, see left.

Fact file

DISTRIBUTION:
Costa Rica; Panama into northern South America; absent in the Andes; in 3 subspecies

HABITAT:
lowland; tropical woodland up to 1,200 m (3,937 ft) in Panama, 1,000 m (3,281 ft) in Venezuela and 1,500 m (4,921 ft) in Colombia; also parks, gardens, plantations, orchards and cultivation

CLUTCH:
2 to 4, sometimes 3 to 5, oval and pointed, white eggs

INCUBATION:
25 to 26 days by the female

FLEDGING:
62 to 63 days

AVERAGE LIFESPAN:
25 years

SEXING:
the female is similar to the male

JUVENILES:
less blue than the adults; mainly green

SIZE:
28 cm (11 in)

Cuba Amazon
Amazona l. leucocephala

Fact file

DISTRIBUTION:
eastern and central Cuba;
in 5 subspecies; CITES
Appendix I: threatened

HABITAT:
pine forests; broad-leaved
woodland; palm groves,
mangroves and plantations;
cultivation; parks and gardens;
in pairs or family groups

CLUTCH:
3 to 5, generally 4, rounded,
white eggs

INCUBATION:
25 to 28 days by the female

FLEDGING:
58 to 60 days

AVERAGE LIFESPAN:
40 years

SEXING:
the female is similar to the male;
the male of the subspecies
A. l. caymanensis is usually
larger and brighter in colour
than the female; the latter
subspecies is rare in aviculture

JUVENILES:
fewer black feather
edges and less vinaceous
on the abdomen
than the adults

SIZE:
32 cm (12½ in)

Known for its intelligence, the Cuba Amazon has been placed on Appendix I of the Convention on International Trade in Endangered Species (CITES) as it is threatened with extinction. But its numbers seem to be recovering slowly, but surely, for importation is a thing of the past and most birds are captive-bred.

This Amazon is a hardy and gentle bird and a fair talker and mimic. Breeding it is relatively easy. It is interesting to note that the first hybrids (*leucocephala* x *aestiva*) were reported as early as the summer of 1885 by a lady in Karlsruhe, Germany. Three chicks hatched from four eggs, but only one young survived. The pair bred again in 1886, and of the three eggs, one was placed under a breeding pair of grand eclectus, thanks to P Hieronymous, a dentist who then had to assist in freeing the chick from the egg.

This bird can be kept as a companion, but should be housed in a large cage with strong, metal bars running horizontally. The cage's shape must be rectangular as the birds (like all species of *Amazona*) become nervous in round ones. Most Amazons are rather destructive, so house them in strongly built aviaries constructed with 14G-gauge wire (mesh size 25 x 25 mm/1 x 1 in), a draught-free night shelter and an open run at least 4.2 m (13¾ ft) long. Supply a hollow tree trunk, barrel or box of hard timber measuring 30 x 30 x 142 cm (11¾ x 11¾ x 56 in), with an entrance 10 cm (4 in) in diameter. In front of the entrance, attach some strong branches; on the inside, fasten some mesh or large staples so that the birds can leave the nest easily.

Feeding: about 30 per cent of the birds' daily menu should consist of fresh fruits and vegetables. Provide willow branches, dandelions, a reputable parrot-seed mixture, germinated sunflower seeds, safflower, weed and grass seeds, cooked corn and corn on the cob, pulses, old cheese, various nuts (pine, walnut and some peanuts), pellets mixed through seed (in a 40:60 ratio), a cooked chicken bone with meat, grit (free choice) and fresh water daily.

SPECTACLED or WHITE-FRONTED AMAZON
Amazona a. albifrons

The members of this species are much smaller than most Amazon parrots, but are very self-possessed and will stand up to the largest, most intimidating rival.

Not much is known about this bird. Old breeding records are available, but real breeding successes have been extremely rare. Nevertheless, these birds are very common in aviculture as they are rather quiet and easily sexed (the female lacks the male's red wing edge, or alula). Solitary, they can be excellent pets and good talkers, especially when purchased young. Old birds remain noisy and will constantly raise their nape feathers when excited.

The only way to accomplish breeding success is by placing several birds together in a large aviary so that they can choose their own partners. Pairs should then be separated and placed in their own, roomy aviary (they are skilful fliers). Provide hollow tree trunks, barrels, or nest boxes of thick hardwood timber measuring 35 x 35 x 50 cm (13¾ x 13¾ x 19¾ in), with an entrance-hole diameter of 10 cm (4 in).

There is a lutino specimen in the United States, namely at Houston Zoo in Texas.

Feeding: as for the Cuba Amazon, see left.

Fact file

DISTRIBUTION:
north-western Mexico through northern Guatemala and Belize, western El Salvador, north-western Costa Rica and Nicaragua; in 3 subspecies

HABITAT:
wooded areas; open country with trees; pine woodland; gallery forests; savannah; coconut plantations; cultivation

CLUTCH:
3 to 4 rounded, white eggs

INCUBATION:
24 to 26 days by the female

FLEDGING:
49 to 56 days

AVERAGE LIFESPAN:
40 years

SEXING:
the female has green primary coverts and alula; some males may show a vague red colouration

JUVENILES:
similar to the female; the forecrown is tinged with yellow

SIZE:
27 cm (10½ in)

Fact file

DISTRIBUTION:
north-eastern Mexico; feral populations near Los Angeles (California), Brownsville (Texas), Oahu (Hawaiian Islands) and Puerto Rico

HABITAT:
dry forests; brushland; other semi-arid areas

CLUTCH:
2 to 4 rounded, white eggs

INCUBATION:
28 days by the female

FLEDGING:
63 days

AVERAGE LIFESPAN:
40 years

SEXING:
the female usually has less red on the head than the male

JUVENILES:
less red on the head than the adults; some blue-banded feathers on the crown and over the eyes

SIZE:
33 cm (13 in)

MEXICAN RED-HEADED or GREEN-CHEEKED AMAZON
Amazona viridigenalis

A familiar member of the large *Amazona* genus, the Mexican red-headed or green-cheeked Amazon is characterised by its pleasant and gentle personality. These Amazons are very popular with aviculturists. Their courtship behaviour (performed in March in the wild) is accompanied by much shrieking and pecking at one another. Hybridising with *A. a. albifrons* succeeded in 1934, when three of the four young survived. Because this bird is placed on Appendix I of the Convention on International Trade in Endangered Species (CITES), hybridisation is strongly discouraged, however. House a pair in a good-sized aviary and provide a roomy barrel or nest box measuring 30 x 30 x 60 cm (11¾ x 11¾ x 23½ in), with an entrance-hole diameter of 12 cm (4¾ in).

Feeding: as for the Cuba Amazon, see page 172. During the breeding season, boiled corn, some hemp, oats and wheat, peanuts, walnuts, hazelnuts and various berries (such as rowan berries, blackcurrants, bilberries, gooseberries and strawberries) are essential.

Finsch's Amazon
Amazona f. finschi

This parrot, which is also called the lilac-crowned Amazon, is widely known. It is distinguished by the striking colour and markings around its crown and lore. This Amazon was bred in the USA as early as 1949, by J Mercer. R E McPeek, of Ontario, Canada, raised three young in 1972, three in 1973 and two in 1975. In that same year, Mr Greenblatt, of Poer Bird Farm in Arizona, the USA, raised two chicks. During the past ten years, breeding successes have been numerous. Pairs should be placed in large aviaries and given a nest box measuring 30 x 30 x 60 cm (11¾ x 11¾ x 23½ in), with an entrance-hole diameter of 12 cm (4¾ in). Finsch's Amazon is not that suited to keeping in a large cage, although hand-raised birds can become quite tame and affectionate.

There are also many so-called 'bleached' specimens in California, which originated in Mexico, where they are known as 'Lady Clairols'. The subspecies *A. f. woodi* (Somora, Chihuahua and Sinaloa) is unknown in aviculture, and is much greener, especially the underparts and tail feathers.

Feeding: as for the Cuba Amazon, see page 172.

Fact file

DISTRIBUTION:
western Mexico; in 2 subspecies;
a small feral population around
Los Angeles, the USA

HABITAT:
wooded hills and mountains
(including canyons), up to
2,225 m (7,300 ft)

CLUTCH:
3 rounded, white eggs

INCUBATION:
26 days by the female

FLEDGING:
54 to 60 days

AVERAGE LIFESPAN:
40 years

SEXING:
the female is similar to the male

JUVENILES:
similar to their parents,
but less red;
dark-brown iris

SIZE:
32 cm (12½ in)

Fact file

DISTRIBUTION:
from Mexico south into
Amazon, Nicaragua, Costa Rica,
Panama, north-western
Colombia, Ecuador, Belize,
Guatemala and Honduras;
in 4 subspecies

HABITAT:
wooded and open areas with
trees; mangroves; wooded
swamps; gallery forests;
cultivation; up to 915 m (3,002
ft); in pairs or small family groups

CLUTCH:
3 rounded, white eggs

INCUBATION:
26 days by the female

FLEDGING:
58 to 63 days

AVERAGE LIFESPAN:
40 years

SEXING:
the female is similar
to the male

JUVENILES:
unlike their parents, less
or no yellow and red in
the face; brown iris

SIZE:
35 cm (13³/₄ in)

PRIMROSE-CHEEKED or YELLOW-CHEEKED AMAZON
Amazona a. autumnalis

The three remaining subspecies are quite common in aviculture, as is *A. a. salvini*, or the Salvin's Amazon, which lacks the yellow cheek colour of, and is somewhat larger than, the nominate. *A. a. lilacina*, from western Ecuador and generally called the Ecuador Amazon, which has a blue-violet crown and green ear region, while its beak is whitish and grey. *A. a. diadema*, or the diademed Amazon (which lives near rivers in Brazil), looks much like the Salvin's Amazon, but differs mainly in having thick, red, hair-like feathers in its nose area.

All of these birds can be kept in large cages as companion birds, as well as in roomy aviaries. Hand-raised birds are easily tamed and have an agreeable manner. Their speaking ability is not impressive, and their natural cries are piercing and monotonous.

These birds like either a closed barrel with a nest opening of 25 cm (9³/₄ in) in diameter as their 'maternity room' or a nest log measuring 50 x 50 x 70 cm (19¹/₂ x 19¹/₂ x 27¹/₂ in), with a nest-entrance diameter of 15 cm (6 in).

Feeding: as for the Cuba Amazon, see page 172.

BLUE-FRONTED AMAZON
Amazona a. aestiva

One of the most popular companion birds, with an excellent talking and mimicking ability, the blue-fronted Amazon becomes very tame and affectionate. There are various colour mutations, the best-known being pied-yellow, blue and lutino. The subspecies *A. a. xanthopteryx*, or yellow-winged blue-fronted Amazon, differs from the nominate by being greener and having more yellow on its face and yellow edges, mixed with red, on its wings; in some birds, the red is completely replaced by yellow. The yellow-winged blue-fronted Amazon ranges from the northern parts of Bolivia through eastern Brazil, Paraguay and northern Argentina to northern most Buenos Aires. This subspecies is reasonably common, and is often mistaken for the nominate form; it is likely that many such birds are owned by people who are unaware of their pets' true identity!

In aviculture, the bird has proved to be robust and hardy, although the natural sounds that it makes are impossible to ignore. Although friendly outside the breeding season, these birds' behaviour often changes drastically when they are brooding, especially when dealing with sexually mature birds. They may even start false brooding (especially when housed in cages), may make neurotic movements and may pick one another's feathers.

Sex determination through DNA has made pair formation easy; the difference in eye colouration (males have orange irises, females, red ones) is far from reliable. We house our pairs in large aviaries and offer them a hollow log or nest box measuring 50 x 50 x 70 cm (19$\frac{1}{2}$ x 19$\frac{1}{2}$ x 27$\frac{1}{2}$ in), entrance diameter 12 cm (4$\frac{3}{4}$ in), containing a layer of peat moss.

Feeding: as for the Cuba Amazon, see page 172. During the breeding season, a variety of fruits, berries and greens, corn on the cob and germinated sunflower seeds are essential.

Fact file

DISTRIBUTION:
eastern Brazil to southern Mato Grosso; in 2 subspecies; *A. a. xanthopteryx:* eastern Bolivia, Paraguay, northern Argentina and south-western Brazil

HABITAT:
wooded areas and open country with trees; savannah; caaratinga gallery woodland; palm groves; cultivation

CLUTCH:
3 to 4 ovate, white eggs

INCUBATION:
28 days by the female

FLEDGING:
56 to 63 days

AVERAGE LIFESPAN:
40 years

SEXING:
the female is similar to the male

JUVENILES:
less yellow and blue on the head than the adults; in *A. a. xanthopteryx*, barely any yellow on the bend of the wing

SIZE:
36 to 38 cm (14 to 15 in)

Fact file

DISTRIBUTION:
central and South America, south to eastern Brazil and northern Bolivia; in 4 subspecies

HABITAT:
open woodland; gallery woodland; forest edges; savannah; swamps in rainforests; cultivation and human habitation; always close to water

CLUTCH:
3 ovate, glossy, white eggs

INCUBATION:
26 days by the female

FLEDGING:
63 days

AVERAGE LIFESPAN:
40 years

SEXING:
the female is similar to the male

JUVENILES:
a smaller yellow head patch than their parents; dark-brown beak and iris

SIZE:
40 cm (15³/₄ in)

YELLOW-CROWNED or YELLOW-FRONTED AMAZON
Amazona o. ochrocephala

The nominate of this species becomes very tame and is seldom malicious. It likes human company and is a very good talker and imitator, although not all specimens are intelligent. Breeding successes are regularly obtained, especially when breeding pairs are housed in large aviaries without their fellows or other Amazon species. Supply sturdy nest boxes measuring 45 x 45 x 75 cm (17³/₄ x 17³/₄ x 29¹/₂ in), with an entrance diameter of 14 cm (5¹/₂ in). There is an almost pure lutino in captivity, as well as a beautiful blue mutation (with a white forehead) of the subspecies *A. o. panamensis*. This Panama yellow-headed Amazon is from western Panama and the tropical lowlands of northern Colombia; it has a yellow forehead, a horn-coloured beak, with a dark tip on the upper mandible, and flesh-coloured legs and feet; at 33 cm (13 in), it is somewhat smaller than the nominate.

The second subspecies, *A. o. auropalliata*, or yellow-naped or golden-naped Amazon, also strongly resembles the nominate. It has a yellow nape, a grey upper mandible and horn-coloured, grey lower mandible, a grey eye-ring and flesh-coloured legs and feet; it is 39 cm (15¹/₄ in) in size. Its range is central America, from south-western Mexico in the north to Costa Rica in the south.

The largest subspecies, at 41 cm (16 in), is *A. o. oratrix*, or the double yellow-fronted Amazon, from Mexico. It, too, looks very like the nominate, but its head and nape are yellow, its bill is horn-coloured and its legs and feet are a bright flesh colour. *A. o. belizensis*, or the double yellow-headed Amazon, from British Honduras, is very similar to *A. o. oratrix*, but with some yellow on its head.

All require the same care and management as previously mentioned Amazons.

Feeding: as for the Cuba Amazon, see page 172.

Double yellow-fronted Amazon
Amazona ochrocephala oratrix

This Amazon, which has already been mentioned under the nominate *A. o. ochrocephala* (left), is often considered a full species: *Amazona oratrix*. This beautiful parrot is frequently kept and bred in captivity. It requires a spacious aviary, and pairs should have their own, large housing. A breeding pair should have access to a deep nest box measuring 45 x 45 x 75 cm (17³/₄ x 17³/₄ x 29¹/₂ in), with an entrance diameter of 14 cm (5¹/₂ in). Keep an eye on them because they may become aggressive.

The yellow on the head is often used for sexing, but the amount of yellow is not a clear indication of gender, nor is the overall colour: a healthy female is often brighter in colour than a healthy male.

This Amazon is highly valued, both as a breeder and as a companion bird. Like most Amazons, this species is an excellent mimic: we have heard it laugh, sneeze, whistle, imitate grandfather's smoker's cough or a squeaky door and swear in many different languages! However, it never loses its somewhat harsh, natural voice, especially if it is left to its own devices.

Amazon parrots are relatively easy to keep. Do not buy a bird on impulse: remember that you are purchasing a friend for life. Check the bird's nostrils for signs of discharge. If they appear enlarged or blocked, this may indicate a respiratory infection to which Amazon parrots are susceptible; contact an avian veterinarian immediately because this infection is difficult to cure.

Feeding: as for the Cuba Amazon, see page 172.

Fact file

DISTRIBUTION:
the coast of Mexico;
in 4 subspecies

HABITAT:
savannah; tropical deciduous forests; thorn forests; swamps (along the Pacific coast); various woodlands and cultivation

CLUTCH:
2 to 4, generally 3, ovate, glossy, white eggs

INCUBATION:
26 days by the female

FLEDGING:
63 days

AVERAGE LIFESPAN:
40 years

SEXING:
the female is similar to the male

JUVENILES:
little or no yellow on the forehead and crown; all yellow and red in the adults' wings lacking; dark-brown iris; adult colouration achieved in about 5 years

SIZE:
41 cm (16 in)

The Handbook of Cage and Aviary Birds

Fact file

DISTRIBUTION:
from southern Mexico to
Nicaragua and north-western
Costa Rica; in 3 subspecies; *A.
o. parvipes*: Honduras and
north-eastern Nicaragua

HABITAT:
open woodland; close to water;
grassland; mountain slopes

CLUTCH:
2 to 3 ovate, glossy, white eggs

INCUBATION:
26 days by the female

FLEDGING:
77 days

AVERAGE LIFESPAN:
40 years

SEXING:
the female is similar to the male

JUVENILES:
some yellow feathers in the
green nape; brown iris; grey
upper mandible; in *A. o.
parvipes*, the lower mandible
is horn-coloured

SIZE:
39 cm (15¼ in)

YELLOW-NAPED AMAZON
Amazona o. auropalliata

These impressive parrots, also known as golden-naped Amazons,
are very loud birds. As companion birds, they are often good
talkers, and their voices closely resemble the human voice.
Popular pets in the USA, there are also lutino and blue mutations.
These birds are far from bashful and like to associate with people.

Their breeding parallels that of other Amazon parrots. They
require a roomy, outdoor aviary and a nest box measuring
50 x 50 x 70 cm (19½ x 19½ x 27½ in), with an entrance hole
12 cm (4¾ in) in diameter, containing a layer of peat moss. It
takes approximately 4 years before the young develop their full
adult plumage. The best breeding results may be accomplished
when a pair is 4 to 5 years old. These birds may become
somewhat aggressive during the breeding season, so it is advisable
to allocate each large, outdoor flight to one pair. Cover the nest
box with some willow branches for privacy.

Feeding: as for the Cuba Amazon,
see page 172.

ORANGE-WINGED AMAZON
Amazona amazonica amazonia

Although very similar to the well-known blue-fronted Amazon (see page 177), this species is much smaller and slimmer. The speculum of the wing and patch of the tail feathers are also orange, instead of red. This charming bird, which makes an excellent companion bird, is very loud (much too loud to be kept indoors).

The orange-winged Amazon, a popular bird in aviculture, was regularly bred in the United States at Bush Gardens, Tampa, Florida, and still is at San Diego Zoo. In England, Rode Tropical Bird Gardens became well known for its pair, which was kept at liberty, returning to its small, outdoor flight every evening and spending the night in a nest box.

Their care and management parallels that of other Amazon parrots.

Feeding: as for the Cuba Amazon, see page 172.

Fact file

DISTRIBUTION:
southern South America, north of the eastern Andes; in 2 subspecies

HABITAT:
lowland forests; gallery woodland; savannah; mangroves; cultivation and human habitation

CLUTCH:
3 to 4 elliptical to ovate, white eggs

INCUBATION:
25 days by the female

FLEDGING:
56 to 60 days

AVERAGE LIFESPAN:
40 years

SEXING:
the female is similar to the male

JUVENILES:
similar to their parents; dark-grey iris

SIZE:
33 cm (13 in)

The Handbook of Cage and Aviary Birds

Fact file

DISTRIBUTION:
northern South America,
north of the Amazon; in 2
subspecies; *D. a. fuscifrons:*
south of the Amazon

HABITAT:
lowland rainforests;
in pairs or small flocks

CLUTCH:
2 to 4 ovate to elliptical,
white eggs

INCUBATION:
25 to 28 days by the female

FLEDGING:
63 days

AVERAGE LIFESPAN:
30 years

SEXING:
the female is similar
to the male

JUVENILES:
similar to their parents, but
duller, and with more green;
horn-coloured lower mandible;
brown iris; whitish skin
surrounding the eyes

SIZE:
35 cm (13³/₄ in)

HAWK-HEADED PARROT
Deroptyus accipitrinus

Closely related to the *Pyrrhura* conures, this is the only known parrot with the ability to raise its head feathers to form a fan or ruff. While the excited bird erects these head and neck feathers, its body sways slowly from side to side, the bird all the while emitting a high-pitched whine. This very expensive bird is something of a rarity in aviculture, but is nevertheless bred regularly, especially in Germany, England and the USA.

This parrot is intelligent, interesting to observe and generally good-natured. Most are charming, playful and usually make excellent companions (if one is able to tolerate their loud voices), but pairs, and especially males, can often be aggressive and ready to attack anyone who dares to pay attention to another bird. Most captive birds are a little nervous and jumpy (often resulting in feather-plucking, biting or self-mutilation).

Pairs are best kept in an outdoor aviary with a permanent, roomy nest box measuring about 50 x 50 x 70 cm (19¹/₂ x 19¹/₂ x 27¹/₂ in), with an entrance hole 12 cm (4³/₄ in) in diameter, in which a pair will not only raise a family, but will roost and sleep throughout the year, especially on cold nights. To offer breeding or resting birds a sense of security, cover the nest box with willow- and fruit-tree branches.

Feeding: besides a reputable parrot-seed mixture, these birds need a daily supply of fresh fruits, including berries (such as hawthorn), and vegetables. During the breeding season, also provide a commercial parrot- or parakeet-rearing food and grit (free choice). Water-soaked wheat bread is welcome throughout the year, but especially during the breeding season.

CANARY
Serinus canaria domesticus

The early history of the domestication of the canary is obscure, but there are a few fairly believable stories, such as the one about the Frenchman, Jean de Bethancourt, who married a girl who came from the Canary Islands. He became fascinated by the songs of the wild canaries (*Serinus canaria*) and began to build small cages in his spare time. He then began to fill them with canaries and shipped them to Spain in Spanish vessels.

Another story tells of how some Spanish ships were caught in a storm off the coast of Italy as they sailed to Livorno. The cargo of one of these ships consisted largely of canaries, for which the sailors felt sorry and which they compassionately released. This is why, it is said, canaries were found on the island of Elba, from which some found their way to the Italian mainland. The Italians caught them in their thousands and sent them via northern Italy to the Tyrol and parts of Germany, where they were successfully bred and marketed. It was not long before they found their way to England and Russia.

Today, the canary is the most popular cage bird in the world, and has been domesticated and established in many colour varieties, shapes, sizes and songs. Popular breeds are the Borders, Norwich, Glosters, Yorkshires and lizards. Fascinating colours are also very popular in canaries, ranging from red through apricot, agate, pastel, ivory, bronze to frosted orange, and inos and phaenos. 'Old' breeds are also gaining in popularity, such as the Lancashire (both copy and plainhead), Scotch fancy and southern Dutch frill, the latter being a continental variety that, together with the Parisian frill, Belgian frill, Milan frill, Muenchener and Padovan frill, to name but a few, are definitely back in fashion. Roller and Waterslager are song canaries.

Fact file

DISTRIBUTION:
originally from the Canary Islands, the Azores and Madeira; now one of the most popular cage and aviary birds the world over

HABITAT:
its 'ancestors' still live in thick bush and scrub, never far from large trees and forested areas

CLUTCH:
4 to 5 light-blue-green eggs, with brown markings (which can be various)

INCUBATION:
12 to 14 days by the female

FLEDGING:
21 to 23 days

AVERAGE LIFESPAN:
10 years

SEXING:
the differences depend on the type, colour or song breed; in general, the female is duller than the male; the male sings; scientific (DNA) sexing is possible

JUVENILES:
similar to their parents; type canary breeds fledge with shorter tails

SIZE:
11 to 17 cm (4¼ to 6½ in)

Green canary.

Red brown canary.

Lizard canary.

Blue opale canary.

Crest canary.

Breeding is mostly done in box or breeding cages, but also in aviaries. Provide the pairs with a nest pan (available from pet shops) and line it with felt. Most fanciers remove each egg and replace it with an artificial (plastic) one until the clutch has been completed. The real eggs are stored (end up) in a cool place in an open drawer filled with a layer of bran or another soft material.

Feeding: provide a reputable, standard canary-seed mixture and green food (fed early in the day, and always in small quantities), such as chickweed, lettuce, spinach, cress, dandelion leaves and pieces of carrot. Also provide canary-egg and -rearing food, cuttlefish bone, sprouted seeds, a vitamin-and-mineral supplement and fresh water every day.

Varieties
The red factor was introduced into the canary by pairing it with the hooded siskin or red siskin, *Serinus (Carduelis) cucullata*, from Venezuela and Trinidad (and later introduced to Cuba and Puerto Rico). The male is primarily red, with a black head, and is currently one of the few birds that can be crossed with the canary hen to produce the red-factor colouring. This red colouration is a kind of lipochrome, having some qualities in common with the yellow lipochrome of the canary. (A lipochrome or chromolipid is one of various fat-soluble pigments, such as caratenoid, that occur in natural fats.) The red factor can be used as an under-colour for pigment canaries or to determine the colouring of lipochrome canaries.

Canaries with the red factor must be colour-fed, especially during the moult. Avoid sources of lutein, which are present in various green foods, egg yolk and rape seed, as these foods will add too much yellow to the canary's colouration. Instead, offer groats, Niger seed (ramtil), grated carrot and soft food without xanthophylls and egg food. Many breeders use canthaxanthin, which is derived from cantharel, an edible fungus that seems to have no vitamin value. It works in other organisms, including some insects and fish, as well as flamingo and scarlet-ibis feathers. Pure canthaxanthin is used in a dosage of 0.05 to 0.1 g per 500 g to intensify and hold the red colour in the plumage. There are various other colour foods available on the market, which should be used according to the manufacturer's instructions.

Phaenos canary.

Onyx canary.

Blue agate canary.

Lancashire canary.

The Handbook of Cage and Aviary Birds

Yellow canary.

Red canary.

Red mosaic type-2 canary.

Satinet yellow mosaic type-2 canary.

NORWICH CANARY

This variety probably originated in Flanders and came via Belgium to Britain, where it was further improved in Norwich, hence its modern name.

Old illustrations show that it was very similar to the Waterslager, an excellent song canary that was probably one of its ancestors. This old race was considered a colour variety for some time. The lizard canary may have played a role as this canary was definitely crossbred, as is evident when you look at the silky, shiny feathers of the Norwich. According to the illustrations, the Norwich canary underwent various changes in around 1800, so it is likely that the original type dates back well before this.

A large exhibition in honour of the Norwich canary was held in Norwich, England, in 1890. About 400 entrants are said to have participated, and breed standards were established then, along with a scale of points for form and position. The colour was no longer thought to be a major factor, and the bird became a type rather than a colour canary. With breeding interruptions occurring only during the two world wars, the Norwich has been a very successful breed, with a second form (crest and crest-bred) also becoming popular. The length of the Norwich canary is 16 cm (6¼ in).

SCOTCH FANCY

Little is known about the origin of this breed, but this canary variety probably originated in Scotland. Earlier versions were known as the Glasgow fancy or Glasgow Don. In all probability, the Belgian Bult has a lot to do with its ancestry, and the hooded form of this breed has been further developed into a semi-circular shape. (Due to the canary's posture, it is sometimes called 'the bird o' circle'.) The Scotch fancy's other ancestors are anyone's guess, although the southern Dutch frill may have played a part. Its size is 17 cm (6½ in).

The miniature Japanese Hoso is very similar. The first examples of this race arrived in Europe in 1970, although they were already known in Japan in 1963. The most obvious characteristic of this breed is its half-moon shape, with its tail sticking under the perch like that of the Scotch fancy, forming a clean curve with its body, which should be narrow and cylindrical. The size of the bird is one of its important points: the recommended length is 11 cm (4¼ in), but up to a maximum of 12 cm (4¾ in) is acceptable.

GLOSTER FANCY CANARY

Isabel canary.

Blue Isabel canary.

White canary.

Red mosaic type-
2 grey-winged
canary.

This is a relatively recent addition to the type canary group. It was developed by Mrs Rogerson of Cheltenham (Gloucestershire, England) in 1925. Its popularity was enhanced by J McLey, a Scottish show judge. It was probably produced by crossing the Norwich with a small Border and then selecting the smallest individuals for further breeding. Through constant selection, Mrs Rogerson produced specimens that were shown at the exhibition at Crystal Palace, London, in 1925. There are two types of Gloster: the Gloster corona, which has a crest or crown, and the Gloster consort, which is uncrested. As crest x crest produces a 25 per cent lethal factor, both types must be used for breeding. Gloster canaries are often called 'buff birds' in reference to their coarse feathers. Some Glosters' plumage displays a combination of dark and light colours, and they are therefore often called variegated Glosters. The Gloster's length is 10 cm (4 in).

Fact file

DISTRIBUTION:
Africa, from Senegal across to the Sudan and Ethiopia

HABITAT:
dry, open bush; human habitation; cultivation

CLUTCH:
3 to 4 white, or very pale-green, eggs, with little, black markings

INCUBATION:
13 to 15 days by the female

FLEDGING:
14 to 21 days; both parents feed the young

AVERAGE LIFESPAN:
10 years

SEXING:
the female is similar to the male, although her flanks are sometimes a little darker streaked

JUVENILES:
similar to their parents, but more heavily streaked

SIZE:
11 cm (4¼ in)

GREY SINGING FINCH
Serinus leucopygus

This species, which is also called the white-rumped seed-eater or African songbird, is a great favourite with aviculturists. It is lively and energetic, of amiable disposition and an exquisite songster. The strength of its voice and the energy with which it pours out its song are quite astonishing, and the little bird will sit on a branch and sing away almost incessantly hour after hour. Very hardy, it is an ideal bird for a garden aviary among such companions as waxbills, mannikins and the like. The sexes look similar, but the free-singing males are easily picked out from the silent hens. This bird sometimes quarrels with its fellows, but is generally of a playful nature.

These finches breed readily, preferring an ordinary canary nest pan in which to build their nest. They will hybridise with canaries, and although the results of such a cross are neither striking nor recommended, they make nice pets and excellent songsters.

Feeding: as for the canary, see page 184. Extra thistle and millet spray are welcome.

GOLDEN SONG SPARROW
Auripasser luteus

This pretty sparrow is found in flocks numbering approximately 20 to 50 birds, and frequents open country. It is shy in disposition and, when flying, makes a linnet-like note; it chirps like a house sparrow when in trees. It is sometimes spiteful in an aviary, but generally likes cosy, community-style living, a trait that is clear from its community-breeding in colonies. (We have seen groups of 50 or more nests close together in just a few trees.) In the aviary, these birds prefer to build their nests in thick bushes, although they will also use nest boxes measuring 15 x 20 x 15 cm (6 x 7¾ x 6 in), with an entrance-hole diameter of 2 cm (¾ in). The nesting boxes should not be hung higher than 2 m (6½ ft) above the ground. The breeding period lasts from between May and November. The birds usually have two or three broods per season.

Crossbreeding with the house sparrow (*Passer d. domesticus*) is known. These are popular birds due to their pleasant song, lively nature and tolerance, even during the breeding season.

Feeding: give these birds a seed mixture consisting of various millet seeds, canary, hemp and weed seeds and oats (a canary-seed mixture will do nicely), chickweed, spinach, egg and/or rearing food (especially during the breeding season), universal food (with animal protein) and a few insects daily. Provide some grit (free choice), cuttlefish bone and fresh drinking water, too.

Fact file

DISTRIBUTION:
northern Nigeria to Darfur, eastern Sudan, the Ethiopian coast, Somaliland and south-western Arabia

HABITAT:
arid, thornbush country; steppes and cultivation (garden, parks)

CLUTCH:
3 to 4 greenish-white eggs, with grey and brown spots

INCUBATION:
10 to 13 days

FLEDGING:
14 to 16 days

AVERAGE LIFESPAN:
5 years

SEXING:
the female has a buff-brown head, mantle and rump and a greyish-white underside

JUVENILES:
look much like the female

SIZE:
14 cm (5½ in)

The Handbook of Cage and Aviary Birds

Fact file

DISTRIBUTION:
Peru; Ecuador; Colombia; Venezuela; the Guianas; introduced to Jamaica in around 1823

HABITAT:
shrubbery; palm groves; campos; parks and gardens

CLUTCH:
3 to 4 white eggs, with a few sparse, black or grey markings

INCUBATION:
13 to 14 days by the female

FLEDGING:
14 days

AVERAGE LIFESPAN:
10 years

SEXING:
the female is similar to the male, but duller, especially her yellow and orange colours

JUVENILES:
similar to the female, but streaked above; a whitish underside, with yellow on the breast, flanks and under-tail coverts

SIZE:
15 cm (6 in)

SAFFRON or BRAZILIAN SAFFRON FINCH
Sicalis flaveola

Although it is sometimes spiteful and tempestuous with weaker birds, this beautiful bird is a popular aviary bird and a suitable companion for weavers, Java sparrows, cut-throat finches and other strong species. It is hardy and easy to cater for. These birds usually build their nests in tree hollows in the wild, which is why they should be supplied with closed-type nesting boxes in a roomy aviary. It is not unusual for them to inspect the nests of other birds, which is why it is best to keep just one pair per aviary. Its song is hardy, but not particularly melodious.

The Pelzeln's saffron finch (*S. f. pelzelni*), which is less often seen on the market, originates in Brazil, Paraguay and Argentina. The hen is coloured differently to the cock. The cock is yellowish-green, streaked with black on the back, with black, yellow-edged wings and tail. His lower back is dull yellow, his forehead is orange, and the sides of his head and below are bright yellow. There are some dark streaks on his flanks; his beak is dark horn in colour; his feet are brownish and his eyes, brown. The hen is dull-brownish, with dark-mottled-grey above and dirty-white underparts and dusky streaks on her breast. This bird's habits do not differ much from those of the saffron finch.

Feeding: as for the golden song sparrow (page 189). During the breeding season, a variety of insects and greens, a rearing food for soft-billed birds and bread soaked in water are vital.

RED-WINGED PYTILIA
or AURORA FINCH
Pytilia phoenicoptera

Fact file

DISTRIBUTION:
Gambia to northern Congo,
Uganda and southern Sudan;
in 2 subspecies

HABITAT:
bush; tall grass;
wooded country

CLUTCH:
3 to 6 white eggs

INCUBATION:
12 to 14 days, probably by both
sexes; during the night, however,
the male often sleeps alongside
the female on the nest

FLEDGING:
18 to 21 days

AVERAGE LIFESPAN:
6 years

SEXING:
the female is slightly browner
than the male, with less grey; she
has smaller and paler-red areas

JUVENILES:
similar to the female, but
browner; brown bill

SIZE:
11.5 cm (4½ in)

This beautiful species is large for a waxbill, and more like a large lavender finch. It does not have much of a song, but utters a peculiar little flute-like phrase of three notes, the middle one being vibrant and prolonged. It is not nervous by disposition, but likes to hide among bushes in a naturally planted aviary; and this is the ideal place in which to breed it. In a suitable aviary, most pairs (especially aviary-bred ones) will start nesting as soon as they have had time to settle down. But the results are often erratic: some pairs will rear their young for a week or so, then leave them and start nesting again.

Auroras are not particular as to the site of their nests, but will build in a bush, dead brushwood or a nest box. The free nest is of the typical, dome-shaped type, and is lined with feathers and so on when these are available. The female is a steady breeder who is not easily flushed from her nest.

Feeding: as for the golden song sparrow, see page 189. It is not easy to rear auroras without live food, and a regular supply of gentles (blowfly maggots) and rearing food for soft-billed birds should be provided for the best results. Mealworms should be given sparingly as they are very stimulating.

Fact file

DISTRIBUTION:
southern and eastern Africa;
in 13 subspecies

HABITAT:
dry thornveld; thickets;
neglected cultivation;
always near water

CLUTCH:
2 to 6 white eggs

INCUBATION:
12 to 13 days by both sexes;
during the night exclusively
by the female, but the male
remains in the nest

FLEDGING:
18 to 21 days; both sexes
feed the young

AVERAGE LIFESPAN:
6 years

SEXING:
the female is duller, with a grey
head; she lacks the male's orange
wing panels

JUVENILES:
like the female, but the upper parts
are darker; no bars and spots;
sepia beak

SIZE:
12.5 cm (5 in)

MELBA FINCH
Pytilia melba melba

The Melba finch is a very desirable bird. It is fairly hardy, but it's best to provide some artificial heat during the colder months of the year. The cock has a not unpleasant song.

This species is usually quite aggressive towards other birds, so it is advisable to keep only one pair in a community aviary. These birds spend a lot of time on the floor, looking for small insects, spiders, seeds and such like. They build a little domed nest in a small bush; seldom do they use a commercial, wooden nest box. The parents sometimes throw 23-day-old young out of the nest, even when the food is right. The only way to avert this is to provide a rich variety of insects and small seeds (millet spray, grass and weed seeds) and hope for the best. The young birds should be separated from their parents as soon as they become independent, and only one pair should remain in the same enclosure.

Feeding: as for the golden song sparrow, see page 189; see also above.

GREEN-BACKED TWINSPOT

Mandingoa n. nitidula

This twinspot is a lively, hardy bird that feeds mainly on the ground. A thickly planted aviary is necessary. This species is usually friendly towards other birds and is hence excellent for a community aviary. During the breeding season, these birds sometimes behave in a quarrelsome fashion towards small finches, however.

The green-backed twinspot uses half-open nest boxes. After the young have left the nest, they will return to it for the first few days for up to a week to spend the night there. Sometimes young males can be observed carrying nesting materials at 2½ to 3 months of age. Recently imported birds must be housed inside, at a temperature of approximately 25°C (77°F). During warm, sunny summers they may be housed in a garden aviary.

Feeding: grass and weed seeds, ant pupae and other insects should be available throughout the year. For more details, see the Melba finch (left).

Fact file

DISTRIBUTION:
through equatorial and southern tropical Africa; in 4 subspecies

HABITAT:
evergreen-forest edges; coastal bush; plantations

CLUTCH:
3 to 6 white eggs

INCUBATION:
12 to 14 days by both sexes

FLEDGING:
17 to 21 days

AVERAGE LIFESPAN:
6 years

SEXING:
the female is paler, with pale orange or yellow on her chin and around her eyes

JUVENILES:
paler than the female, with an olive-grey underside; buff chin and sides of the face

SIZE:
10 to 11 cm (4 to 4¼ in)

The Handbook of Cage and Aviary Birds

Fact file

DISTRIBUTION:
from Kenya to Congo,
Angola and Mozambique;
in 5 subspecies

HABITAT:
forest edges and bush;
always near water

CLUTCH:
3 to 6 white eggs; host of
the twinspot widafinch
(*Vidua codringtoni*)

INCUBATION:
12 to 14 days by both sexes

FLEDGING:
18 to 22 days

AVERAGE LIFESPAN:
6 years

SEXING:
the sides of the
female's head are greyish brown;
her red areas are paler than the
male's; her upper-tail coverts are
buff; her underparts are dark
grey, with white spots

JUVENILES:
similar to the female, but with a
paler head, chin and breast

SIZE:
11.5 cm (4½ in)

PETER'S TWINSPOT
Hypargos n. niveoguttatus

In the wild, this magnificent finch frequents dense bush and
thorn tangles on river banks, and spends most of its time on the
ground in thick undergrowth (bear this in mind when planting a
garden aviary).

Members of this species are excellent aviary birds of hardy
condition that are friendly towards their keeper and small birds.
They have to be carefully acclimatised at a temperature of
approximately 25°C (77°F). After about six weeks, the temperature
may be lowered to about 20°C (68°F). These birds will not
withstand cold nights, and sleeping boxes must therefore be
provided all year round. They are best housed indoors at room
temperature during the autumn and winter. When their facilities
are well planted, breeding successes are possible, but they will not
tolerate disturbances. Their freestanding, globular nests, which
have a short tunnel, are constructed in a bush or half-open nest
box of grass, vegetable fibres and moss and are then lined with fine
grass and some small feathers. During the breeding season, a pair
may sometimes be aggressive towards other small finches.

Feeding: as for the Melba finch, see page 192. A variety of small
insects, such as white worms, cut-up mealworms, small maggots,
fruit flies and ant pupae, as well as a fine-grade, commercial
insectivorous mixture are essential throughout the year, but
especially during the breeding season.

RED-BILLED FIRE FINCH
Lagonosticta senegala

This is one of the most popular of the waxbills. Although newly imported birds are very delicate, when they have been properly established, they are not difficult birds to breed. Birds received in winter should be kept in a cage at about 25°C (77°F). Established birds housed in garden aviaries are fairly free breeders. The nest is mostly built by the cock, who will use a finch nest box or brushwood in the aviary shelter.

When rearing, these birds require seeding grasses, any available insects, ant pupae, gentles, aphids and sprouted seeds. Many successful breeders with large, open flights place a tin of rotten fruit or horse dung covered with mesh in the aviary to attract small insects, which these little finches quickly catch as soon as they fly away from the mesh cover. During cold spells, a hen who is about to lay must be carefully watched because these birds are somewhat prone to egg-binding.

Fire finches generally get on with other small birds, but some cocks may prove vicious to others of their own kind. One pair to an enclosure is the best rule.

Feeding: all small millet varieties; spray millet; a reputable commercial seed mixture for finches; grass and weed seeds; fresh, sprouted and germinated greens, such as chickweed, spinach and dandelions; small insects (see above), white worms and spiders; egg and rearing finch food; rearing food for soft-billed birds; cuttlefish bone; a vitamin-and-mineral supplement; fresh water every day.

Fact file

DISTRIBUTION:
Africa south of the Sahara (except for the extreme south); in 9 subspecies

HABITAT:
thornveld; cultivation; habitation; mostly near water

CLUTCH:
2 to 4 white eggs

INCUBATION:
11 to 14 days by both sexes; host of the village indigo bird (*Vidua chalybeata*)

FLEDGING:
18 to 20 days; both sexes feed the young

AVERAGE LIFESPAN:
5 years

SEXING:
the female is grey or earth-brown, finely spotted on her upper parts with white; she has a pinkish-red forehead and upper-tail coverts

JUVENILES:
similar to the female, but without the reddish forehead and white spots on the underside

SIZE:
9 cm (3½ in)

Fact file

DISTRIBUTION:
Africa, from Congo and Tanzania to Natal; introduced to eastern Africa (formerly Zanzibar) and Sao Thomé; in 4 subspecies

HABITAT:
low herbage; thornveld; mixed woodland; cultivation; often near human dwellings

CLUTCH:
3 to 6 white eggs

INCUBATION:
11 to 14 days by both sexes

FLEDGING:
17 to 19 days; nestlings are mainly insectivorous

AVERAGE LIFESPAN:
8 years

SEXING:
the female is very similar to the male; her upper parts are often a lighter blue; her underparts are pinkish-buff

JUVENILES:
similar to the female, but paler; blackish bill

SIZE:
12 cm (4³/₄ in)

BLUE-BREASTED WAXBILL or ANGOLAN CORDON BLEU
Uraeginthus a. angolensis

This dainty, little waxbill is less common in captivity than the red-cheeked cordon bleu (see right), but is fairly plentiful in its native land. In the spring, both sexes have a pleasant song; the normal alarm note is a shrill twittering.

The nest is built in low bushes from 90 cm to 2.4 m (3 to 8 ft) high, and consists of a ball of grasses, with a small side entrance, lined with fine grass and feathers.

This waxbill is most desirable as an aviary bird, being much more readily established than the red-cheeked cordon bleu and hardier, too, besides being a free breeder. The young are fed on insects. In a mixed collection, this species is inclined to be antagonistic only towards the red-cheeked cordon bleu, and seldom fights other birds unless attacked, whereupon it is able to rout most birds of its own size. Although sudden temperature changes can chill these birds, they resist lower temperatures far better than the red-cheeked cordon bleu. This species belongs indoors during the autumn and winter, at a minimum temperature of 18°C (64.4°F).

Feeding: as for the red-cheeked cordon bleu, see right.

Red-cheeked Cordon Bleu
Uraeginthus b. bengalus

This beautiful waxbill is a great favourite with fanciers, being a lively little bird, a good mixer and a fairly free breeder. The main problem is acclimatising imported specimens, and members of this species are undoubtedly delicate when they first arrive in colder climates. Newly imported birds should be caged and kept in a warm room at a fairly steady temperature; do not turn them out into a garden aviary until early summer. One need not take such trouble with aviary-bred birds since they are reasonably hardy. Even imported birds have wintered successfully in an outdoor aviary without heat in the south of England. These charming birds will breed when about six months old, and it is their natural inclination to breed all year round. This should only be permitted for those living in warm countries, however, as hens that are allowed to breed year-round in colder climates are susceptible to egg-binding. Cordons build a somewhat frail nest of fine grasses, and line it with feathers if they are available. These birds are not spiteful towards other birds, but will defend their nest vigorously against intruders, so do not house more than one pair in an aviary.

Feeding: Cordons are very fond of the aphids that gather on beans, roses and other plants during the summer. They will also pick up minute insects from newly turned (aviary) soil. Ant pupae make excellent food, and may be given freely in regions where termites are found. Spray millet and the seeding heads of grasses must be supplied regularly, along with a reputable seed mixture for finches, cuttlefish bone and fresh water every day. During the breeding season, it is vital to provide commercial egg and rearing food.

Fact file

DISTRIBUTION:
from Senegal through a semi-arid belt to Ethiopia, and south through eastern Africa to Shaba and Zambia; in 7 subspecies

HABITAT:
open country; cultivation

CLUTCH:
4 to 7 oval, white eggs

INCUBATION:
12 to 13 days by both sexes

FLEDGING:
11 to 13 days

AVERAGE LIFESPAN:
8 years

SEXING:
the sexes are very similar, but the female's face is often lighter blue; her underparts are pinkish-buff; she lacks the male's red cheeks

JUVENILES:
similar to the female, but paler; blackish bill

SIZE:
11.5 to 13 cm (4½ in to 5 in)

The Handbook of Cage and Aviary Birds

Fact file

DISTRIBUTION:
from southern Somalia
and Ethiopia to Tanzania;
in 2 subspecies

HABITAT:
arid regions with acacia varieties

CLUTCH:
4 to 6 white eggs

INCUBATION:
11 to 13 days by both sexes

FLEDGING:
17 to 19 days

AVERAGE LIFESPAN:
8 years

SEXING:
the female is paler than the male,
with a buff-brown forehead,
crown and nape

JUVENILES:
similar to the female, but paler

SIZE:
11.5 to 13 cm (4½ to 5 in)

BLUE-CAPPED CORDON BLEU
Uraeginthus cyanocephalus cyanocephalus

The male of this species is very similar to the blue-breasted waxbill (see page 196). There is a smaller subspecies (*U. c. muelleri*), with duller colours, that is found in northern Kenya and in bordering Somalia and Ethiopia. The blue-capped cordon bleu is found in arid, grass and thornbush country. The birds search primarily for grass and weed seeds, small insects and spiders. Their nests are mostly constructed in thorny bushes, often close to wasps' nests.

This species is somewhat shyer than the blue-breasted waxbill. If acclimatised properly, this beautiful bird will breed regularly in a large, well-planted aviary. For more details, see the blue-breasted waxbill.

Feeding: see the red-cheeked cordon bleu, page 197.

VIOLET-EARED WAXBILL
Uraeginthus (Granatina) g. granatina

Most fanciers consider this species to be the finest, and most beautiful, of all of the waxbills. It has been known in continental Europe for a long time, having first been brought there in 1754. It has never been common, although small numbers arrive fairly regularly on the market. It is a rather costly species.

Unfortunately, this lovely waxbill is rather difficult to keep and will not survive temperatures below 10°C (50°F). The usual practice in England and Western Europe is to keep them in an outdoor aviary during the summer, and indoors at living-room temperature, that is, at approximately 18°C (64.4°F), during the winter. It should be remembered that this bird is insectivorous and is also extremely fond of grass seeds. It is an ideal exhibition bird.

Its nest is globular, with a side entrance, and made of grasses. In the wild, it is usually built in a thorn bush 90 cm to 1.8 m (3 to 6 ft) above the ground. In an outdoor aviary, some thick and high thorn bushes are much appreciated when planted in a covered run. Supply enough nesting material, including wool, grass, coconut fibres and such like, as well as some small feathers, which the male likes to play with while sitting on the nest.

Feeding: provide a commercial seed mixture for finches; grass and weed seeds; Senegal millet; and spray millet. During the breeding season, provide small insects; brown bread soaked in water; and finch egg and rearing food. Throughout the year, provide cuttlefish bone, small grit (free choice) and fresh water every day. See also above and the red-cheeked cordon bleu, page 197.

Fact file

DISTRIBUTION:
Africa: Angola and Zambia (not in the extreme south, although observed in Kwa-Zulu-Natal); in 2 subspecies

HABITAT:
dry, thorn scrub and tall grass

CLUTCH:
3 to 6 white eggs

INCUBATION:
11 to 13 days by both sexes

FLEDGING:
16 to 22 days; during the nestling period, the young are fed by both parents

AVERAGE LIFESPAN:
8 years

SEXING:
the female has paler markings than the male, although they are similar

JUVENILES:
the males resemble the adult female except for the sides of the face, ear coverts, chin and belly; the females resemble the adult female, but with buff sides of the face and ear coverts

SIZE:
14 cm (5½ in)

Fact file

DISTRIBUTION:
western Africa, from Senegal
to northern Cameroon and
south-western Chad

HABITAT:
grassland; bush; cultivation;
parks and gardens

CLUTCH:
3 to 6 white eggs

INCUBATION:
14 to 16 days by both sexes

FLEDGING:
18 to 20 days

AVERAGE LIFESPAN:
5 years

SEXING:
the sexes are similar, although the
female's rump and tail are not
wine red, but rusty red

JUVENILES:
duller than their parents; they
lack the white spots on the
adults' flanks; light-slate-grey bill

SIZE:
11 cm (4¼ in)

LAVENDER WAXBILL
Estrilda (Glaucestrilda) caerulescens

This beautiful species is rather fragile. The birds never look very robust when they arrive from overseas, and always require special attention, but develop quite nicely in heated vitrines and indoor aviaries.

The members of this species are among the best acrobats of the bird world. They are uniformly cheerful and lively, and are always ready to perform their simple song. The mating call of the male distinguishes the sexes, which are otherwise somewhat hard to tell apart, especially when they are young. These waxbills perform a pleasant nighttime routine: once the sun has set, the male and female sit close together in their usual roosting place, then nod goodnight, using definite head movements, and utter a monotonous, but pleasant-sounding, 'chew-chew-chew'. The summoning calls differ between the sexes. The male calls with a 'shee-tooey', while the hen utters 'shee-shee'. If you separate the two, these summoning calls can be constantly heard.

In the wild, as well as in the aviary, lavender waxbills build a round nest with a small, narrow entrance near the bottom. This species needs adequate space: placing these birds in cages that are too small often results in them losing their head and neck feathers as a result of plucking one another. The same problem also occurs when one ships the birds to shows.

This species does very well in a group setting, but be sure to furnish the birds with separate sleeping nests and baskets. Put some nesting material inside so that they have some protection against the cold at night.
Feeding: as for the violet-eared waxbill, see page 199. Also offer them greens, such as endives, chicory, chickweed and dandelions, and millet spray. In addition, these birds like hummingbird-nectar mixtures throughout the year, but especially during the breeding season.

ORANGE-CHEEKED WAXBILL
Estrilda m. melpoda

Fact file

DISTRIBUTION:
Senegal to Congo, northern Angola and around Lake Chad; introduced to Puerto Rico in 3 subspecies

HABITAT:
grassland; forest clearings; cultivation; mostly in mountainous areas

CLUTCH:
3 to 7 white eggs

INCUBATION:
11 to 12 days alternately by both sexes, but at night only by the female, although the male often stays in the nest

FLEDGING:
20 to 21 days

AVERAGE LIFESPAN:
5 years

SEXING:
the sexes are similar; some females are paler; none have a black face

JUVENILES:
lighter-greyish-brown upper parts and a paler-buff underside than the adults; blackish bill

SIZE:
10 cm (4 in)

Orange-cheeked waxbills are favourites with beginners. They have much to commend them, being pretty, though not gaudy, inexpensive and quite hardy in Britain, Western Europe and similar climates. Keep any newly purchased birds indoors if they were bought in winter, and turn them outside during May. As breeders, these waxbills are fairly prolific, and the best results are obtained in outdoor aviaries with planted flights, where the birds will build a nest in a shrub or creeper about 1.2 m (4 ft) above the ground. The nest is constructed of grass, and they like to use feathers or teased cotton wool as lining material. These birds will also make use of a finch nest box.

One difficulty for breeders is sexing the birds because they are coloured alike. Hens generally have rather less orange about the cheeks and in smaller area, but this is variable. Once orange-cheeked waxbills breed, they are devoted parents and work hard to satisfy their brood's requirements for food. Young birds are dull-looking replicas of their parents, and do not assume the full adult plumage until after the first moult.

Feeding: as for the violet-eared waxbill, see page 199. They also like greens, as well as sprouted and germinated seeds (especially grass and weed seeds).

Fact file

DISTRIBUTION:
from Senegal to Sudan
and northern Ethiopia

HABITAT:
savannah woodland;
swamp; riparian thickets;
rice cultivations

CLUTCH:
2 to 7 white eggs

INCUBATION:
11 to 14 days by both sexes

FLEDGING:
17 to 21 days

AVERAGE LIFESPAN:
5 years

SEXING:
the sexes are similar

JUVENILES:
like the parents, but without
the eye stripe; black bill

SIZE:
9 cm (3¹/₂ in)

RED-EARED WAXBILL
Estrilda troglodytes

This waxbill is an excellent, lively cage and aviary bird that is especially at home in large facilities. It is friendly towards other finches. The female uses a nest box or constructs a freestanding, bullet-shaped nest in a bush from grass, wool, moss, fibres and small feathers. During the breeding period, the male's colour becomes a more intense red and his eyebrows become darker. He then goes through his display, holding a blade of grass or something similar in his beak and dancing in circles around the female. As soon as the breeding season starts, it is advisable to separate the various pairs and to give them each their own aviary, which must be well planted. The partners communicate with a harsh 'pee-chee, pee-chee'. During the autumn and winter, the birds must be housed indoors at a minimum temperature of 25°C (77°F).

Feeding: as for the violet-eared waxbill, see page 199, and orange-cheeked waxbill, see page 201.

St Helena or
Common Waxbill
Estrilda astrild astrild

This waxbill may be described as a more strongly marked edition of the red-eared waxbill (see left), but is also larger, and has dark feathers under its tail. It is one of the most popular of the *Estrilda* family, being hardy and a fairly free breeder. Although not normally quarrelsome, a pair inclined to nest can prove rather aggressive and may attack other birds that encroach on their nesting site. Generally speaking, most aviculturists grossly overcrowd their waxbill aviaries. These birds may be small creatures, but need a reasonable amount of space. More than one pair of St Helenas will usually agree in a reasonably large aviary that is not overcrowded. However, never keep two pairs in the same cage or aviary, always one, three or more.

While courting, the cock performs a curious kind of dance in which he jumps up and down holding a piece of straw or grass in his beak to attract his mate.

Like other waxbills, the St Helena will use a covered nest box or construct a spherical nest in a bush. The nest is made of interwoven grasses and has a bottleneck-shaped side entrance. Large quantities of feathers are used as a lining. The birds do not like any interference with their nest, when they will desert it rather rapidly. The hens are somewhat subject to egg-binding if allowed to nest during inclement weather.

Feeding: as for the red-eared waxbill (see left). When breeding, the birds should be supplied with millet spray, soaked for a day or so, plenty of live ants' eggs, chopped mealworms, houseflies, gentles and even very small earthworms. Cuttlefish bone should be available, and the birds have been known to carry small pieces to their nest, probably for hygroscopic reasons. Seeding grasses, chickweed and so on should also be supplied.

Fact file

DISTRIBUTION:
much of Africa south of the Sahara; introduced to many islands (like New Caledonia) and to the Cape Verde Islands, Portugal; in 17 subspecies

HABITAT:
woodland; grassland; cultivation; near, or along, rivers and in reed beds

CLUTCH:
3 to 6 white eggs

INCUBATION:
11 to 12 days by both sexes

FLEDGING:
18 to 21 days

AVERAGE LIFESPAN:
5 years

SEXING:
the female is paler than the male, with less extensive areas of crimson red on the breast and belly

JUVENILES:
similar to the female, with barred underparts; pinkish breast and belly; blackish bill

SIZE:
11 cm (4¼ in)

RED-HEADED WAXBILL
Estrilda (Krimhilda) a. atricapilla

Fact file

DISTRIBUTION:
south-eastern Nigeria;
southern Cameroon;
Gabon; north-eastern
Zaire; in 5 subspecies

HABITAT:
forest edges; grass clearings
in forest belts and bamboo,
and up to 3,500 m
(11,483 ft) in grassland

CLUTCH:
2 to 5 white eggs

INCUBATION:
11 to 12 days by both sexes

FLEDGING:
19 to 20 days

AVERAGE LIFESPAN:
6 years

SEXING:
the female has a browner
mantle and back, the male's
crimson colour is paler in her

JUVENILES:
dusky-brown mantle and back;
the adults' crimson colour is
lacking; black bill

SIZE:
10 cm (4 in)

This species looks very similar to the black-crowned waxbill (*E.*, or *K., n. nonnula*), a species that hails from eastern Cameroon through to Sudan, Kenya and Tanzania, but with less, or no, red on the flanks, especially after the birds have been living in captivity for some time. It is a pity that both species are rarely seen in aviculture, although they are popular in South Africa.

The red-headed waxbill, as well as its cousin, the black-crowned waxbill, is an excellent and lively bird for large cages or well-planted aviaries, where it is friendly towards most other small African finches. During the breeding season, it is sometimes somewhat quarrelsome, however. Both species are best housed in an indoor facility with an average room temperature during the autumn and winter.

Feeding: as for the St Helena waxbill, see page 203. It is vital to provide a diet that is rich in animal protein during the breeding season.

BLACK-CHEEKED WAXBILL
Estrilda (Brunhilda) e. erythronotos

This species is one of the foster parents of the pintailed whydah (*Vidua macroura*) and Senegal combassou (*Hypochera*, or *Vidua, hypocherina*); in other words, these species lay their eggs in the nests of the black-cheeked waxbill and various other waxbill species. This is a classic example of brood parasitism.

Although not common, these waxbills are popular among aviculturists. It is difficult to sex them, so make sure that you arrange with the breeder or seller to make an exchange if you find that you have not acquired a true pair. You can tell the male by his mating dance and piercing contact call: 'tooooeyt-tooooeyt'. The birds can be kept in an aviary or large cage. They build a keg-shaped nest in an outdoor aviary or roomy, indoor one.

These birds love to sit in the sun for hours, holding their wings low. If you want to raise them indoors, you must definitely use infrared lamps. This species is particularly sensitive to dampness, so during the winter months, house the birds in a lightly heated facility, preferably with an infrared lamp. It is best to keep the birds at a temperature of about 24°C (75.2°F), even during the summer, especially if they have recently arrived from Africa. (You can gradually drop the temperature to 20°C (68°F).) An outdoor aviary should have a draught-free night shelter or coop.

These waxbills are quite trusting and can therefore be kept indoors. You cannot be certain of successful breeding, however. They build free nests and also make use of nest boxes and baskets. The problem is that after several days of steadily brooding, they may abandon their eggs; alternatively, they may stop feeding their young when they are half-raised. Peaceful surroundings are therefore of the utmost importance, as is a proper diet.

Feeding: as for the St Helena waxbill, see page 203.

Fact file

DISTRIBUTION:
eastern and southern Africa, from southern Kenya to south-eastern Angola and Cape Province (but not in the extreme south); in 3 subspecies

HABITAT:
rocky scrub; dry, acacia thornveld

CLUTCH:
3 to 6 white eggs

INCUBATION:
11 to 12 days by both sexes

FLEDGING:
22 to 24 days

AVERAGE LIFESPAN:
5 years

SEXING:
the female is slightly paler than the male, especially on the belly and flanks

JUVENILES:
similar to the female; a greyish throat and belly; brown iris; light-horn-coloured bill

SIZE:
11.5 to 12.5 cm (4½ to 5 in)

Fact file

The Handbook of Cage and Aviary Birds

DISTRIBUTION:
India; Pakistan; southern Nepal; Yunnan; south-east Asia (except Malaya): Java, Bali, Lombok, Flores, Sumba, Timor; introduced to Singapore, Malaysia, Sumatra, the Philippines, Fuji, Reunion, Mauritius, Spain, Portugal, Italy, Israel, Egypt and elsewhere; in 3 subspecies

HABITAT:
scrub jungle; reeds; sugar-cane fields; tall-grass areas along bodies of water; cultivation

CLUTCH:
5 to 6 white eggs

INCUBATION:
11 to 13 days by the female

FLEDGING:
18 to 21 days

AVERAGE LIFESPAN:
8 years

SEXING:
the female (and non-breeding male) has grey-brownish upper parts and paler underparts; the wings are darker grey-brown, with white spots; the rump and upper-tail coverts are red

JUVENILES:
mainly dark grey-brown, with beige underparts and a grey breast; blackish bill

SIZE:
10 cm (4 in)

RED AVADAVAT or TIGER FINCH
Amandava a. amandava

This species is very popular, in part because of its colourful appearance. Novice fanciers can expect good results from these birds, including active breeding. Both sexes have an attractive song, although the female does not trill as loudly as the male. The mating dance is also interesting because the male stretches out his head and walks around with a drooping, spread tail.

These birds are likely to build free nests, although they also use half-open nest boxes. Such free nests are keg- or bag-shaped, with one or two entrances about 10 cm (4 in) in diameter. Provide a quiet environment for breeding birds because these are nervous breeders that can quickly decide to leave the nest to start again elsewhere. Don't house them in an overly large collection. The male defends the nest aggressively, and if he considers the nest to be endangered, often by other birds in the vicinity, the pair will become so upset that nothing much will come of their breeding.

Outside the breeding season, the male is not easy to distinguish from the hen, but for his breeding colour, he attains a beautiful red with little white dots, which is why this species is often called strawberry finch. The male is out of colour from December until March; during this time, you can find all kinds of gradations between the normal, 'off-colour' and the 'fancy', in-season, red colour, hence few males resemble one another. Many have large amounts of yellow in their plumage, while others have red or brown.

Feeding: as for the St Helena waxbill, see page 203. Animal proteins (insects, rearing food for soft-billed birds and so on) are vital, especially during the breeding season.

GREEN AVADAVAT
Amandava (Stictospiza)
formosa

This bird is now often offered in the trade, in part because of its friendly disposition and attractive colours. We have consistently found it a quiet aviary bird, one without complicated demands that breeds well, provided that it is properly cared for. It will not cause any problems for other birds during the breeding season. In a group aviary, it does not associate much with other birds, but tends to stay on the ground, under bushes and in grass clumps.

In the wild, it builds a large, round nest in cane fields or long-grass tussocks, but in captivity it seldom builds a free nest. It likes half-open nest boxes in a well-planted aviary. Do not disturb these birds during the breeding process. The female in particular is quite nervous, and will leave the nest at the slightest disturbance (she will, however, return once everything has become peaceful and safe again). This nervousness is one reason why this species is not very well suited to being a cage bird.

Recently imported birds, even from European breeders, must at first be housed in a warm, roomy, indoor aviary at 22°C (71.6°F). After about six weeks, they can be placed in a well-planted outdoor aviary. During the autumn and winter, however, they must be housed indoors again; during the winter, they require a lightly heated facility.

When courting, the cock sings a one-note song, at the end of which he tilts his head backwards, then bringing it around in an arc as low as the perch at full stretch, with his beak wide open, as though he intended to regurgitate, while emitting a very low-pitched, gurgling sound. Sometimes the pair faces one another on the ground, both nodding their heads and circling around each other, with their tails held at almost right angles to their bodies.

Feeding: various millets, spray millet and canary grass seed, seeding grass and weed plants, as well as germinated millets. Also as for the St Helena waxbill, see page 203.

Fact file

DISTRIBUTION:
central India; eastern Pakistan

HABITAT:
grassland; cultivation

CLUTCH:
4 to 7 white eggs

INCUBATION:
11 to 12 days by presumably only the female, although both sexes stay in the nest during the night

FLEDGING:
20 to 21 days

AVERAGE LIFESPAN:
8 years

SEXING:
the female is paler than the male; she also has more distinct barring on her flanks

JUVENILES:
pale grey-green; black bill

SIZE:
10 to 11 cm (4 to 4$\frac{1}{4}$ in)

The Handbook of Cage and Aviary Birds

Fact file

DISTRIBUTION:
much of Africa south of the
Sahara, except for the extreme
south; in 4 subspecies

HABITAT:
grassland; marches; reeds;
cultivation; usually near water;
in large flocks

CLUTCH:
4 to 6 white eggs

INCUBATION:
11 to 14 days by both sexes;
both parents feed the young

FLEDGING:
18 to 21 days

AVERAGE LIFESPAN:
8 years

SEXING:
the female lacks the
male's crimson eye stripe;
she is paler overall and
has a yellow belly

JUVENILES:
earth-brown upper parts;
no eye stripe; pale-brown
tail coverts washed with
crimson; the flanks lack
bars; blackish bill

SIZE:
9 cm (3½ in)

GOLDEN-BREASTED WAXBILL *Amandava (Sporaeginthus) s. subflava*

This easy-to-keep bird has a rich colour, loving disposition and good breeding record. The subspecies differ only slightly, and are often mixed up with one another. Newly arrived birds should be placed in quarantine for at least 30 days, and should then be gradually acclimatised to the local outside average temperature. They must spend the winter in warm conditions, at around 18°C (64.4°F). Members of this species are usually pleasant towards other finches, but may be slightly quarrelsome with other birds during the breeding season. If the aviary is not too densely populated, and there is enough plant life to provide hiding places for those birds that want or need it, there should be no difficulty.

Generally, all of the subspecies will move into a closed nest box before breeding, although a pair will build a nest in a bush at times. The nest will look quite ramshackle, but despite its rough, unattractive appearance and construction, it is totally safe. A free nest is round and enclosed, with a small, narrow entrance. When the young have become independent, remove them from their parents to stimulate the female to start a new clutch.

These birds sing a reasonably pleasant song without interruption. They are continually cheerful and friendly, and treat one another pleasantly. They do especially well in large cages or vitrines.

Feeding: as for the green avadavat, page 207, and the St Helena waxbill, page 203. Animal protein is essential during the breeding season.

African or Common Quail Finch
Ortygospiza atricollis atricollis

Quail finches are strange, little, short-tailed, terrestrial birds that resemble quails in their habit of running about in the grass. The floor of the cage is best covered with granulated peat moss or shortly clipped turf. These birds' feet must not be allowed to become dirty as they are comparatively weak. The nest is built in clumps of grass.

These shy birds often fly perpendicularly, so it is necessary to attach some soft fabric to the inside of the cage's roof.

Feeding: provide a reputable commercial seed mixture for tropical finches; seeding grass; and ants' eggs, greenfly and so on. See also the Bengalese finch, page 230.

Fact file

DISTRIBUTION:
Africa, from south of the Sahara to Angola and Damaraland; in 10 subspecies

HABITAT:
open grassland; swamp; tussock bog; cultivation

CLUTCH:
4 to 6 white eggs

INCUBATION:
11 to 14 days by both sexes, but only the female feeds the young

FLEDGING:
19 to 21 days

AVERAGE LIFESPAN:
8 years

SEXING:
the female is paler and lacks the black on the male's face

JUVENILES:
similar to the female; no bars the breast; creamy-white bars on the flanks; blackish bill

SIZE:
9 cm (3½ in)

Fact file

DISTRIBUTION:
eastern and south-
eastern Australia

HABITAT:
savannah; mallee
(dwarf eucalyptus brushwood)

CLUTCH:
4 to 6 white eggs

INCUBATION:
11 to 13 days by presumably only
the female, although both sexes
stay in the nest during the night

FLEDGING:
21 to 25 days

AVERAGE LIFESPAN:
8 years

SEXING:
the female has a brownish lore
and coral-pink bill

JUVENILES:
duller than their parents, with an
indistinct chest bar; black bill

SIZE:
11.5 cm (4½ in)

DIAMOND FIRETAIL FINCH
Zonaeginthus guttatus or *Staganopleura guttata*

The diamond firetail or diamond sparrow finch was one of the first birds to attract the attention of the earlier settlers in Australia, and paintings of it date back to 1790.

In captivity, it is a hardy grass finch that is easy to keep, but not particularly easy to breed. These birds like to have a nest box lined with hay in which to sleep. They sometimes roost in this during cold days or inclement weather. If not provided with plenty of boxes from which to choose, they are apt to camp in the nests of other birds in the aviary. This can, of course, be disastrous, but the diamond firetail is not at all pugnacious, merely boldly assertive.

To get these birds into breeding condition, it is advisable to give them plenty of grass seeds, both green and dry. If the grass is gathered when green and abundant, and is then placed in a loosely woven bag, it will dry out, and the seed may then be shaken loose and stored.

This finch is active in an aviary, but old birds are apt to become rather phlegmatic in a small cage, and to eat until they become fat. It is an ardent and amusing wooer, the cock's antics when dancing before the hen being extremely entertaining.

Cinnamon yellow-billed diamond firetail finch.

Cinnamon diamond
firetail finch.

Dilute or pastel diamond firetail
finch (autosomal recessive).

Yellow-billed diamond firetail
finch (autosomal recessive).

Normal-coloured
diamond firetail finch.

Various colour mutations are currently known. In the recessive yellow, the conspicuous, red rump of the normal form is replaced with orange. Another mutation is the sex-linked fawn, and a third is the yellow split for fawn (yellow/fawn).

Feeding: provide a commercial seed mixture for finches, with extra grass and weed seeds (ripe seed heads will be taken greedily if you place them in bottles of water and set them on the floor). Also provide green food (like spinach, chickweed, endives and chicory), commercial egg food and (although many birds may not eat them) various small insects (ant pupae, small, cut-up mealworms, encytrae, maggots, spiders and similar); fruit flies (*Drosophila* spp.) are often avidly taken. Finally, provide cuttlefish bone, a mineral block, a salt wheel (available commercially), oyster-shell grit, some charcoal, a vitamin-and-mineral supplement, and, during the breeding season, stale wholegrain bread soaked in water twice a week (but look out for mould).

Painted firetail finch
Emblema picta

Fact file

DISTRIBUTION:
central Australia

HABITAT:
porcupine grass (spinifex plains)

CLUTCH:
4 to 6 white eggs

INCUBATION:
15 to 19 days (the latter during the winter brood); the female incubates for the first 3 days, after which the male broods about every other hour; during the night, only the female incubates

FLEDGING:
19 to 22 days

AVERAGE LIFESPAN:
6 years

SEXING:
the male's red is more limited and duller in the female; she has a red lore, rump and bill; the spots on her flanks are larger; she has a black upper beak, with a red tip; her lower mandible has a bluish base

JUVENILES:
duller than the female; only the rump is red

SIZE:
10 cm (4 in)

This lovely grass finch is regularly bred in captivity, in Australia and in other countries. An ideal aviary bird, it is very tame in disposition and quite harmless to other birds. In the wild, these birds build their nests in spinifex or porcupine grass. During the rainy season, this grows so rapidly that a nest built in it would be pushed out of shape. To prevent this, the birds' natural habit is to make a platform using earth, pieces of charcoal or clods from a white-ants' nest; they will even collect the equivalent of a small bucketful of such materials. They then construct the nest proper out of grass in the usual finch pattern on this platform. Once fledged, the young birds are apt to squat on the bare ground, and adult birds often do this, too, sunning themselves like fowl. This finch does best in a wood-floored aviary whose entire roof is covered. It is essential that no long, wet grass be allowed to grow if the birds have access to an open flight because they are subject to chills in such conditions.

The male's song is a loud twittering.

Feeding: provide a reputable mixture for finches; extra grass and weed seeds are welcome. These birds take little or no interest in live food, although some may be taken when they have young to feed. See also the diamond firetail finch, pages 210–211.

RED-BROWED or SYDNEY FINCH

Aegintha t. temporalis

This pretty bird has been known as a cage and aviary bird in Europe and the United States for many years, but is seldom either cheap or plentiful. This species does not thrive in regular cages and indoor vitrines, but does best in a good-sized, outdoor aviary. This finch is extremely sensitive to cold, so ensure that the temperature never drops below 18°C (64.4°F). It is also sensitive to high levels of humidity, which means that it may need to be housed in a roomy, indoor aviary during the fall. Males and females share in nest-building, although the hen concentrates more on the nest cup. They generally like a half-open or enclosed nest box or a coconut-type nest. They often build a free, bottle-shaped nest in a bush using freshly cut and dry grass, hair, moss, wool, coconut fibres, small feathers and similar materials.

The male has an interesting, clear and monotonous, but still appealing, whistle that he utters before mating. He also makes amusing steps during the mating dance, which he performs with his body held erect and tail tilted. He usually carries a long stalk in his beak.

Feeding: provide a reputable commercial seed mixture for finches. During the breeding season, provide a rich variety of insects, egg and rearing food, germinated seeds, greens, grit, cuttlefish bone, a vitamin-and-mineral supplement and fresh drinking (and bath) water every day. Indoor birds should be sprayed with a mister daily.

Fact file

DISTRIBUTION:
eastern and south-eastern Australia (northern Queensland); introduced to Tahiti; in 3 subspecies

HABITAT:
mangroves, forests and dense shrubland interspersed with open, grassy country; cultivation

CLUTCH:
4 to 6 white eggs

INCUBATION:
13 to 14 days by both sexes

FLEDGING:
20 to 21 days

AVERAGE LIFESPAN:
6 years

SEXING:
the sexes are similar

JUVENILES:
duller than their parents, with shorter eyebrows; black bill

SIZE:
12 cm (4³/₄ in)

CRIMSON FINCH
Neochmia p. phaeton

Fact file

DISTRIBUTION:
coastal areas of northern and
north-eastern Australia;
in 4 subspecies

HABITAT:
grassy margins of inland waters;
cane fields

CLUTCH:
5 to 8 white eggs

INCUBATION:
14 to 15 days by both sexes

FLEDGING:
21 to 22 days

AVERAGE LIFESPAN:
4 years

SEXING:
the female is a duller crimson
than the male; her nape, back
and rump are washed in
brownish-olive; the centre of her
belly is a pale creamy-fawn

JUVENILES:
duller than the female; black bill

SIZE:
13 to 14 cm (5 to 5½ in)

This species is not polygamous and will accept alternative mates for different seasons. As a general rule, these birds should only be kept in single pairs with no other birds as they have a reputation for being extremely pugnacious. However, some are less truculent than others and can be kept in either a colony or mixed-species aviary, provided that the other occupants are equally robust. When the temperature drops below 15°C (59°F), they must be housed indoors at room temperature. This species is very nervous while breeding, and thus susceptible to disturbances. These birds like to use canary baskets as their nests, although we have had more success by offering them large nest boxes measuring 25 x 25 x 25 cm (9¾ x 9¾ x 9¾ in), with a half-open front, positioned as high as possible in thick bushes. Their free nests are constructed from coarse grasses, wool, pieces of bark and moss, with a lining of soft feathers, preferably white. These free nests are bold structures about 15 cm (6 in) long, 10 cm (4 in) high and 15 cm (6 in) wide, built mainly by the female. The birds may use the nest at various times, but be warned that hygiene is not their biggest virtue!

The cock's mating display is impressive, and when performed in full sunlight, his plumage seems to be on fire. He spreads out his tail like a fan, holds his body very erect, makes a curious, low sound and moves his head slowly from side to side in an odd, but dignified, manner.

Feeding: see the Bengalese, page 231.

CHERRY FINCH
Aidemosyne modesta

These rather timid and passive birds have become popular in recent years, but are still very expensive. They can be kept in a mixed collection and are eminently suitable for colony-breeding. The acclimatisation of imported birds, such as those from Japan, for example, can cause difficulties, and only experienced finch-hobbyists should take them on.

These birds build a tidy, closely woven-round nest lined with small feathers, often in bushes, but also in canary nest boxes and the like. To avoid breeding problems, one could use either Bengalese (see page 230) or African silverbills (see page 233) as breeders and foster parents. Personally, we prefer to use the latter because they are close relatives of the cherry finch; in fact, the two species have frequently been hybridised.

Breeding cherry finches in cold and even mild areas is best done indoors. The birds like heat and don't do well in temperatures below 18˚C (64.4˚F). Their aviary should have ample plantings because they tend to be shy, particularly during the breeding season. In order to obtain good breeding pairs, give the birds the chance to choose their own partners; colony-breeding (with 6 to 12 pairs) is usually very successful. As soon as the nest is complete, remove most of the excess building material. The same applies when the birds are using nest boxes as these finches tend to continue to refine their nests, often at the expense of egg-laying!

Feeding: as for the Bengalese, see page 231. Extra small berries, greens, sprouted millets and ripe and half-ripe grass and weed seeds are always welcome.

Fact file

DISTRIBUTION:
the eastern savannah belt of Australia

HABITAT:
riverine scrub; open woodland

CLUTCH:
4 to 7 white eggs

INCUBATION:
11 to 12 days by both sexes, although the female does most of the brooding

FLEDGING:
21 to 22 days

AVERAGE LIFESPAN:
7 years

SEXING:
the female lacks the male's claret forehead and chin spot and has a thin white line above, and to the rear of, her eyes

JUVENILES:
olive-brown plumage, without any red markings on the head; greyish underside, often with some vague barring

SIZE:
10 to 11 cm (4 to 4¼ in)

Fact file

DISTRIBUTION:
Australian interior, except
Cape York peninsula and Tasmania;
1 subspecies (Timor)

HABITAT:
woodland and savannah;
always near food and water

CLUTCH:
3 to 6 white eggs

INCUBATION:
14 days by both sexes; domesticated
birds will breed all year round

FLEDGING:
21 to 24 days; able to breed at
about 10 weeks of age

AVERAGE LIFESPAN:
8 years

SEXING:
the female lacks the male's breast
barring, orange cheek patches and
chestnut flanks; her bill is less red

JUVENILES:
similar to the female; the black stripe
under the adults' eyes is lacking;
blackish bill

SIZE:
10 to 11 cm (4 to 4^1/$_4$ in)

ZEBRA FINCH
Poephila guttata castanotis

The best-known of all Australian grass finches, the zebra finch is a perky, hardy and pompous little bird, with a song that sounds like the piping of a toy whistle. Several pairs (but never two) will live amicably together and will breed in an aviary, but make sure that there are nest boxes to spare, otherwise pairs may select the same box and waste most of the breeding season bickering over its ownership. The most suitable size of nest box for this small finch is about 15 x 15 x 10 cm (6 x 6 x 4 in) from back to front, with a 5 cm (2 in) opening all along the upper front. Hang the nest box near the roof of the cage to prevent the birds from making a nest on top of it. Grass and hay are suitable nesting materials, and they will line the nest with feathers. A suitable cage for breeding would measure about 120 x 45 x 50 cm (47^1/$_4$ x 17^3/$_4$ 19^1/$_2$ in).

Both parents share the duties of incubation. As soon as the young are self-supporting, they should be separated from their parents, otherwise they will disturb the old birds by crowding into the nest boxes.

Male dilute normal zebra finch.

Male orange-breast grey zebra finch.

Male pastel grey or silver zebra finch.

Male pied zebra finch.

Male brown zebra finch.

Varieties

Dr Carl Russ, the German aviculturist of the 19th century, mentioned some colour mutations, but attached no importance to them and did not attempt to retain them by line-breeding. New colour mutations are always being recorded, however, and at the time of writing (2004), about 50 had been established, the white one being the first. These were first bred by A J Woods of Sydney, Australia, who reared three young ones in an aviary containing a mixed collection in 1921. They were later established by another Sydney fancier, H Lyons. The pied mutation is grey, with white flight feathers and body patches varying from 25 to 50 per cent. The fawn pied is similar, except that its patches are fawn instead of grey. In the marked white, the body colour is white, with chestnut flanks and a faintly black-barred chest. For more details on colour mutations, consult the many publications published by various national and international zebra-finch clubs and societies.

Feeding: as for the Bengalese, see page 231. Note that zebra finches are very fond of green food; they should also be supplied with the heads of small, annual, meadow grasses.

Fact file

DISTRIBUTION:
north-western, northern
and north-eastern Australia;
in 2 subspecies

HABITAT:
grassy margins of rivers, creeks
and swamps; mangroves and
around brackish water

CLUTCH:
3 to 7 white eggs

INCUBATION:
12 to 14 days by both sexes

FLEDGING:
20 to 25 days

AVERAGE LIFESPAN:
8 years

SEXING:
the female is duller than the
male, with red only on her
forehead and lore

JUVENILES:
brownish-olive; black bill

SIZE:
10 to 11.5 cm (4 to 4½ in)

STAR FINCH
Bathilda (Neochmia) ruficauda

Being bold and venturesome by nature, this species is quite popular the world over. These birds are easy to breed, provided that they are kept in a quiet, well-planted aviary. For plantings, select tall grasses, reeds, ivy and dense bushes. The birds will quickly select a display area where the cocks will perch and sing, thereby presenting their owners with many hours of enjoyment. The birds are exceptionally friendly to fellow aviary inhabitants.

Star finches must be housed indoors at room temperature during the autumn and winter. A minimum temperature of 15°C (59°F) is essential as the species does not normally roost in a nest or nest box. It is advisable to separate pairs outside the breeding season to prevent any untimely attempts at nesting, resulting in a possible loss of the hen through egg-binding.

In roomy, outdoor aviaries, they will usually build a free nest in a little bush. (Don't disturb them there as they are quite sensitive.) The male carries the nesting material and the hen constructs a nest in long grass or reeds, or else in a half-open nest box. We like to place a canary nest pan, half-filled with grass and other fibres, in the box to act as a base.

Feeding: during the breeding season, a rich variety of insects and their larvae, sprouted seeds, greens, commercial egg and rearing food, grit, cuttlefish bone and vitamins and minerals must be available at all times (the birds tend to throw their young from the nest when the food is not to their liking.) They should have constant access to clean bath and drinking water.

BICHENOS FINCH
Stizoptera (Poephila) bichenovii

This Australian grass finch is an extremely friendly and peaceful aviary bird that must be housed indoors during the autumn and winter. These birds are often found on the ground, and it is advisable to establish a leaf-mould compost heap in one of the corners of the aviary. This compost heap should give the birds the opportunity to look for insects, satisfying their urge to scratch.

Members of this species should choose their own partners. They build little nests from grass and small feathers in thick shrubbery or use a nesting box. During the night, both parents sit on the nest.

There is a subspecies, often named the ringed finch (*S. b. annulosa*), in which the rump is entirely black (instead of white, as in the *S. b. bichenovii*). It is mostly found in the most northern part of Northern Territory and central Australia.

Feeding: as for the zebra finch, see page 217. In addition to insects, supply standard egg and rearing food for finches throughout the year, particularly during the breeding season. Limit the feeding of small mealworms to only two per day per bird, and to only one per chick in the nest. These birds drink by sucking, as do zebra finches.

Fact file

DISTRIBUTION:
northern, north-western and eastern Australia, including Northern Territory and various offshore islands; in 2 subspecies: *S. b. bichenovii* (which has a white rump) and *S. b. annulosa* (from Northern Territory, which has a black rump)

HABITAT:
varied: savannah; open forest; grassland; often near creeks

CLUTCH:
3 to 7 white eggs

INCUBATION:
11 to 14 days by both sexes; during the night, both are in the nest

FLEDGING:
19 to 25 days

AVERAGE LIFESPAN:
8 years

SEXING:
the female's breast is slightly paler than the male's; she has blackish-grey wing coverts (the male's are jet black)

JUVENILES:
the adults' transverse band is lacking; overall, sooty-grey above and sooty-white underneath

SIZE:
8 to 10 cm (3 to 4 in)

MASKED FINCH
Poephila p. personata

Fact file

DISTRIBUTION:
northern Australia; in 2 subspecies:
P. p. personata (which has
rosy-brown cheeks) and *P. p.
leucotis* (which has white cheeks)

HABITAT:
dry savannah; open woodland
with a grassy understorey

CLUTCH:
4 to 6 white eggs

INCUBATION:
13 to 14 days by both sexes

FLEDGING:
21 to 22 days

AVERAGE LIFESPAN:
6 years

SEXING:
the sexes are similar, but the
female is usually a bit smaller

JUVENILES:
the adults' black face mask is
lacking; muddy-brown overall
impression; black bill

SIZE:
13 to 14 cm (5 to 5½ in)

This excellent, sociable, but somewhat noisy bird, which needs a large, well-planted aviary, is very popular. These birds live mainly on the ground, where they search for food, but spend their mating season high up, between the branches of dead shrubs and trees. They are generally very good breeders, with some pairs being more prolific than others. Some will desert their nest if disturbed, so do not interfere with sitting birds. The nest is a flask-shaped ball made of dry grass, built in either nest boxes, brushwood or growing shrubs in the aviary. The cock shares the tasks of building the nest and incubating the eggs. In the wild, this bird has a curious habit of putting small bits of charcoal into its nest, most likely for hygroscopic reasons.

The white-eared grass finch (*P. p. leucotis*) is found in the extreme north of Queensland. Because of its rather remote habitat, it has always been rare in collections. The birds now available are all captive-bred. The subspecies has a much lighter, richer, cinnamon-brown colour than the masked finch, also having white ear coverts and white below the black of the throat. Its beak is much paler yellow, too. In Australia, this grass finch is very popular as an aviary bird. For more details, see the other *Poephila* species in this book.

Feeding: as for the zebra finch, see page 217, and the Bichenos finch, see page 219.

LONG-TAILED FINCH
Poephila a. acuticauda

This grass finch is extremely sociable in the wild, but can be troublesome in an aviary. These birds are best kept with larger birds in a well-planted aviary, and must be housed indoors during the autumn and winter. A spacious area encourages the growth of the two long, central, tail feathers. Offer the birds as many different nest boxes as possible; these must be positioned high and far apart, behind natural cover. The birds will construct roosting nests as well, so be sure to provide enough building materials. Different pairs will sometimes sleep together in these nests.

Stimulate breeding by supplying grass and weed seeds, as well as live food. Restrict a pair from breeding after two or three clutches. The hen should be at least one year old before being placed in a breeding programme. The courtship display of the male begins with frequent bowing and head-bobbing towards the female, often with a stem of grass in his beak, like African waxbills. During this dance, his body feathers are fluffed out, particularly accentuating his black throat patch. The female responds with similar head-bobbing and bowing. The male then sings his little song, which has been described as ascending to a louder and clearer series of soft notes. The female accepts his advances by leaning forwards and quivering her tail to solicit copulation. After mating, the pair usually indulge in further bobbing and mutual preening.

Feeding: as for the zebra finch, see page 217, and the Bichenos finch, see page 219.

Fact file

DISTRIBUTION:
northern Australia and parts of Queensland; in 2 subspecies: *P. a. acuticauda* (yellow bill) and *P. a. hecki* (reddish bill)

HABITAT:
open forest and woodland; usually near creeks

CLUTCH:
5 to 6 white eggs

INCUBATION:
13 to 14 days by both sexes

FLEDGING:
21 to 23 days

AVERAGE LIFESPAN:
6 years

SEXING:
the female is similar to the male, but may be slightly smaller; most wild females have a smaller heart-shaped throat patch (bib)

JUVENILES:
duller than the female, but with the same markings as their parents; black bill

SIZE:
18 cm (7 in)

The Handbook of Cage and Aviary Birds

Fact file

DISTRIBUTION:
Australia: Queensland and
northern New South Wales;
in 3 subspecies

HABITAT:
open forest; woodland; scrubby
country; near watercourses and
open plains

CLUTCH:
5 to 9 white eggs

INCUBATION:
13 to 14 days by both sexes

FLEDGING:
21 to 22 days

AVERAGE LIFESPAN:
8 years

SEXING:
the female is similar to the male;
in the wild, the female's bib is
often somewhat smaller

JUVENILES:
duller, but similar to their
parents; black bill

SIZE:
10 cm (4 in)

PARSON FINCH
Poephila c. cincta

In captivity, these are sociable, but sometimes aggressive, birds.
They need space, making a large, well-planted aviary necessary.
Keeping several pairs (at least three, but never only two) together
stimulates social behaviour and nest-construction. They build a
bottle-like nest of grass, feathers and plant fibres with an entrance
tunnel, but prefer using a nest box or the old nests of other birds.
They like a choice, so supply lots of nesting facilities. This species
has acquired an unjust reputation as a bit of a busybody that
interferes with other birds' nests. But it is natural for these birds to
have a nest to hand in which to spend the night. They will soon
utilise a nest box stuffed with hay to sleep in, and will eventually
use it for breeding purposes.

This bird can be safely kept in a garden aviary from May until
September, after which it is best caged in a spot where the
temperature does not fall below 10°C (50°F).

Feeding: as for the zebra finch, see
page 217. They are very fond of
insects and should also be
supplied with gentles and
a few mealworms.

Red-headed parrot finch

Amblynura (Erythrura) psittacea

This is a really bright-coloured bird that is exceptionally well suited to a roomy aviary with lots of plants. It must not be exposed to temperatures below 18°C (64.4°F), and must therefore be moved to a heated facility during the winter months. It is perfectly harmless in relation to other small birds.

When in breeding condition, the cock begins to utter a curious little song: a loud, prolonged 'chee', followed by a creaky trill resembling someone winding up a clock. For breeding purposes, it will adopt almost any kind of nesting receptacle, but prefers a wooden box with a hole in the side or a hollow log. The cock builds the nest and sits in it during the day, while the hen incubates in the evening and at night. After the young fly out of the nest, they sleep close together in low vegetation. There is no problem with keeping grown-up young with their parents, as long as the family is housed in an aviary. In cages, the father tends to chase after the youngsters, especially when the female has a new clutch.

These birds are fond of bathing, which helps to keep their plumage in good condition.

Feeding: provide a reputable seed mixture for tropical finches, with extra canary grass seed and millet varieties, Niger and poppy seed, ripe and unripe grass and weed seeds and oats. Also provide greens (like spinach, dandelions and chickweed), fruits (like figs, dates, oranges and bananas) and insects (like cut-up mealworms, ant pupae, white worms, wax moths, tubifex, water flies and other water insects), plus a good brand of egg and rearing food rich in animal protein. These birds are very fond of sweet apples.

Fact file

DISTRIBUTION:
New Caledonia

HABITAT:
grassland with bush growth

CLUTCH:
3 to 6 white eggs

INCUBATION:
13 to 14 days by the female

FLEDGING:
21 to 22 days

AVERAGE LIFESPAN:
7 years

SEXING:
the female is similar to the male, but somewhat duller, and with less red on her head

JUVENILES:
similar to the female, but without any red

SIZE:
12 cm (4³/₄ in)

PIN-TAILED PARROT FINCH
Erythrura p. prasina

Fact file

DISTRIBUTION:
Thailand south-east to Malaysia,
Sumatra, Java and Borneo;
in 2 subspecies: *E. p. prasina*
(which has less red underneath)
and *E. p. coelica* (whose breast
and belly are partly red)

HABITAT:
forests; bamboo thickets; cultivation;
up to 2,012 m (6,600 ft) high
in the mountains

CLUTCH:
2 to 5 white eggs

INCUBATION:
13 to 14 days by the female

FLEDGING:
20 to 22 days

AVERAGE LIFESPAN:
7 years

SEXING:
the female is duller than the male;
she has a greenish head, lacks the
male's blue on the forehead and
throat, and all of the red on the
underside, although some may
have a little red on the breast

JUVENILES:
like the female, but with no, or only
a little, red; dark-horn-coloured bill

SIZE:
14 to 15 cm (5½ to 6 in)

This beautiful bird is best suited to experienced fanciers only. It is difficult to keep alive and in good condition, and its successful acclimatisation requires much effort and experience. Until recently, birds shipped from their native land were fed principally on paddy rice during the journey, and new arrivals suffered from this one-sided feeding; they require a far more balanced diet, especially vitamins B and D. Immediately after arrival, these wonderful birds must be housed in a roomy flight, with their (breeding) cages being kept at a constant minimum temperature of 25°C (77°F). The cages must be equipped with infrared lamps. Once the birds recover, which will take at least a few weeks, the temperature can be reduced to 20°C (68°F).

Breeding is a real challenge, especially considering that the birds moult twice a year. Although the moult doesn't last for long, that of both partners should coincide in order to achieve copulation. The mating dance is well worth studying. The male repeatedly races towards the female while making small bows with his body and beating his tail from left to right. Sometimes he runs sideways, like a crab, for several paces. The couple builds a sizeable nest from fibres, grass leaves, skeleton leaves and the like. They rarely use nest boxes, but prefer to build a free nest in thick bushes, broom branches or tufts of tall, thick grass.

Feeding: as for the red-headed parrot finch, see page 223.

BLUE-FACED PARROT FINCH

Amblynura (Erythrura) t. trichroa

This beautiful parrot finch is readily available in the trade. It requires roughly the same care as the red-headed parrot finch (see page 223). We personally believe that breeding successes can easily be obtained in a roomy aviary that contains enough thick bushes and other plants; successes are far less frequent in cages. Once it has been properly acclimatised, this bird is better able to withstand colder climates than many other parrot finches. The blue-faced parrot finch is rather active and a good flyer, even though it spends a good deal of its time on the ground. It is an excellent breeder, and prefers a half-open nest box. This species is known to breed continuously if not stopped by the removal of its nesting facilities. Only three broods per season should be allowed.

This species does not tolerate temperatures lower than 18°C (64.4°F), so it is important to move the birds to a heated facility for the autumn and winter months.

Various colour mutations of this, as well as of the red-headed and pin-tailed parrot finch, are known: lutino and sea green are seen regularly.

Feeding: as for the red-headed parrot finch, see page 223.

Fact file

DISTRIBUTION:
Celebes; Moluccas; New Guinea and adjacent islands; Bismarck archipelago; north-eastern Australia; Palau islands; Caroline islands; Guadalcanal; Bank islands; New Hebrides and Loyalty islands; in 10 subspecies

HABITAT:
the edges of mangroves and rainforests

CLUTCH:
4 to 5 white eggs

INCUBATION:
14 to 15 days by the female

FLEDGING:
21 to 22 days

AVERAGE LIFESPAN:
7 years

SEXING:
the female is duller than the male; the blue in her face often runs near, or just past, her eyes

JUVENILES:
similar to the female, but without the blue

SIZE:
11.5 to 12 cm (4½ to 4¾ in)

Fact file

DISTRIBUTION:
northern Australia, especially
the Kimberley district; in 3 colour
variations (red-, black- and
yellow-headed)

HABITAT:
savannah; grassland;
open woodland

CLUTCH:
5 to 6 oval-shaped, slightly glossy,
white eggs

INCUBATION:
14 to 16 days by both sexes; at
night, only the female broods

FLEDGING:
23 to 26 days

AVERAGE LIFESPAN:
7 years

SEXING:
the female is similar to the male, but
her breast is more mauve and her
underparts are duller

JUVENILES:
mainly olive-green above, with much
grey in the tail and wings; the upper
tail feathers are grey washed with
blue; whitish chin, throat, most of
the belly and underside of the tail;
horn-coloured bill

SIZE:
12.5 to 14 cm (5 to 5^1/$_2$ in)

GOULDIAN FINCH
Chloebia gouldiae

Gouldians are famous for their remarkable, almost unnaturally
coloured, plumage. Although they are not recommended for bird
fanciers with little or no avicultural experience, they are one of the
most satisfying cage birds to keep, providing, of course, that they
receive all that they require in order to remain in top condition.
Once accustomed to their new surroundings after spending a few
weeks in a roomy cage or an aviary, these birds will remain
unflappable. The key is to treat them with the respect that they
deserve. If approached calmly and kindly, they will respond in a
similar manner.

A single pair can be induced to breed in a roomy cage, but
breeding successes can also be achieved in a garden or indoor
aviary. Several pairs can be housed together in an aviary: the
minimum is three, the maximum, five. They require a nest box
measuring at least 15 x 15 x 25 cm (6 x 6 x 9^3/$_4$ in), with an entry
hole 5 cm (2 in) in diameter; alternatively, the nest box should be
half-open. These birds use either dry or fresh grass for nesting
material, and seem especially to prefer hay, skeleton leaves, sisal
rope and coconut fibres. In order to prevent the birds from
becoming entangled, make sure that such
material is no longer than 10 cm (4 in).
Supply ample amounts of nesting
material because some birds like
to build large nests.

*Yellow-headed, yellow-
bodied, white-breasted, male
Gouldian finch.*

Yellow- and red-headed Gouldian finches..

Female black-headed, white-breasted Gouldian finch.

Red-headed normal, male Gouldian finch.

Young female black-headed Gouldian finch.

These birds cannot tolerate low temperatures. The best breeding results occur at temperatures above 25°C (77°F). To achieve a good moult, the temperature should never drop below 22°C (71.6°F). Sick birds should be isolated and kept at a temperature of at least 25°C (77°F). However, in our experience, a constant 30°C (86°F) is best for these situations. During the moult, the birds are very sensitive to temperature changes, and will even stop moulting if the temperature drops below 21°C (69.8°F). Humidity is also extremely important; at a temperature of 25°C (77°F), the humidity should be kept at 70 per cent. You should have a good thermometer and hygrometer with which to monitor the environment.

Note: some pairs are prolific breeders, but Bengalese finches (see page 230) must be used as foster parents for others.

*Female black-headed
Gouldian finch.*

*Male red-headed, yellow-bodied,
white-breasted Gouldian finch.*

*Yellow-headed normal
Gouldian finch.*

Some mutations

White-breasted: this mutation, probably the most beautiful of all of the established mutations, is inherited recessively, and it is possible to breed it in all three mask colours. A particularly recommended pairing is split white-breasted crossed with white-breasted, which produces strong, lively offspring.

Lilac- or rose-breasted: in this mutation, the males have a lilac, rather than a purple, chest band. The mutation arose from crossings of split white-breasted x split white-breasted and split white-breasted x white-breasted. The mutation is possible in all three head colours. Experiments have shown that this mutation is dominant in white-breasted, and recessive in the three normal, or purple-breasted, finches. Lilac-breasted x normal therefore gives normal split for lilac-breasted.

Blue-breasted: this dominant mutation dates from the mid-1970s. It is not an easy mutation to breed and maintain. The cock has a medium-blue breast, whereas the hen's is a soft or light blue.

Blue: this mutation originated in 1960s' Australia. The mutation is inherited recessively by the three normals. There are thus normal Gouldians that are split for blue. These split birds can sometimes be recognised in that they may possess a sprinkling of blue feathers.

Yellow or lutino: this mutation occurs in red-headed and yellow-headed forms; they are beautiful birds: yellow, with a red mask. The mutation appeared in Australia during the 1960s; it is autosomal recessive and now well established.

White or albino: along with the yellow Gouldian finch, this mutation was well established by the Dutch breeder G Megers. The albino was established during the 1960s, although the exact genetic explanation has yet to be discovered. It has been concluded that crossings of lutinos with pastel colours can lead to white offspring (in pastel birds, there is a general dilution of colours, a phenomenon that occurs now and again in all three normal colours).

Feeding: as for the zebra finch, see page 217.

White Gouldian finch.

SPICE FINCH
Lonchura p. punctulata

This bird is practically always available in the trade, and was first imported into Europe in 1758. Modest in its demands, this species is suitable for garden aviaries, large cages and indoor flights. In the winter, these birds must be housed indoors in a frost-free area, but this doesn't mean that they cannot tolerate low temperature zones. If the birds are given an outside aviary with a sturdily built night enclosure containing felt-lined nest boxes, which also serve as sleeping places, they can spend the winter outdoors.

A pair builds a rather large, round nest in a thick bush; these birds seldom use nest boxes. However, the spice finch (also called the nutmeg finch) is not a ready breeder in captivity, although hybrids between it and other *Lonchura* finches have been produced. All in all, this finch is an attractive bird that may safely associate with any small finch, provided they are not overcrowded.

Feeding: keep these birds in excellent health by giving them a variety of insects throughout the year, as well as weed seeds and a tropical mix, some cod-liver oil and stale bread soaked in water. For more nutritional information, see the Bengalese, page 231.

Fact file

DISTRIBUTION:
Sri Lanka; India south of the Punjab and Assam; southern Nepal; Bhutan; Bangladesh; Burma; eastwards to southern China; Hainan; Taiwan; south-east to Thailand; Indochina; the Malay peninsula; Sumatra; Java; Bali; Lesser Sundas; Celebes; Philippines; introduced to eastern Australia (*L. p. topela*); in 12 subspecies

HABITAT:
grassland; rice paddies; reed and bamboo areas; along rivers and streams; along forest edges; usually near human habitation

CLUTCH:
4 to 5, sometimes 7 to 10, white eggs

INCUBATION:
13 to 14 days by both sexes

FLEDGING:
21 days

AVERAGE LIFESPAN:
5 years

SEXING:
similar in appearance; the male sings

JUVENILES:
similar to their parents, although somewhat duller; adult colour is attained in about 5 months

SIZE:
11.5 to 13 cm (4½ to 5 in)

Fact file

DISTRIBUTION:
domesticated; not in the wild;
various colour mutations available

HABITAT:
captivity only: best kept and
bred in cages instead of aviaries
as these are very sociable birds

CLUTCH:
4 to 6 white eggs, and often
more: females deposit their eggs
in the same nest

INCUBATION:
12 to 13 days by both sexes

FLEDGING:
24 to 25 days

AVERAGE LIFESPAN:
5 years

SEXING:
the female is similar to the male;
the male sings and fans his tail
during courtship

JUVENILES:
duller than their parents; the
intensity, shade and distribution
of colours may vary widely

SIZE:
10 cm (4 in)

BENGALESE or SOCIETY FINCH
Lonchura striata var. *domestica*

The Bengalese is a domesticated bird that exists in many varieties,
for instance: chocolate and white; fawn and white; self chocolate;
self fawn; self white; dilute fawn and white; dilute chocolate and
white; crested (in all colour varieties); frilled; albino; ino-grey;
red-grey; and pastel.

This finch was originally produced centuries ago by the Chinese,
and is believed to have resulted from a cross between the striated
finch and sharp-tailed finch. The striated finch (*L. striata*) comes
from southern India and Sri Lanka, and is also known as the
white-rumped mannikin. The sharp-tailed finch (*L. acuticauda*) is a
native of India, Burma and Sumatra. It is hardy and long-lived, but
not as easy to breed as the Bengalese, except when crossed with it.

A quietly fascinating little bird, unpretentious in both mannerisms
and colouring, the Bengalese has certain pleasing traits that make
it an extremely popular cage bird. It is one of the few foreign birds
that will breed better in a cage than in an aviary, for example, and
is also a valuable foster parent for the hatching and rearing of the
young of Australian grass finches (such as
Gouldians). It is hardy and can be kept
in either a cage or a well-planted aviary.
If kept caged indoors at ordinary
living-room temperature, it may
be allowed to breed at any time
of year, but if it is kept in
an unheated aviary, it is
best to keep the sexes
separated during the
winter to avert
the danger of
egg-binding.

*Original black-brown-
('wild-') form Bengalese finch.*

Crested
Bengalese finch.

Unfortunately, the sexes look alike, and the cocks can only be determined when they are seen displaying to the hens. They do this with an amusing, bowing motion while uttering their harsh, squeaky little song. Bengalese are sociable and of an amiable temperament, be it with their own kind or other species.

Feeding: provide millet varieties, millet spray, canary grass seed, rape seed, flax, poppy seed, hulled oats or oat groats, raw apple, stale wheat bread soaked in water, cracker meal, cracked peanuts, spinach, cracked sunflower seeds, weed and grass seeds and wheat germ. During the breeding season, provide commercial egg food (offer various brands and let the birds decide which they like best), fine-grade softbill meal, insectivorous food, finch pellets, gentles (the cleaned larvae of blowflies or bluebottles), small flies (2 to 4 per bird per day; 4 to 6 during the breeding season), small, cut-up mealworms, spiders, ant pupae, white worms and germinated and sprouted seeds. Provide the following (listed in order of importance) on a daily basis: water, vitamins and minerals, cuttlefish bone, crushed oyster shells, baked chicken eggshells, mineral grit and millet spray.

Fact file

DISTRIBUTION:
Sri Lanka; India; Bangladesh; Assam;
Burma; south-west China; northern
Thailand; Indochina; Malaysia; Java;
Sumatra; Greater Sundas; Celebes;
Philippines; Kalimantan; Hainan;
Palawan; Sulawesi; Natura islands;
Luzon; Taiwan; introduced to the
Moloccas; in 11 subspecies

HABITAT:
grassy country; rice paddies

CLUTCH:
3 to 5, sometimes 7, white eggs

INCUBATION:
12 to 13 days, mainly by the female

FLEDGING:
22 days

AVERAGE LIFESPAN:
5 years

SEXING:
similar in appearance; the male sings

JUVENILES:
similar to their parents,
but generally duller;
adult colouration is attained
after about 8 months

SIZE:
11.5 cm (4½ in)

TRI-COLOURED MANNIKIN
Lonchura (Munia) m. malacca

This extremely strong and lively bird is excellent for the beginner. It is, however, far from easy to breed, but in quiet, large, garden aviaries that have been well planted with reeds, corn, grass and dense bushes, it may use the deserted nests of canaries or other finches in which to raise a family. Leave a few flagstones on the aviary floor to keep these birds' nails short and in shape. They will not tolerate inspections during the breeding cycle. Supply them with perches located high up in the aviary, and offer them plenty of insects and rearing food for finches all year round. Stimulate the urge to breed by keeping them in a small group in a roomy aviary. Our *Lonchura* aviary contains bamboo bushes that really encourage these finches to start a family.

Feeding: as for the spice finch, see page 229. Provide these finches with a variety of insects, as well as cuttlefish bone, weed and grass seeds, egg and rearing food for finches, greens and stale bread soaked in water.

African Silverbill
Euodice (Lonchura) c. cantans

This species, formerly considered conspecific with the Indian silverbill (*E. malabarica*), is an excellent bird for large cages and community aviaries. These birds are easy to keep and become steady breeders. The best breeding successes are obtained in well-planted, outdoor aviaries, although these facilities must be located in a quiet place as breeding pairs are very susceptible to disturbances. Therefore avoid inspecting their nests.

The sexes can only be distinguished by the almost inaudible, somewhat muttering, song of the male, and during the mating season, when the cock dances around his bride holding a grass stem in his beak. A true pair will build a free, small nest in a bush or nest box, but these birds also like to use old weaverbird nests, which they furnish with a long and narrow entrance.

Note: the Indian silverbill (*E. malabarica*) comes from India and Sri Lanka, has a white, instead of black, rump and also much larger clutches.

Feeding: as for the tricoloured mannikin, see left. Germinated grass and weed seeds are considered a treat and should be given throughout the year.

Fact file

DISTRIBUTION:
northern Africa south of the Sahara; eastern Africa from Somalia to central Tanzania; south-western Arabia; in 4 subspecies

HABITAT:
savannah; farmland and orchards; rice paddies; human habitation

CLUTCH:
3 to 6 white eggs

INCUBATION:
12 days by both sexes

FLEDGING:
21 to 22 days

AVERAGE LIFESPAN:
5 years

SEXING:
the female may be a bit smaller, with more red in her tail; the male sings in the breeding period

JUVENILES:
similar to their parents; the adult colour is attained after 2 months

SIZE:
10 to 11.5 cm (4 to 4½ in)

JAVA SPARROW
Padda oryzivora

Fact file

DISTRIBUTION:
Indonesia, especially Java and Bali; introduced to many tropical countries, especially in south-east Asia

HABITAT:
grassland; bush; reeds; light woods; cultivation; in small groups

CLUTCH:
4 to 7 white eggs

INCUBATION:
13 to 14 days by both sexes

FLEDGING:
24 to 28 days

AVERAGE LIFESPAN:
7 years

SEXING:
the female is similar to the male; however, the male sings; the female's beak is often paler (and sometimes smaller) than the male's

JUVENILES:
the plumage is streaked on the breast

SIZE:
14 cm (5½ in)

This finch, which is often named the Java rice bird, is one of the birds that can safely associate with budgerigars, but is not really a safe companion for birds smaller than weaverbirds. Several mutations have been developed, including white, calico, grey with black cheek patches, pied and brown. In 1973, we came across a black-headed Java sparrow in Herentals, Belgium.

These birds are ideal for large cages and aviaries. They prefer using half-open nest boxes measuring 30 x 25 x 25 cm (11¾ x 9¾ x 9¾ in) or the beechwood blocks that are often used for budgerigars; the entrance hole should have a diameter of at least 5 cm (2 in). If nothing is done to prevent it, these birds will breed throughout the year, which could lead to egg-binding problems, so limit the breeding period to May through July, with no more than four clutches per season. To discourage fighting, do not hang the breeding boxes close together. Never house two pairs in one cage or aviary; always keep just one pair, or three or more pairs. The white mutation is by far the easiest to breed. The male has a nice, bell-like song.

Feeding: although the Java sparrow sometimes raises its young without much animal protein, it is nevertheless advisable to present the full menu offered to the Bengalese, see page 231. Seeding grasses are stimulating: the parents like to take them and then feed their young with regurgitated seeds.

CUT-THROAT FINCH
Amadina f. fasciata

This popular finch is one of the best-known foreign cage and aviary birds, despite not being a gaudy species. A good breeder in either a cage or aviary, when it starts to build a nest, it should be provided with a covered nest box and some hay and feathers, as well as strips of bark (particularly willow) and plant fibres (such as agave), as nesting materials. Two or three broods are often reared in summer. The hens are very susceptible to egg-binding in cold weather, and this is the one snag inherent in building up a stock of these birds.

The cut-throat finch being hardy, newly imported birds can be put outside at about the end of May; they can then remain there throughout the winter without artificial heat. But if you have room indoors, by all means position them in a room-temperature environment. In order to avoid winter broods, males and females should be housed separately at this time. Females should be at least nine months to a year old before they start to breed.

The cut-throat finch is not much of a songster, but the cock has a low, soft, bubbling warble. The normal note is a sparrow-like chirp.

This species is partial to dust-bathing in the aviary. The birds behave similarly in the wild, where they take daily sand-baths in their rather arid habitats. They have been rightly accused of interfering with other birds' nests and of bullying smaller birds. On the whole, they are suitable birds for a mixed collection of small finches in a large aviary, but it is important that the aviary is not overcrowded. They can be kept and bred in a colony system.

Feeding: as for the Bengalese, see page 231. Live food, soft-billed rearing food and gentles should be offered when young are being reared.

Fact file

DISTRIBUTION:
western Africa to the Red Sea; south as far as Tanzania, Rhodesia, Botswana and Transvaal; in 3 subspecies

HABITAT:
dry acacia savannah and thornbush; near villages and cultivation

CLUTCH:
3 to 5, sometimes up to 9, white eggs

INCUBATION:
12 to 13 days by both sexes

FLEDGING:
21 to 24 days

AVERAGE LIFESPAN:
5 years

SEXING:
the female lacks the male's red throat markings and is paler and browner

JUVENILES:
similar plumage to that of their parents; young males have a paler-red throat band

SIZE:
11.5 to 13 cm (4$\frac{1}{2}$ to 5 in)

The Handbook of Cage and Aviary Birds

Fact file

DISTRIBUTION:
eastern Sudan; Ethiopia; south-eastern Zaire; north-eastern Uganda; Kenya; Angola; Zimbabwe; Botswana; Mozambique; Swaziland; South Africa; in 5 subspecies

HABITAT:
open woodland; dry thornveld; cultivation

CLUTCH:
3 to 4 white eggs, but only 1 to 3 parasite eggs; one female may lay as many as 2 eggs in the host's nest

INCUBATION:
12 to 13 days by the Melba finch and its subspecies

FLEDGING:
16 days

AVERAGE LIFESPAN:
10 years

SEXING:
the female and male's non-breeding plumage is duller, sparrow-like and without the long tail plumes

JUVENILES:
similar to the female; they are reared by their foster parents, Melba species, and in captivity also fire finches (*Lagonosticta s. senegala*)

SIZE:
15 cm (6 in) when out of colour; the male measures 40 cm (15³/₄ in) during the breeding season

PARADISE WHYDAH
Vidua paradisaea

This is one of the most popular aviary birds, while the cock in full plumage is one of the most striking common foreign birds. It is gentle in disposition, hardy, long-lived and harmless to other birds and plants in the aviary. It is a parasite of various species of Melba finch (see page 192) and fire finch (see page 195). The female whydah may lay as many as two eggs in the host's nest.

There are various whydah species that differ chiefly in the width of their tail feathers and shade of chestnut or golden brown around their necks; others have more or less impressive tails. The pintail whydah, for example, has four elongated, black, tail feathers. A habit common to all is that when feeding, they scratch the soil like poultry. They exhibit fascinating courtship behaviour, the cock rising up and down in the air above the hen, flapping his wings with a regular and noisy beat.

The paradise whydah is a suitable companion for waxbills and any other small seed-eaters. Some two hundred years ago, Portuguese sailors brought this species from the African port of Widah to Spain, hence its name. Due to the male's mainly black plumage, this species is also known as the widow bird.

Feeding: as for the Bengalese, see page 231. Extra grass and weed seeds are welcome, especially those from dandelions, docks and various thistles. Small mealworms, moths, fly larvae or maggots and spiders are appreciated throughout the year, but especially during the moult.

Fact file

DISTRIBUTION:
southern Zaire; Zambia;
southern Angola; Mozambique;
north-western Zimbabwe; northern
Namibia; northern and north-eastern
Botswana (the same distribution as
the Orix weaver); in 4 subspecies

HABITAT:
reed beds; bushy
grassland; cultivation

CLUTCH:
2 to 4 white eggs, with dark-green
and black spots, mostly
at the broad end

INCUBATION:
12 to 14 days by the female

FLEDGING:
13 to 28 days

AVERAGE LIFESPAN:
7 years

SEXING:
the female and male's non-breeding
(eclipse) plumage has a light-brown
upper surface, with dark streaking;
buff-white underparts, darker
on the flanks and breast

JUVENILES:
similar plumage to the adult female,
but with darker striations

SIZE:
11 cm (4¼ in)

NAPOLEON or GOLDEN WEAVER
Euplectes a. afer

This is one of the most attractive weavers, the cock in full plumage being a splendid study in black and yellow. In the early days of English aviculture, Dr A G Butler wrote, 'When in colour, the male is very excitable, puffs up its feathers and sings its strange song, which commences with four or five clicks and then goes off into a sort of hacking cough; the bird's plumes are also shown to great advantage in flight, which is short, jerky, abrupt, and very like a clockwork toy; between each flight, usually in pursuit of some other bird, the wings are jerked up and down over the bird in a most mechanical manner'.

The Napoleon weaver is an excellent aviary bird, being amiable, long-lived and very hardy. Both sexes, when out of colour, can be distinguished from Orix weavers in a similar condition by their darker shade of brown and pronounced, yellowish, eyebrow streak.

These weavers construct an oval nest of dried grass, with an entrance in one of the sides, near the top. The nest's entrance is covered by a 'porch'. In the wild, it is constructed from short, matted grass or weeds, and sometimes even rice. Males are usually polygamous, so do not house a cock with only one hen in a well-planted indoor or garden aviary.

Feeding: as for the Orix weaver, see page 237. Mealworms, termites, earwigs, hairless caterpillars, grubs (wasp larvae), fly larvae (maggots) and a commercial softbill-rearing food are also welcome.

ORIX WEAVER
Euplectes o. orix

When out of colour, the Orix-weaver cock is of a similar hue to the female: namely tawny brown, with dark streaks to the feathers.

The Orix weaver, also known as the red bishop, crimson grenadier, grenadier weaver and red coffee tink, among other names, differs from other subspecies by having a chin that is jet black, as are the top and sides of the head. It is polygamous, with each male having about three hens, gregarious and lives and breeds in communities in reed beds in the wild. It feeds on grain and insects, and is therefore regarded as a serious pest to agriculture. Its nest is oval, slung between upright reeds and composed of strips of reed blades, with little lining. It has been bred a number of times, the first time by Mr De Quincey, of England, in 1912. The cock guards the nest, but the hen takes care of the business of feeding and rearing the young. It is advisable to keep more than one hen with a cock as there is otherwise a risk that he will persecute her.

Feeding: provide a reputable seed mixture for tropical finches, grains, grass and weed seeds, flowers and commercial egg and rearing food. A variety of insects is welcome; in the wild, these birds will eat kelp that they find along the seashore, as well as sandhoppers and fly larvae; they even catch flies in mid-air.

Fact file

DISTRIBUTION:
southern Zaire; Zambia; southern Angola; Mozambique; north-western Zimbabwe; northern Namibia; northern and north-eastern Botswana; in 5 subspecies

HABITAT:
thornveld; open grassland; reed beds; cultivation

CLUTCH:
2 to 7, but usually 3, white eggs

INCUBATION:
12 to 16 days by the female

FLEDGING:
15 to 21 days

AVERAGE LIFESPAN:
7 years

SEXING:
the female and male's non-breeding plumage is sparrow-like, with dark-brown striation on the upper surface; the white underparts are washed in buff-brown and are paler towards the abdomen

JUVENILES:
similar to the female, but with the feathers of the underparts having pale-buff edges

SIZE:
15 cm (6 in)

Fact file

DISTRIBUTION:
the primeval forests of
central Africa

HABITAT:
low elevations; highland forests
and mountains at elevations
of between 1,800 and 2,700 m
(5,906 and 8,858 ft)

CLUTCH:
2 white eggs

INCUBATION:
20 to 23 days by the female

FLEDGING:
28 days

AVERAGE LIFESPAN:
12 years

SEXING:
the female is similar to the male;
scientific sexing is required

JUVENILES:
duller plumage than that of their
parents; dull-black beak

SIZE:
41 cm (16 in)

BLACK-BILLED TOURACO
Tauraco schuttii

Touracos are related to cuckoos. Their plumage displays metallic reflections and is dominated by the colours green, purple and red. These colours are not colourfast: when the birds take a water-bath, the water becomes a little reddish. Experiments have shown that their feathers can be faded to a brownish-grey if soaked in sal ammoniac (ammonium chloride), which will completely wash out the colours.

Black-billed touracos prefer thickly wooded areas, which is why their aviary should be well planted. Both sexes construct the nest; provide a shallow basket as a base.

These expensive birds are best kept in pairs in a roomy aviary that should be at least 3 m (9¾ ft) in length. Regularly spray the plants in the aviary to ensure that the air remains humid, which is absolutely essential to the bird's health. When planting the aviary, remember that the birds must be able to find shady spots because they don't like to walk or sit in the sun. A little water pond is very welcome for bathing purposes. With the proper care, they will become tame in a matter of a few weeks. They like to sleep high up, and love to climb during the day, so provide tree perches, as well as artificial, horizontally placed extra perches as necessary. These birds must be housed indoors at room temperature during the winter months.

Feeding: provide a variety of fruits; berries; cooked, dry rice; chopped carrots; pieces of cooked potato; bread soaked in orange juice; pieces of boiled egg; a few mealworms, ant pupae and white worms; and a good brand of universal or chicken-rearing food. It's advisable to provide a fruit mixture consisting of soaked raisins, berries, and pieces of banana, apple, cherries, pear and the like, on a daily basis.

Fire-tufted Barbet
Psilopogon pyrolophus

Some red feathers are sometimes seen behind the beard-like bristles ('barbet' means 'bearded') at the base of this bird's beak, the hallmark of most barbet species. This species is only for the more experienced fancier. These birds are not that popular in the wild because of the almost constant noise that they make, rather like a hammer hitting an anvil. Another unique fact about these birds is that they are often found alone in the wild, in contrast to members of other barbet species, who like to live in groups.

Their nests are constructed in tree hollows in the wild; in captivity, they like a nest box or preferably a hollow log of soft wood so that they can excavate their own nest cavity like a woodpecker. (Barbets are related to woodpeckers.) They will also use a nest box for roosting. Both sexes share the various tasks of the breeding process. During the breeding season, the male often becomes rather aggressive towards its mate, so that a temporary separation is usually required. They cannot tolerate damp and cold weather, so keep them indoors.

Feeding: in the wild, these birds live almost exclusively on insects. They therefore require a rich variety of insects and egg and rearing food for soft-billed birds. Their staple diet is a variety of fruit, berries, insectile mixtures and occasionally a small, dead mouse.

Fact file

DISTRIBUTION:
Malay peninsula;
Sumatra (Indonesia)

HABITAT:
mountain forests; wooded country; open terrain; elevations of up to about 900 m (2,953 ft)

CLUTCH:
2 to 4 white eggs

INCUBATION:
14 to 15 days by both sexes

FLEDGING:
19 to 20 days

AVERAGE LIFESPAN:
8 years

SEXING:
in comparison to the male, the female has duller, maroon-red head markings and nape

JUVENILES:
duller plumage than that of their parents

SIZE:
28 cm (11 in)

Fact File

DISTRIBUTION:
the Guianas; northern, eastern
and southern Brazil; Bolivia;
Paraguay; northern Argentina

HABITAT:
rainforests; wooded areas; in
loose flocks (5 to 10 individuals);
the birds generally keep to the
upper levels of the forest

CLUTCH:
2 to 4 white eggs

INCUBATION:
16 to 18 days by both sexes

FLEDGING:
48 to 50 days; the chicks
develop very slowly

AVERAGE LIFESPAN:
10 years

SEXING:
the female is similar to the male;
she may have a somewhat smaller
body and bill, but this is variable
and cannot be considered a
definite characteristic

JUVENILES:
duller plumage than that of their
parents; the chicks have amazing,
ridged, heel pads that assist them
in moving about the nest cavity

SIZE:
53 cm (20³/₄ in)

TOCO TOUCAN
Ramphastos toco

Toucans, together with toucanets and aracaris (*Ramphastidae*), stand out because of their huge bills, which are partly hollow. These are made of hollow bone cells, which make them very light, with only the edges being hard and serrated. The birds have long tongues that look frayed at the edges. The wings are relatively short and rounded, as is the tail. The birds walk rather poorly because their first and fourth toes are directed backwards.

Provide large parrot nesting boxes (like those used for macaw-like hookbills, see page 137) and hollowed-out palm logs, placed high in the aviary, which will be used for breeding, as well as for roosting. The nest cavity should measure about 25 cm (9³/₄ in) in diameter. These birds feed their young with pink mice, berries and fruit. During the breeding season, pairs can become rather aggressive towards other birds, and could steal their eggs and young.

Toucans are very inquisitive, but also quite calm in their behaviour. They like to have a high aviary, but do not behave well with other species or with small birds, particularly near feeding dishes. In their native habitats, toucans were once hunted for their dark meat, which was considered highly tasty.

These birds love to take frequent baths and need thick perches, with a diameter of about 6 cm (2¹/₄ in), for both resting and sleeping.

Feeding: provide fleshy fruits, berries, insects, pink mice, wheat bread soaked in water, soaked rice, and a commercial softbill food. Most birds will take pellets soaked in orange juice. Virtually all ramphastids are susceptible to iron-storage disease (haemochromatosis), making low-level iron pellets essential.

Fact file

RED-EARED OR RED-WHISKERED BULBUL
Pycnonotus jocosus

Bulbuls belong to the order *Passeriformes* and the family *Pycnonotidae*. They are often beautiful, colourful and decorative birds, and most have a rather pert crest. The red-eared bulbul is an excellent representative of these handsome birds, which rather resemble thrushes in both shape and behaviour.

Red-eared bulbuls like freedom of movement and therefore need a lot of space. Their cages must be at least 70 cm (27¹/₂ in) long. They will be much happier when housed in a roomy aviary with live plants. However, do not house a pair together with either fellow species members or different birds since there is a good possibility that this will lead to serious conflict. During the breeding period, they will even steal the young out of another bird's nest. Their own nests are cup-shaped and are constructed in trees or bushes from grass, moss, dry leaves, hay, coconut fibres, spiders' webs and hair. While the female is breeding the cock does not feed her, but will later forage for his young.

The male sings in a rather remarkable manner, often displaying the red plumage of his underparts, especially during the breeding season.

Like all bulbuls, the red-eared bulbul is initially somewhat timid and withdrawn. This behaviour will soon change, however, and it won't be long before this bird is taking food out of its keeper's hand.

Feeding: provide a variety of fruits, especially berries, and some insects now and then. Universal, egg and rearing food are welcome, while mynah pellets are essential.

PLAIN-BACKED SUNBIRD
Cinnyrus reichenowi

Sunbirds (*Nectariniidae*) are in general characterised by their thin, long, somewhat curved bill that is often very finely serrated along the edges. Their red tongue can be extended quite some distance outside their mouth. The cocks are often very beautifully coloured birds, with brilliant red and iridescent green in a subordinate degree on the head and chin. Their humming flight is fast and a little wavy in pattern. Sunbirds do not generally hover over a flower for very long, but gently set themselves down on it. Their nests, which are located at various levels and made in a variety of dimensions, are nearly always pouch-shaped and hung in the fork of a branch. There is usually a narrow entrance at the side.

Sunbirds are delightful little creatures, although they sometimes display a slightly aggressive side to their natures (but such a display is usually over very quickly). Keep them in a large, well-planted, outdoor aviary equipped with a good-sized night shelter. Avoid overcrowding to keep any squabbles to a minimum. They should be housed inside during the late autumn and winter. Sunbirds, and plain-backed sunbirds in particular, usually become tame very quickly. We have various species (all kept in separate aviaries!) that have become very attached to us, and some will calmly take some insects or little spiders out of our hands without acting in the least bit nervously or timidly.

Feeding: it is essential to provide a variety of small insects (such as live *Drosophila* and other small flies) and their pupae. (Place the flies in a glass jar, cover it with a sheet of stretched clingfilm, poke a twig through the clingfilm and let it protrude so that the flies can crawl up it, and then punch a few little holes in the clingfilm through which the flies can escape before being caught by the birds.) These birds do well on commercial hummingbird mixtures, pure-pollen granules and nectar (contained in bottles for red-tipped hummingbirds), as well as on their natural diet of all kinds of small insects.

Fact file

DISTRIBUTION:
lowland-forest areas of Mozambique, Zimbabwe, southern Kenya and north-eastern Tanganyika.

HABITAT:
almost ubiquitous

CLUTCH:
2 to 3 pale-green-blue eggs, with highly variable markings

INCUBATION:
13 to 15 days by the female

FLEDGING:
14 days

AVERAGE LIFESPAN:
7 years

SEXING:
the upper surface of the female's plumage is grey-brown; the underside is olive-yellow; some grey mottling on the throat

JUVENILES:
similar to the female

SIZE:
14 cm (5½ in)

Fact file

DISTRIBUTION:
from the western Himalayas east
to Burma, Assam, northern
Vietnam and southern China;
introduced to Hawaii;
in 6 subspecies

HABITAT:
wooded areas; in little groups,
and mostly in pairs during the
breeding season

CLUTCH:
3 to 4 light-green-white eggs,
with grey-brown and purple
spots found primarily towards
the blunt end

INCUBATION:
14 days by both sexes

FLEDGING:
14 days

AVERAGE LIFESPAN:
10 years

SEXING:
the female is paler than the male;
her head has greyer lores, but
there remain some variations in
plumage among the subspecies;
the male sings

JUVENILES:
duller plumage than that of
their parents

SIZE:
15 cm (6 in)

PEKIN ROBIN
Leiothrix lutea

In the wild, Pekin robins are rather timid in open fields, preferring heavily wooded areas. They generally live in small groups, and mostly in pairs during the breeding period. Their cup-shaped nests are often located in thick bushes, and are made out of moss, roots, dried leaves and stems. In captivity, they will use canary 'baskets', which must be placed inside half-open nest boxes. They will also build their own nests, which are cup-shaped and made of straw, bark, moss and thin roots and twigs. The boxes should be hung in secluded locations. A pair should be placed in a well-planted aviary. Absolute rest is vital, but not every couple will breed. We recommend keeping only a few seed-eaters of the same size and just a couple of weavers as co-inhabitants of the aviary. (Smaller birds would be constantly terrorised, their nests pulled apart and young destroyed.)

These birds will do well in a cage that is at least 75 x 45 x 65 cm (29$^{1}/_{2}$ x 17$^{3}/_{4}$ x 25$^{1}/_{2}$ in), and their exuberant song and beautiful plumage will enthuse even the most confirmed bird-hater. Do not keep more than one pair in a cage or aviary because housing more than one couple together leads to fighting. The cock and hen are very lovey-dovey as they gently pick at one another's feathers and sleep close together, often with their wings over each other's shoulders.

These birds will become tame very quickly, and will often take a mealworm or a few ants' eggs out of their keeper's hand. (There is no problem with giving them mealworms outside the breeding period, and cage birds that do not breed can also have them; see below.)

These birds may remain in an outdoor aviary during the winter, as long as it is equipped with a night shelter that is wind- and draught-free, securely closed and heatable, with good sleeping nests. The moult takes place from August to September.

Feeding: provide millet varieties, millet spray, canary grass seed, maw seed, some hemp, chopped, boiled egg, ant pupae, berries, banana slices, chopped apples or pears and (once in a while) some soaked raisins. A mixture of universal and rearing food for soft-billed birds should also be on the menu, as well as soaked, stale bread, grit, spinach and chickweed. Never offer mealworms during the breeding season as the parents have a habit of throwing their eggs or young out of the nest. These birds should have daily access to drinking and bathing water, the latter warmed to room temperature.

INDIAN ZOSTEROPS or WHITE EYE
Zosterops palpebrosa

The pleasant, active, white eyes (*Zosteropidae*), members of a family that comprises some one hundred different species, are displayed to full advantage in a vitrine or show cage measuring 70 x 50 x 60 cm (27^1/$_2$ 19^1/$_2$ x 23^1/$_2$ in) or a room aviary. These birds are tolerant towards other species, and become very tame with their keepers, particularly those who are the birds' sole carers.

Of the many species, the Indian white eye is the most readily obtainable. This sombre-coloured bird is both plentiful and inexpensive, as well as one of the easiest and most charming of all small softbills to keep. Always keep them in pairs, however, as solitary birds slowly pine away.

The best chances for successful breeding are in facilities in which absolute peace reigns, preferably in an aviary without other birds. They make a cup-shaped nest (they will sometimes use a little canary nest pan) with blades of grass, coconut fibres, thin strips of bark and wool; they will also use horsehair and small feathers. The youngsters should be separated from their parents as soon as the brood has become independent because the father may sometimes chase them aggressively. Allow these birds to spend the cold winter months indoors, in a lightly heated area. Most species have a fairly pleasant song, although this observation applies only to the cock. Bathing is an absolute must!

Feeding: these birds require variety. It is a good idea to place their food on a small table about 50 cm (19^1/$_2$ in) above the ground because white eyes are rarely on the ground, and usually tumble around in the foliage looking for insects, larvae, berries, fruits, leaf buds and even nectar, which they draw out by piercing a hole in the flower with their pointed beaks. They also like universal food with insects, in addition to soaked or cooked rice and grated apples and carrots. You could give them bananas and dried fruits daily. A mashed-fruit concoction consisting of cherries, apples, pears, apricots, oranges and dates, sweetened with glucose, is also very much enjoyed by these birds.

Fact file

DISTRIBUTION:
eastern Afghanistan; India; Sri Lanka; Indochina; the Greater Sundas; the Himalayas; Bhutan; Nepal

HABITAT:
woods; large gardens and parks; up to 1,700 m (5,577 ft)

CLUTCH:
2 to 4 green-blue eggs

INCUBATION:
18 to 19 days by the female

FLEDGING:
13 to 14 days

AVERAGE LIFESPAN:
10 years

SEXING:
the female is similar to the male

JUVENILES:
the plumage is very similar to that of the parents, but somewhat greener and duller

SIZE:
10 cm (4 in)

Fact file

DISTRIBUTION:
India; Sri Lanka; Burma; Thailand;
Indochina; Malaysia; Java;
Sumatra; Borneo; Bali;
Andamans; Nicobars; Sunda
islands; Palawan; southern China;
Hainan; in 10 subspecies

HABITAT:
forests

CLUTCH:
2 to 3 blue eggs

INCUBATION:
13 to 16 days by both sexes

FLEDGING:
20 to 21 days

AVERAGE LIFESPAN:
8 years

SEXING:
the female and male are
alike in colour

JUVENILES:
duller plumage than that of their
parents; depending on the
subspecies, their wattles may still
be relatively inconspicuous, with
flat areas of yellowish skin
indicating where they will be

SIZE:
23 to 38 cm (9 to 15 in)

GREATER or GLOSSY JAVA HILL MYNAH
Gracula religiosa

This popular species, which is often called the Indian grackle, is one of the most beloved of pet birds if obtained young, its ability to talk being unexcelled, and its rate of learning amazingly rapid. The best talkers are those that have been hand-reared and trained; 'unschooled' birds will be hard to control and will never make good talkers. The bird's plumage is mainly glossy black, with purple reflections; a white patch is visible in the wing primaries. The yellow-orange, bare skin (which varies in shape and size) on the sides of the head and nape are called wattles. In young birds, the wattles are not properly formed, and flat areas of yellowish skin indicate where they will be.

The lesser hill mynah (*G. r. indica*), from south-western India and Sri Lanka, is also very popular, although this species is not renowned for its talking ability. The Nepal or Assam hill mynah (*G. r. intermedia*), also known as the greater hill mynah, lives in northern India, Burma, Thailand and Indonesia and measures 25 to 28 cm ($9^{3/4}$ to 11 in). Its yellow wattles are separated only by a small area of black feathers behind the eyes, and end in a broad, pendant lobe on the nape.

To achieve breeding success, place a starling's nest box in a well-planted aviary. The parents may become aggressive during the breeding season, so don't house them with other species. During the winter, all mynahs should be housed indoors, in a slightly heated room at a minimum temperature of 12°C (53.6°F).

Feeding: various commercial mynah-bird pellets are available, but most are too high in iron. Besides live food, offer universal food, raw minced beef, all kinds of insects (especially mealworms, white worms, ant pupae, grasshoppers and so on), peanuts (shelled, but not roasted), raisins, sultanas, berries, cheese, all kinds of fruit and so on. If you are planning on taking in a mynah, you will be guaranteed a sweet tooth to feed. Note that it is essential to provide live food while the young are being reared.

Fact file

DISTRIBUTION:
the Himalayas, south-east to
Burma, parts of Thailand,
Indochina, south-western China,
Sumatra and Hainan

HABITAT:
mountain forests

CLUTCH:
4 to 5, sometimes 6, white eggs

INCUBATION:
14 days by both sexes

FLEDGING:
21 days

AVERAGE LIFESPAN:
10 years

SEXING:
the female is similar to the male in
colouration, although she can
often be distinguished by her
smaller, somewhat greyer, crest

JUVENILES:
duller plumage than that of
their parents

SIZE:
30 cm (11¾ in)

WHITE-CRESTED LAUGHING-JAY THRUSH
Garrulax leucolophus

The genus *Garrulax* has an important place among the babblers (*Timaliinae*). These are sturdy birds, with long beaks and fairly large nostrils that are mostly covered with feathers. The wings are short and rounded, and the tail is as long as the wings. In the wild, they live harmoniously together in little groups. In captivity, they should be housed in a large, planted aviary as they are far too restless for a cage. The cup-shaped nest, which is hung between thin twigs, is fairly loosely built of grass, fibres, hair, moss, roots, bamboo stalks and the like, and is lined with little roots and twigs. These birds breed in captivity, but should be kept away from other birds as they will kill and eat them. They are constantly on the go and hop about in a rather comical fashion, both on the ground and over feeders. They are very inquisitive, but difficult to tame. The whistling tones of the cock are full and pleasant to the ear. When they go to sleep, they often cover one another with their wings. They love to bathe, and do so frequently. During the winter months, they must be brought indoors into an unheated area.

Feeding: besides commercial thrush food, provide juicy fruits and greens (like lettuce, endives, chickweed and spinach), various insects (beetles, ant pupae, mealworms and so on) and finely minced raw or cooked beef. They also enjoy various seeds (hemp, millet varieties, canary grass seed and so on) and chicken-rearing food, and will much appreciate being given a dead mouse now and then.

BLUE-NECKED TANAGER
Tanagara cyanicollis

Because of their preferred, basically sweet and juicy, food, the droppings of tanagers (*Thraupidae*) are watery. The bottom of their cages and show vitrines should therefore be covered with kitchen paper or a few layers of newspaper. It is essential to clean out their cages or aviaries daily in order to avert disease. Also ensure that the birds always have access to washing facilities, which should be cleaned and refilled with boiled, then cooled, water a few times a day. After it has become acclimatised, the blue-necked tanager is easily managed, but should be housed indoors during the winter.

A single pair should be housed in a cage measuring 150 x 80 x 60 cm (59 x 31½ x 23½ in). Breeding successes occur only sporadically, however, and housing the birds in a large, garden aviary will improve the odds. The birds prefer to breed as high up as possible, in a variety of nest boxes that already contain nesting materials (coconut fibres, dead and fresh grass, leaves, moss, pieces of bark, wool and such like). The birds also construct free nests in thick shrubs. Assist tanagers in their nest-building by offering them a few 'nest shells' bent from chicken wire into the shape of a little bowl (watch out for sharp edges!)

Feeding: this species seldom eats seeds and universal foods, and prefers various types of fruits and berries, especially soaked, dried currants and raisins, grapes, cut-up pears and apples, sliced tomatoes, dates, figs, bananas and halved oranges. Insects, cut-up mealworms, soaked coconut biscuits and finely shredded carrots are also most welcome. Colour foods, such as the ones used for colour canaries, can be mixed with their food in very small quantities, but only after the moult is completely finished. Better still, offer the birds a well-balanced and complete diet that eliminates the need for such additives. Never serve honey water in open dishes because the birds may take a bath in it.

Fact file

DISTRIBUTION:
north-western Venezuela;
western Colombia; Ecuador;
western Peru; northern Bolivia

HABITAT:
forest

CLUTCH:
5 pale or white eggs, with
dark blotches

INCUBATION:
14 to 15 days by the female

FLEDGING:
20 to 22 days

AVERAGE LIFESPAN:
8 years

SEXING:
the female is similar to the male;
all tanagers are dimorphic

JUVENILES:
duller plumage than that of
their parents

SIZE:
13 cm (5 in)

Fact file

DISTRIBUTION:
south-western Africa

HABITAT:
acacia thornveld; reed beds;
cultivation; in pairs when
breeding, otherwise in
little troops

CLUTCH:
2 to 3 pale-blue, sparingly
umber- or brown-speckled eggs,
or else with a few large spots,
mostly on the large end

INCUBATION:
15 to 16 days by the female

FLEDGING:
21 days

AVERAGE LIFESPAN:
10 years

SEXING:
the female is similar to the male

JUVENILES:
duller plumage than that of
their parents

SIZE:
24 cm (9½ in)

PURPLE GLOSSY STARLING
Lamprotornis purpureus

Starlings (*Sturnidae*) have become very popular aviary birds in recent years, and special feeders like those designed for Pekin robins have even been introduced for keeping them. In addition, their care is not at all complicated, so even an unspecialised bird-fancier can succeed in keeping them, as long as he or she has enough space and time.

In the wild, these birds form little troops that follow herds of cattle and flocks of sheep, for understandable reasons. In captivity, they soon lose their timid nature and remain extremely active. The cock sings during the early morning and evening hours, but is seldom heard during the rest of the day. During the breeding season, they require a suitable-sized nest box; the nest itself is bulky, and is constructed from little twigs, plant fibres, wool, hair and such like.

Feeding: it is essential to provide such live food as fly pupae, small locusts, crickets, white worms and mealworms, especially during the breeding season, as well as a rich variety of fruits, minced raw meat and beef heart, shelled shrimps, hard-boiled egg, dry cheese, fish roe, grated carrots and a commercial insectivorous food. Sprinkle a multi-vitamin preparation over some of the food every day.

PILEATED or PLUSH CRESTED JAY
Cyanocorax chrysops

This species is easily managed and reasonably easy to breed. These birds should be kept in pairs, but cannot be housed with smaller birds as they are rather aggressive. They should be stationed indoors (at room temperature) during the winter months.

This species belongs to the omnivorous *Corvidae* family (that of magpies, jays and crows). Due to the large amount of droppings that they produce, cleanliness is vital, and bathing is absolutely essential to them. With good care, they will quickly become tame and will entertain their owners with their pranks and often astonishing rendition of the human voice (as well as of other pleasant, and perhaps not so pleasant, sounds). They are intelligent and highly amusing birds, and usually good breeders. Provide open nest boxes; their own nest is a flimsy platform made of little twigs and lined with grass. During the breeding season, live food is a must, for if insufficient, the parents may eat or reject their young.

Feeding: provide live food like locusts, grasshoppers, white worms, mealworms, crickets, small beetles and insects during the year, but especially during the breeding season; also supply dead mice, raw beef, hard-boiled eggs, dry cheese, fish roe, insectivorous foods, grated carrots, nuts, and especially acorns.

Fact file

DISTRIBUTION:
Brazil, south of the Amazon; eastern Bolivia; Paraguay; Uruguay; northern Argentina

HABITAT:
forests; groves; cerrados

CLUTCH:
4 to 7 blue-white eggs, with brown markings

INCUBATION:
18 to 21 days by the female

FLEDGING:
21 days

AVERAGE LIFESPAN:
10 years

SEXING:
the female is similar to the male

JUVENILES:
similar to their parents, but duller, with shorter tails and a lighter-coloured bill and feet

SIZE:
33 cm (13 in)

INDEX

A

Abyssinian lovebird, see *Agapornis t. taranta*
Aegintha t. temporalis 213
African grey parrot, see *Psittacus e. erithacus*
African quail finch, see *Ortygospiza atricollis atricollis*
African silverbill, see *Euodice (Lonchura) c. cantans*
Agapornis c. cana 117
Agapornis personata fischeri 127
Agapornis personata lilianae 129
Agapornis personata nigrigenis 128
Agapornis p. personata or *personatus* 124–26
Agapornis p. pullaria or *pullarius* 123
Agapornis r. roseicollis 120–22
Agapornis t. taranta 118–19
Aidemosyne modesta 215
Alexandrine parakeet, see *Psittacula e. eupatria*
Alisterus s. scapulari 88–89
Amadina f. fasciata 235
Amandava a. amandava 206
Amandava (Sporaeginthus) s. subflava 208
Amandava (Stictospiza) formosa 207
Amazona a. aestiva 177
Amazona a. albifrons 173
Amazona a. autumnalis 176
Amazona amazonica amazonia 181
Amazona f. finschi 175
Amazona l. leucocephala 172
Amazona o. auropalliata 180
Amazona ochrocephala oratrix 179
Amazona o. ochrocephala 178
Amazona viridigenalis 174
Amblynura (Erythrura) psittacea 223
Amblynura (Erythrura) t. trichroa 225
Angola lovebird, see *Agapornis p. pullaria* or *pullarius*
Angolan cordon bleu, see *Uraeginthus a. angolensis*
Anodorhynchus hyacinthinus 138–39
Ara ararauna 137
Ara m. macao 141
Ara m. militaris 140
Ara (Propyrrhura) auricollis 142
Aratinga a. acudicaudata 144
Aratinga a. aurea 151
Aratinga a. auricapilla 147
Aratinga (auricapillus) solstitialis 148
Aratinga cactorum cactorum 150
Aratinga c. canicularis 149
Aratinga e. leucopthalmus 145
Aratinga erythrogenys 146
Aratinga (Nandayus) nenday 152
Auripasser luteus 189
aurora finch, see *Pytilia phoenicoptera*
Austral conure, see *Enicognathus f. ferrugineus*
Australian king parrot, see *Alisterus s. scapulari*

B

Barbary dove, see *Streptopelia roseogrisea*, var. *arisoria*
bare-eyed cockatoo, see *Cacatua s. sanguinea*
Barnardius barnardi 136
Barnardius zonarius 94
Barnard's parakeet, see *Barnardius barnardi*
Barraband's parakeet, see *Polytelis swainsonii*
barred ground dove, see *Geopelia s. striata*
barred parakeet, see *Bolborhynchus lineola*
Bathilda leucotis ruficauda 218
Bengalese finch, see *Lonchura striata* var. *domestica*
Bichenos finch, see *Stizoptera (Poephila) bichenovii*
black-billed touraco, see *Ramphastos toco*
black-capped lory, see *Lorius lory*
black-cheeked lovebird, see *Agapornis personata nigrigenis*
black-cheeked waxbill, see *Estrilda (Brunhilda) e. erythronotos*
black lory, see *Chalcopsitta atra*
black-tailed conure, see *Pyrrhura m. melanura*

black-winged lovebird, see *Agapornis t. taranta*
blue and gold macaw, see *Ara ararauna*
blue and yellow macaw, see *Ara ararauna*
blue-breasted waxbill, see *Uraeginthus a. angolensis*
blue-capped cordon bleu, see *Uraeginthus cyanocephalus cyanocephalus*
blue-crowned conure, see *Aratinga a. acudicaudata*
blue-crowned hanging parrot, see *Loriculus galgulus*
blue-faced parrot finch, see *Amblynura (Erythrura) t. trichroa*
blue-fronted Amazon, see *Amazona a. aestiva*
blue-headed parrot, see *Pionus m. menstruus*
blue-mountain lory, see *Trichoglossus h. moluccanus*
blue-necked tanager, see *Tanagara cyanicollis*
blue-winged grass parakeet, see *Neophema chrysostoma*
Bolborhynchus lineola 164
Bourke's parakeet, see *Neophema bourkii*
Brazilian saffron finch, see *Sicalis flaveola*
Brotogeris chiriri 169
brown-headed parrot, see *Poicephalus cryptoxanthus*
budgerigar, see *Melopsittacus undulates*

C

Cacatua alba 81
Cacatua galerita 79
Cacatua goffini 82
Cacatua leadbeateri 77
Cacatua moluccensis 80
Cacatua s. sanguinea 83
Cacatua sulphurea 78
cactus conure, see *Aratinga cactorum cactorum*
Californian quail, see *Callipepla (Lophortyx) california*
Callipepla (Lophortyx) california 53
canary, see *Serinus canaria domesticus*
canary-winged parakeet, see *Brotogeris chiriri*
Cape dove, see *Oena c. capensis*
Cape parrot, see *Poicephalus robustus*
celestial parrotlet, see *Forpus c. coelestis*
Chalcopsitta atra 64
Chalcopsitta duivenbodei 63
Chalcopsitta scintillata 65
Charmosyna papou goliathina 73
chattering lory, see *Lorius garrulus*
cherry finch, see *Aidemosyne modesta*
Chinese painted quail, see *Coturnix chinensis*
Chloebia gouldiae 226–28
Cinnyris reichenowi 245
cockatiel, see *Nymphicus hollandicus*
collared dove, see *Streptopelia decaocto*
common quail finch, see *Ortygospiza atricollis atricollis*
common waxbill, see *Estrilda astrild astrild*
Coturnix chinensis 52
crimson-bellied conure, see *Pyrrhura perlata*
crimson finch, see *Neochmia p. phaeton*
Cuba Amazon, see *Amazona l. leucocephala*
cut-throat finch, see *Amadina f. fasciata*
Cyanocorax chrysops 253
Cyanoliseus p. patagonus 153
Cyanoramphus novaezelandiae 107

D

Deroptyus accipitrinus 182
diamond dove, see *Geopelia c. cuneata*
diamond firetail finch, see *Zonaeginthus guttatus*
Diopsttaca (Ara) n. nobilis 143
double yellow-fronted Amazon, see *Amazona ochrocephala oratrix*
Duivenbode's lory, see *Chalcopsitta duivenbodei*
dusky lory, see *Pseudeos fuscata*

E

eastern rosella, see *Platycercus eximius*
eclectus parrot, see *Eclectus r. roratus*
Eclectus r. roratus 86–87
elegant grass parakeet, see *Neophema elegans*
Elophus (Cacatua) roseicapillus 76

Emblema picta 212
Enicognathus f. ferrugineus 160
Eos borneo 66
Erythrura p. prasina 224
Estrilda astrild astrild 203
Estrilda (Brunhilda) e. erythronotos 205
Estrilda (Glaucestrilda) caerulescens 200
Estrilda (Krimhilda) a. atricapilla 204
Estrilda m. melpoda 201
Estrilda troglodytes 202
Euodice (Lonchura) c. cantans 233
Euplectes a. afer 238
Euplectes o. orix 239

F

Finsch's Amazon, see *Amazona f. finschi*
fire-tufted barbet, see *Psilopogon pyrolophus*
Fischer's lovebird, see *Agapornis personata fischeri*
Forpus c. coelestis 166
Forpus c. conspicillatus 165
Forpus p. passerinus 168
Forpus xanthops 167

G

Galah cockatoo, see *Elophus (Cacatua) roseicapillus*
Garrulax leucolophus 250
Geopelia c. cuneata 58
Geopelia s. striata 59
glossy Java hill mynah, see *Gracula religiosa*
Goffin's cockatoo, see *Cacatua goffini*
golden-breasted waxbill, see *Amandava (Sporaeginthus) s. subflava*
golden-capped conure, see *Aratinga a. auricapilla*
golden-crowned conure, see *Aratinga a. aurea*
golden song sparrow, see *Auripasser luteus*
golden weaver, see *Euplectes a. afer*
Goldie's lorikeet, see *Trichoglossus goldiei*
Gouldian finch, see *Chloebia gouldiae*
Gracula religiosa 248
greater Java hill mynah, see *Gracula religiosa*
greater sulphur-crested cockatoo, see *Cacatua galerita*
green avadavat, see *Amandava (Stictospiza) formosa*
green-backed twinspot, see *Mandingoa n. nitidula*
green-cheeked Amazon, see *Amazona viridigenalis*
green-cheeked conure, see *Pyrrhura m. molinae*
green-naped lory, see *Trichoglossus h. haematodus*
green-rumped parrotlet, see *Forpus p. passerinus*
grey singing finch, see *Serinus leucopygus*

H

Hahn's macaw, see *Diopsttaca (Ara) n. nobilis*
hawk-headed parrot, see *Deroptyus accipitrinus*
hyacinth macaw, see *Anodorhynchus hyacinthinus*
hyacinthine macaw, see *Anodorhynchus hyacinthinus*
Hypargos n. niveoguttatus 194

I

Indian ringneck parakeet, see *Psittacula krameri malillensis*
Indian zosterops, see *Zosterops palpebrosa*

J

Jardine's parrot, see *Poicephalus gulielmi*
Java sparrow, see *Padda oryzivora*

L

Lagonosticta senegala 195
Lamprotornis purpureus 252
laughing dove, see *Streptopelia senegalensis*
lavender waxbill, see *Estrilda (Glaucestrilda) caerulescens*
Leadbeater cockatoo, see *Cacatua leadbeateri*
Leiothrix lutea 246
lesser Patagonian conure, see *Cyanoliseus p. patagonus*
lesser sulphur-crested cockatoo, see *Cacatua sulphurea*
lineolated parakeet, see *Bolborhynchus lineola*
little corella, see *Cacatua s. sanguinea*

Lonchura (Munia) m. malacca   232
Lonchura p. punctulata   229
Lonchura striata var. domestica   230–31
long-tailed finch, see *Poephila a. acuticauda*
Loriculus galgulus   130–31
Lorius garrulus   72
Lorius lory   71

M

Madagascar lovebird, see *Agapornis c. cana*
Magellan conure, see *Enicognathus f. ferrugineus*
Mallee ringneck parakeet, see *Barnardius barnardi*
Mandingoa n. nitidula   193
maroon-bellied conure, see *Pyrrhura f. frontalis*
maroon conure, see *Pyrrhura m. melanura*
masked dove, see *Oena c. capensis*
masked finch, see *Poephila p. personata*
masked lovebird, see *Agapornis p. personata* or *personatus*
Maximilian's parrot, see *Pionus m. maximiliani*
Melba finch, see *Pytilia melba melba*
Melopsittacus undulates   60–62
Mexican red-headed Amazon, see *Amazona viridigenalis*
Meyer's parrot, see *Poicephalus meyeri*
military macaw, see *Ara m. militaris*
Mitchell's cockatoo, see *Cacatua leadbeateri*
Molina's conure, see *Pyrrhura m. molinae*
Moluccan cockatoo, see *Cacatua moluccensis*
Moluccan lory, see *Eos borneo*
monk parakeet, see *Myiopsitta monachus*
Musschenbroek's lorikeet, see *Neopsittacus musschenbroekii*
Myiopsitta monachus   162–63

N

Nanday conure, see *Aratinga (Nandayus) nenday*
Napoleon weaver, see *Euplectes a. afer*
Neochmia p. phaeton   214
Neophema bourkii   102–3
Neophema chrysostoma   104
Neophema elegans   101
Neophema pulchella   106
Neophema splendida   105
Neopsittacus musschenbroekii   74
Nyasa lovebird, see *Agapornis personata lilianae*
Nymphicus hollandicus   84–85

O

Oena c. capensis   57
orange-cheeked waxbill, see *Estrilda m. melpoda*
orange-fronted conure, see *Aratinga a. canicularis*
orange-winged Amazon, see *Amazona amazonica amazonia*
Orix weaver, see *Euplectes o. orix*
Ortygospiza atricollis atricollis   209

P

Pacific parrotlet, see *Forpus c. coelestis*
Padda oryzivora   234
painted conure, see *Pyrrhura p. picta*
painted firetail finch, see *Emblema picta*
palm cockatoo, see *Probosciger aterrimus*
paradise whydah, see *Vidua paradisaea*
parakeet, see *Melopsittacus undulates*
parson finch, see *Poephila c. cincta*
peach-faced lovebird, see *Agapornis r. roseicollis*
peach-fronted conure, see *Aratinga a. aurea*
Pekin robin, see *Leiothrix lutea*
Pennant's parakeet, see *Platycercus elegans*
Peter's twinspot, see *Hypargos n. niveoguttatus*
Petz conure, see *Aratinga a. canicularis*
pileated jay, see *Cyanocorax chrysops*
pin-tailed parrot finch, see *Erythrura p. prasina*
Pionus m. maximiliani   170
Pionus m. menstruus   171
plain-backed sunbird, see *Cinnyrus reichenowi*
Platycercus elegans   96–97
Platycercus eximius   98–99

Platycercus icterotis   95
plum-headed parakeet, see *Psittacula c. cyanocephala*
plush-crested jay, see *Cyanocorax chrysops*
Poephila a. acuticauda   221
Poephila c. cincta   222
Poephila guttata castanotis   216–17
Poephila p. personata   220
Poicephalus cryptoxanthus   115
Poicephalus gulielmi   111
Poicephalus meyeri   113
Poicephalus robustus   110
Poicephalus rueppellii   114
Poicephalus rufiventris   116
Poicephalus senegalus   112
Polytelis alexandrae   92–93
Polytelis anthopeplus   91
Polytelis swainsonii   90
Port Lincoln parakeet, see *Barnardius zonarius*
primrose-cheeked Amazon, see *Amazona a. autumnalis*
Princess of Wales parakeet, see *Polytelis alexandrae*
Probosciger aterrimus   75
Psephotus haematonotus   100
Pseudeos fuscata   67
Psilopogon pyrolophus   241
Psittacula c. cyanocephala   133
Psittacula e. eupatria   132
Psittacula krameri malillensis   134–35
Psittacus e. erithacus   108–9
purple glossy starling, see *Lamprotornis purpureus*
Pycnonotus jocosus   244
Pyrrhura f. frontalis   154
Pyrrhura l. leucotis   157
Pyrrhura m. melanura   159
Pyrrhura m. molinae   156
Pyrrhura perlata   155
Pyrrhura p. picta   158
Pytilia melba melba   192
Pytilia phoenicoptera   191

Q

quaker parakeet, see *Myiopsitta monachus*

R

Ramphastos toco   242-243
red avadavat, see *Amandava a. amandava*
red-bellied conure, see *Pyrrhura f. frontalis*
red-bellied parrot, see *Poicephalus rufiventris*
red-billed fire finch, see *Lagonosticta senegala*
red-browed finch, see *Aegintha t. temporalis*
red-cheeked cordon bleu, see *Uraeginthus b. bengalus*
red-eared bulbul, see *Pycnonotus jocosus*
red-eared waxbill, see *Estrilda troglodytes*
red-faced lovebird, see *Agapornis p. pullaria* or *pullarius*
red-fronted kakariki, see *Cyanoramphus novaezelandiae*
red-headed parrot finch, see *Amblynura (Erythrura) psittacea*
red-headed waxbill, see *Estrilda (Krimhilda) a. atricapilla*
red lory, see *Eos borneo*
red-masked conure, see *Aratinga erythrogenys*
red-rumped parakeet, see *Psephotus haematonotus*
red-shouldered macaw, see *Diopsittaca (Ara) n. nobilis*
red-whiskered bulbul, see *Pycnonotus jocosus*
red-winged pytilia, see *Pytilia phoenicoptera*
Rhynchopsitta pachyrhynchus   161
rock pebbler, see *Polytelis anthopeplus*
rose-breasted cockatoo, see *Elophus (Cacatua) roseicapillus*
Rüppell's parrot, see *Poicephalus rueppellii*

S

saffron finch, see *Sicalis flaveola*
salmon-crested parrot, see *Cacatua moluccensis*
scaly-headed parrot, see *Pionus m. maximiliani*
scarlet macaw, see *Ara m. macao*
Senegal dove, see *Streptopelia senegalensis*
Senegal parrot, see *Poicephalus senegalus*
Serinus canaria domesticus   183–87

Serinus leucopygus   188
sharp-tailed conure, see *Aratinga a. acudicaudata*
Sicalis flaveola   190
society finch, see *Lonchura striata var. domestica*
spectacled Amazon, see *Amazona a. albifrons*
spectacled parrotlet, see *Forpus c. conspicillatus*
spice finch, see *Lonchura p. punctulata*
splendid grass parakeet, see *Neophema splendida*
Staganopleura guttata   210–11
Stanley rosella, see *Platycercus icterotis*
star finch, see *Bathilda (Neochmia) ruficauda*
stella lorikeet, see *Charmosyna papou goliathina*
St Helena waxbill, see *Estrilda astrild astrild*
Stizoptera (Poephila) bichenovii   219
Streptopelia decaocto   54
Streptopelia roseogrisea, var. *arisoria*   55
Streptopelia senegalensis   56
sun conure, see *Aratinga (auricapillus) solstitialis*
Swainson's rainbow lory, see *Trichoglossus h. moluccanus*
Sydney finch, see *Aegintha t. temporalis*

T

Tanagara cyanicollis   251
Tauraco schuttii   240
thick-billed parrot, see *Rhynchopsitta pachyrhynchus*
tiger finch, see *Amandava a. amandava*
toco toucan, see *Ramphastos toco*
Trichoglossus goldiei   70
Trichoglossus h. haematodus   69
Trichoglossus h. moluccanus   68
tri-coloured lory, see *Lorius lory*
tri-coloured mannikin, see *Lonchura (Munia) m. malacca*
turquoise grass parakeet, see *Neophema pulchella*

U

umbrella cockatoo, see *Cacatua alba*
Uraeginthus a. angolensis   196
Uraeginthus b. bengalus   197
Uraeginthus cyanocephalus cyanocephalus   198
Uraeginthus (Granatina) g. granatina   199

V

Vidua paradisaea   236-237
violet-eared waxbill, see *Uraeginthus (Granatina) g. granatina*

W

western rosella, see *Platycercus icterotis*
white-crested cockatoo, see *Cacatua alba*
white-crested laughing-jay thrush, see *Garrulax leucolophus*
white-eared conure, see *Pyrrhura l. leucotis*
white eye, see *Zosterops palpebrosa*
white-eyed conure, see *Aratinga a. leucophthalmus*
white-fronted Amazon, see *Amazona a. albifrons*

Y

yellow-cheeked Amazon, see *Amazona a. autumnalis*
yellow-collared macaw, see *Ara (Propyrrhura) auricollis*
yellow-crowned Amazon, see *Amazona o. ochrocephala*
yellow-faced parrotlet, see *Forpus xanthops*
yellow-fronted Amazon, see *Amazona o. ochrocephala*
yellow-naped Amazon, see *Amazona o. auropalliata*
yellow-streaked lory, see *Chalcopsitta scintillata*

Z

zebra dove, see *Geopelia s. striata*
zebra finch, see *Poephila guttata castanotis*
Zonaeginthus guttatus   210–11
Zosterops palpebrosa   247

ACKNOWLEDGEMENTS

This book is dedicated to Eddie, Kimy and Korrina.

The authors and publisher would like to thank Kimberly Laura DeMeyer and Edward Heming III for their assistance.

Note: CITES is the Convention on International Trade in Endangered Species' register.

MATTHEW M VRIENDS

Matthew M Vriends, professor of biology at Suffolk County Community College, Long Island, New York (USA), is a Dutch biologist and ornithologist who holds several advanced degrees (an MA and MEd), including a PhD, in zoology. He has written over one hundred books on birds, mammals and many other animals. His detailed works on parrotlets, Australian parakeets, finches and doves are well known.

TANYA M HEMING-VRIENDS

Tanya M Heming-Vriends was born in The Hague, in The Netherlands, and went to the United States in 1977. She is a graduate of the University of Cincinnati, Ohio, and this is the tenth book that she has worked on with her father.

This, the result of their collaboration, is an authoritative book that will be a valuable addition to every aviculturist's library, and a volume that is fully comprehensible to readers with no prior knowledge of aviculture.